How the Yankees Explain New York

How the Yankees Explain New York

Chris Donnelly

TRIUMPH
BOOKS

Copyright © 2014 by Chris Donnelly

Library of Congress Cataloging-in-Publication Data

Donnelly, Chris.
  How the Yankees explain New York / Chris Donnelly ; [foreword by] Paul O'Neill.
      pages cm. — (How...explain)
  ISBN 978-1-60078-920-5 (pbk.)
  1. New York Yankees (Baseball team) 2. Baseball—New York (State)—New York. I. Title.
  GV875.N4D67 2014
  796.357'647471—dc23

                              2013040078

This book is available in quantity at special discounts for your group or organization. For further information, contact:

Triumph Books LLC
814 North Franklin Street
Chicago, Illinois 60610
(312) 337-0747
www.triumphbooks.com

Printed in U.S.A.
ISBN: 978-1-60078-920-5
Design by Patricia Frey
Photos courtesy of Getty Images unless otherwise indicated

To Jamie Leigh, whose brains and beauty are all the inspiration I need to keep writing books.

To Erin Elisabeth, you make Daddy prouder and happier with each passing minute.

Another book that Christopher Martin Singer would have loved. Still missing you buddy.

Contents

Foreword

It was early November 1992, and I was out mowing the lawn of my southern Ohio home. Just shy of my 30th birthday, I'd spent most of those 30 years in Ohio to that point. I was born and raised there, spending my youth rooting for the Big Red Machine. Eventually, I was fortunate enough to play for my hometown Reds for parts of eight seasons. When I got in from finishing my yard duties, there was a message on my machine informing me that I'd been traded to the New York Yankees.

My wife and I were devastated. New York seemed like it was another world away. Outside of games at Shea Stadium, I hadn't spent any time in the city and didn't know much about it. I just knew that it was a huge place with millions of people who were rabid about their sports. I also knew I was going to a team that, even with all its tradition and history, had not been to the postseason in a long time. *This is not going to be an easy transition*, I thought to myself.

Instead the nine seasons I spent playing right field for the Yankees were the best and most magical experience in my life. It taught me the meaning of being a Yankee and appreciating the honor and tradition that goes with it. The idea of playing in New York could have overwhelmed me and my family, but instead I was fortunate to be part of creating a winning atmosphere that would rival the Yankees dynasties of old. It is the same can-do spirit we see from New York City time and again.

That spirit was, of course, best exemplified in the aftermath of the September 11th attacks. The city very easily could have given in to fear. New Yorkers, however, rose up as one community. They supported one another. They persevered. During that same period, I got to see just how much the Yankees mean to the city. While we weren't able to win the championship that year, I could never possibly forget the emotion, the passion, and the energy of the fans during that playoff run. In times of great tragedy, baseball can seem so trivial. But for the entirety of that postseason, we really felt like we were playing for the hope and pride of New York.

I was also fortunate to be a part of the team during a period of resurgence both with the organization and with New York City. I was thrown in with an amazing group of talented individuals to both play and work with from the front office folks to my managers, the coaching staffs, and, of course, the guys I took the field with. You don't see guys like Derek Jeter, Andy Pettitte, Jorge Posada, and Mariano Rivera pop up just everyday. And to be able to have them on the same team, surrounded by a Bernie Williams or a Tino Martinez, was more then anyone could ask for. And, of course, it was an honor to play alongside Don Mattingly, who became my first good friend on the Yankees.

Throughout the years, there were countless examples of how the Yankees and everything surrounding the team represented all aspects of the city. Chris Donnelly does a great job of illustrating that by pointing to the creativity and vibrant energy of New York and how it can be seen in the Bleacher Creatures, or how the architecture and makeup of the city is reflected in both the old and the new Yankee Stadium. He deftly examines how no team draws more media attention than the Yankees, a reflection of the media presence and constant pressure and attention that is New York City. Donnelly nails that feeling of hearing Bob Sheppard and seeing Yankee Stadium for the first time while also talking about the excitement and hope generated each New Year's in Times Square.

And, as he notes, perhaps the most beautiful aspect of New York City is the idea that if you can make it there, you can make it anywhere. I was fortunate enough to have that happen and to get to witness it with players like Shane Spencer and Luis Sojo.

New Yorkers are a tough, gritty bunch, but they are also kind, caring, and compassionate. I experienced that tenderness firsthand during Game 5 of the 2001 World Series. Standing in right field at the top of the ninth inning, I began to hear the crowd chanting my name from all pockets of the stadium. It was an overwhelming, extremely emotional moment. Who would have thought that the message on my answering machine nine years earlier, which I thought was such bad news, would have turned into this wonderful moment? I also experienced that tenderness two years earlier when, in the middle of the 1999 World Series, my father passed away. People, many of whom I had never met, were so unbelievably kind and supportive of me. Words cannot accurately describe how that support helped get me through such a difficult time.

It all adds up to New York being a special place and the Yankees being a unique, unprecedented organization. Despite spending nearly all of my life in Ohio, most people, especially New Yorkers, associate me with the Yankees. And as I have come to learn and as Donnelly makes clear in the following pages, it is true: the Yankees really do explain New York.

—Paul O'Neill

1

The Boss Steinbrenner and Boss Tweed

Outside of its literal meaning, the term "boss" has several connotations. Generally, none of them are positive. Nobody likes the person in charge, and even if they do, they always think they can do a better job. In politics "boss" has become a derogatory term slapped onto those who use money and power to influence their political party and the functions of government. In business the "boss" is the person who keeps you late, who doesn't pay you enough, who never thanks you, always steals credit for your ideas, and always blames you when their ideas don't work out.

New Yorkers have bestowed the title of boss on three prominent individuals. One is Bruce Springsteen. (To avoid getting heckled in my Garden State home, I must point out that New Jerseyans played a pretty significant role here.) But Springsteen's nickname is given out of love and admiration for a rock star—not out of anger or spite. The other two men, however, were not given their titles out of respect, admiration, or love. They fit into the two derogatory terms outlined above. One was a politician; the other was a businessman. They were William "Boss" Tweed and George "The Boss" Steinbrenner.

Tweed ruled over the city's famous Tammany Hall faction, stealing millions from the city treasurer and becoming the symbol for political corruption. But he also pushed for the creation of hospitals, bridges, and museums and donated enormous sums of money to charity. Steinbrenner owned the Yankees for 37 years. He was suspended once and even banned from baseball in 1990 (before getting reinstated prior to the 1993 season) because of illegal or downright bizarre behavior. He could be extremely cruel to those who worked for him, particularly general managers, managers, and coaches. He recklessly attacked those who dared utter an unkind word about the Yankees, even implying that an umpire was purposely helping the Seattle Mariners during the 1995 postseason because he grew up in Oregon. "[An] egomaniac wrapped in a bully inside an asshole," as author and illustrator Bruce McCall described him. "And ultimate confirmation that villainy and the New York Yankees would be synonymous for all time."

But speak to the players whom he employed, and you will hear about a wonderful man who started charities, kept people on the payroll after firing them, signed players down on their luck, and made sure to visit the afflicted in the hospital. Depending on who you talked to, Boss Tweed and The Boss Steinbrenner were devil, angel, or both. They were big men—literally and figuratively—who knew the benefit of good media relations and an occasional publicity stunt. They hobnobbed with the social elite, pushed boundaries, broke the law, were targeted for vicious attacks by cartoonists and columnists, and were ultimately brought down by forces of their own making. They lived eerily similar lives that had a profound and everlasting impact on New York City.

By 1973 the Yankees organization was in shambles. The team hadn't made the World Series since 1964 and had failed to make the playoffs once—even under the new expanded format. Its star players—Mickey Mantle, Whitey Ford, Roger Maris, Yogi Berra, and Elston Howard—had all retired. The team's resistance to signing black and Latino players had caught up to it, as the minor league system was void of much talent. Fans had left in droves, and attendance fell from more than 1.3 million in 1964 to just more than 966,000 in 1972. The entertainment on the field was lacking while across town the Miracle Mets were thrilling New Yorkers with young, exciting players like Tom Seaver, Jerry Koosman, and Cleon Jones. CBS had bought the Yankees in 1964 with the idea that owning the most prominent franchise in sports would be a gold mine. Now they just wanted out.

Knowing that they were looking to sell, Michael Burke gathered a group of investors, including Steinbrenner, to pony up $8.7 million for the team. It was the biggest theft in New York City since Manhattan Island was sold for roughly $1,000. At a press conference announcing the sale, Steinbrenner said perhaps the most famous words he ever publicly uttered: "We plan absentee ownership as far as running the Yankees is concerned."

Early on, it became clear Steinbrenner had no intention of living up to his proclamation. On the first day of the season in 1973, he made note of which players wore their hair too long for his taste and immediately demanded they get it cut. (He was so new to the team that he wrote down the uniform numbers of the players because he didn't know their names.) For many it was the first sign of things to come, and before the month was over, co-owner Burke had had enough and sold his shares to Steinbrenner.

But hair length would soon be the least of Steinbrenner's problems. Not long after he purchased the team, news broke that Steinbrenner was linked to the Watergate crimes that had brought down the Richard Nixon presidency. Steinbrenner had illegally funneled money from his Cleveland shipbuilding company through several employees in order to make contributions to Nixon's reelection campaign. He'd also been less than honest about the whole affair. In 1974 he pled guilty to making illegal contributions and to a count of obstruction of justice. He was given a fine but spared jail time. Baseball commissioner Bowie Kuhn immediately suspended Steinbrenner from the game for two years, though it was later reduced to 15 months, meaning The Boss was absent from the team for the entire 1975 season.

When Steinbrenner returned in 1976, the Yankees, through a combination of key trades and big free-agent signings, were now the dominant force in the American League East. They made the playoffs for the first time in 12 years, won an intense five-game AL Championship Series against the Kansas City Royals on a walk-off home run by Chris Chambliss, and marched on to the World Series. But in the Fall Classic, the Yankees were swept by the Cincinnati Reds. As manager Billy Martin sat crying in the trainer's room, which was off-limits to the press, Steinbrenner came in and berated the sobbing manager for embarrassing him. It was just one of many cruel moments in what became one of the strangest relationships in baseball history with Steinbrenner playing the role of mentally abusive spouse and Martin the victim, thinking his better half would change. Over a 13-year period, Steinbrenner would hire and fire Martin five times, and there was a strong possibility there would have been a sixth time had Martin not died in a car accident on Christmas Day 1989.

The Yankees won the World Series in 1977 and 1978, and Steinbrenner took credit for restoring the team to its former glory. But 1978 would be the last title for nearly two decades, as the same attributes that created Steinbrenner and the team's success helped bring him and the Yankees down. Throughout the 1980s, The Boss made numerous erratic and bad decisions that would eventually plummet the team into last place. He traded away nearly every prospect of value for aging, washed-up veterans. He overpaid for mediocre players in nearly every free-agent signing of that decade, and when signings were successful, like with Dave Winfield, he made life hell for them. During the decade the team changed managers 14 times, pitching coaches 19 times, and general managers eight times. The result of all this chaos was that by 1990 the team was shockingly mediocre, finishing in last place. That team failed to have a single starting pitcher with more than nine wins, and only one full-time player managed to bat better than .260.

What made much of this even more maddening was the Jekyll and Hyde personality behind Steinbrenner. He treated players, managers, and his own staff like shit. He believed these folks, earning a living off of his money, were indebted to him. While Tammany Hall crushed their political opponents with unfair and

George Steinbrenner often ruled his team in tyrannical fashion during his more than 30 years as Yankees owner.

illegal tactics, Steinbrenner used the media, whisper campaigns, and outright cruelty to get his revenge. He publicly chided players for their weight, once referring to pitcher Hideki Irabu as a "fat, pussy toad." He chided them for their character, famously calling Dave Winfield "Mr. May" for his perceived inability to deliver big hits late in the '85 season. He chided them for their performance, once saying he was going to send poorly performing pitcher Doyle Alexander to see a doctor because he was afraid his players would get injured playing behind him. Steinbrenner's football mentality caused him to think that this kind of behavior spurred winning. Instead of creating motivation, it just made players more resentful. In one instance a player, believed to be Graig Nettles, stated he was glad Steinbrenner had an increasing airline flight schedule because it meant there was a greater chance he would perish in a plane crash. It got to the point where players came up with a term for anyone who'd gotten publicly called out by The Boss. If that happened, you'd been "Georged."

Managers and staff had it even worse. Steinbrenner was openly critical of the field managers he hired, and when he was angry with them for any sort of trivial matter, he would shut off all communication between himself and his staff and the manager in question. It was a tactic he used on Gene Michael and Lou Piniella, even though both were considered near and dear to Steinbrenner's heart. It was childish and mean. He publicly promised Yogi Berra that he would be the Yankees manager for the entire 1985 season and then fired him after 16 games when the injury-riddled team got off to a poor start. He once fired the Yankees public relations director, Rob Butcher, three days before Christmas. Butcher's crime? He'd left for the holiday to see his family the day the Yankees re-signed David Cone, though Butcher hadn't known if the signing was actually going to happen. "You have to remember that anyone who works for George is reminded daily, constantly of what a privilege it is, and he damn well better perform and do what George wants or he's out on his ear. Induced terror, if you will," said Jack Melcher, a former attorney for Steinbrenner whom The Boss tried to have disbarred after the Watergate-related crimes.

When baseball devised a new collective bargaining agreement aimed squarely at the Yankees, Steinbrenner decided he would slash the team's payroll by cutting the hours of the Yankee Stadium elevator operators, firing a few scouts and some additional employees, and cutting the dental plan of the team's secretaries and janitors. The public backlash caused him to rethink the measures. According to *The Yankee Years*, members of the Yankees' scouting system, who were so critical to the team's success in the late '90s, had received World Series rings after the '96 and '98 championships. They did not get their rings for the '99 championship until after the 2000 World Series—and they turned out to be fake. The scouts did not receive any rings for the 2000 championship, a cruel measure that reeked of a "what have you done for me lately." Anyone who had been with the team for a short period of time knew immediately when The Boss was around because everyone on staff would be on edge. "You didn't have to see Mr. Steinbrenner to know that he was in town," said former Yankees catcher Mike Stanley. "People changed their attitudes and changed the way they went about their business. So you were like, 'Oh, Mr. Steinbrenner must be in town.'" And these stories don't even touch on the cruel manner in which he handled Martin, a man who clearly had a drinking problem and whom Steinbrenner treated well only when Martin wasn't in his employ.

But for all the horror stories there are about Steinbrenner, there are hundreds of random acts of kindness. "Honestly, I am not sure that he liked the spotlight as much as people think he did," said former Yankees pitcher Dennis Rasmussen. "I lived in Tampa after my career was over, and he did a lot of things that I knew about, that the public didn't necessarily know who was responsible (for): high school programs and a lot of different philanthropic endeavors in his hometown." Steinbrenner contributed $1 million to a fund for the families of the 2007 Virginia Tech shooting. He set up a charity to pay for the college tuition of the children of police officers killed in the line of duty. When people were ill, he paid their hospital bills and spent hours checking up on them. "When I was 40 years old, I had leukemia and was going through chemotherapy," said former Yankees infielder Brian Doyle. "He called me up I don't know how many times, constantly encouraging me. It was just really nice of him to do that."

Yankees broadcaster John Sterling saw Steinbrenner act in a similar way. "I was talking with a guy who was a coach with the Yankees, and his wife had been very, very sick with cancer," Sterling said. "George told this guy to just 'Go home and take care of your wife. Your job will be waiting for you, and I'll take care of everything.' So that's George."

Nearly every manager he ever fired remained on the Yankees payroll in some form or another, including Bob Lemon, who still received a paycheck from the Yankees until his death—18 years after Steinbrenner fired him. In 1983 the Yankees decided it was time to finally bring up Don Mattingly once and for all. That meant Bobby Murcer, a fan favorite, was going to have to retire. Instead of just dumping him, Steinbrenner put him in the broadcast booth and made sure he was paid amply for being there. Murcer remained a broadcaster until his death from brain cancer in 2008.

"There were times that he would air me out about something, and later in the day, he would call me into his suite in front of other people, apologizing," said Rick Cerrone, the team's former public relations director. He would say, 'I am embarrassed by the way I behaved.' We had a very volatile but almost loving relationship. I truly loved the man. I really did."

When a teenager named Ray Negron was caught by Steinbrenner spray-painting the walls of Yankee Stadium, The Boss made him a bat boy. Negron eventually became a special advisor and dear friend to Steinbrenner. The Boss had a particular soft spot for players enduring personal problems that had led them astray from the game. He signed pitcher Steve Howe after the pitcher had been suspended from the game numerous times for drug problems. He took on Dwight Gooden and Darryl Strawberry despite their substance abuse problems. In 2007 former Yankee Jim Leyritz was involved in a late-night car crash that took the life of another driver. (Both had been drinking.) "George was the first one to pick up the phone and let me know that if I needed anything that he would be there for me," Leyritz said.

Though Steinbrenner could be downright brutal to his players, he also went out of his way to protect them. During the 2000 Subway Series, The Boss was disgusted with the visiting clubhouse accommodations at Shea Stadium. "So he gets a moving van to move all the furniture from the Yankee clubhouse and he moves it in," Sterling said. "Then some leak occurred (in the clubhouse), and he is there bailing water out of the grungy clubhouse."

Like Boss Tweed, as his lust for power exceeded the bounds of decency and sanity, the press turned on Steinbrenner and so did the public. Steinbrenner's Thomas Nast, the editorial cartoonist who excoriated the politician, was the *New York Daily News'* Mike Lupica, who savaged The Boss in column after column for his pettiness and was the one who coined the phrase "The Boss."

And like Tweed, The Boss was done in by someone within his organization. Winfield had feuded with Steinbrenner since the day he'd signed with the Yankees. The outfielder had a cost of living adjustment in his contract that Steinbrenner hadn't seemed aware of. It was an embarrassing moment for The Boss, who never appeared to forgive Winfield for getting the best of him. As the '80s went on, the two feuded over payments Steinbrenner was supposed to make to Winfield's charity, a condition of his contract. Steinbrenner said the charity was poorly run and rife with fraud. Eventually, Steinbrenner paid Howard Spira, a gambler who had done some minor work for the foundation, $40,000 to get some dirt on Winfield. Spira then turned on The Boss when Steinbrenner came to his senses and refused to pay more extortion money. When the story broke, baseball commissioner Fay Vincent took action. He planned on suspending Steinbrenner for two years. But claiming he was fed up with the game, Steinbrenner asked for and received a lifetime ban from the sport. He was to have nothing to do with the Yankees ever again. (He later realized he missed being involved with the game and wanted back in.) But July 1990 should have seen the end of Steinbrenner. When word broke out at Yankee Stadium that Steinbrenner had been banished, the hometown crowd stood and applauded. Like Tweed, Steinbrenner had been cast aside.

Rather than fade out, like Tweed had done, Steinbrenner rose up and rebuilt his reputation. After his death in 2010, fans and the media were actually longing for the days of The Boss. It began when Vincent lifted Steinbrenner's lifetime ban to a suspension and reinstated him before spring training in 1993. Steinbrenner got the parole Boss Tweed never received. A somewhat more mellow Steinbrenner returned. His absence had allowed the club to load up on key prospects. Coupling the youth with a new attitude toward free agents that emphasized on-base percentage over flash, the rebuilt Yankees became the dominant AL force again, winning six pennants and four world championships over an eight-year span. Instead of becoming infuriating and tiresome, Steinbrenner's rants became endearing. When he challenged other owners for not being willing to spend money on their teams, Yankees fans applauded. They loved that The Boss, unlike other owners, sunk every penny he could find into the team and not himself. They appreciated that Steinbrenner personally went hat in hand and on bended knee to land free agents. Had Steinbrenner not reached out to Cone from a pay phone outside a hospital (where he was visiting a sick friend) to implore him to come back to the Yankees, Cone would have signed with the Baltimore Orioles for the 1996 season, a scenario that could have ended the Yankees' latest dynasty before it started.

But it wasn't just the winning that reinvigorated The Boss' image. He benefited from several unique opportunities that generated enormous amounts of free positive publicity. In 1994 he appeared in the film *The Scout*, a movie about an amazingly talented baseball player discovered in Latin America who signs to play for the Yankees. Appearing as himself, Steinbrenner lampooned his image as a crazy-spending, take-credit-for-all-things-good owner. In one scene he smiles as the media lauds him for an idea he didn't come up with. When the man standing next to him derisively wonders aloud whose idea it really was, a stone-cold Steinbrenner responds, "Well, it's mine now, stupid." In that same year, the hit television show *Seinfeld* began using Steinbrenner as a recurring character. Voiced by show creator Larry David, the Steinbrenner character was a hit, portraying The Boss as a zany caricature of his real self. Steinbrenner, himself, gave the idea his blessing, showing he had a sense of humor. He even appeared in one episode, doing an imitation of the persona his character had taken on. (His scenes were eventually cut.)

Some people even began to stand up to him, including the president of the United States. In 2001 the Yankees visited the White House as reigning World Series champions. In a private meeting later in the Oval Office, President Bush was addressing the team about the importance of being role models. At that point, according to Bush's press secretary Ari Fleischer, The Boss interrupted and started talking. "George," Bush said, "not even The Boss gets to interrupt the president." The players loved it.

Like Tweed, Steinbrenner faced a variety of ailments over his final years that greatly reduced his vigor. Outside of a few appearances, he was hardly seen publicly during the last years of his life. Cerrone recalls having to head over to the team's Tampa complex late in the 2006 season to discuss some marketing issues. He asked someone if Steinbrenner was in his office because he would like to pay him a visit. "He said, 'Yeah, he's up there,'" Cerrone said. "Before I left he said to me, 'Boy, isn't it amazing how things have changed? There was a time you would have come up here, or anybody would have, and they would consider it a good day if they could get out of here without running into him. And now you actually are asking to see him.'"

When The Boss died shortly after his 80th birthday in July 2010, there was an immense sadness surrounding his passing. A gigantic memorial was unveiled at Yankee Stadium. Had Steinbrenner died in 1990, it's hard to imagine the public response would have been anything near resembling what it was in 2010. His image underwent a stunning transformation. But unlike Tweed, whose sympathy after his death was more the result of people feeling sorry for an old, feeble man, Steinbrenner had personally worked to rebuild, recraft, and reshape his image. By the time of his death, The Boss no longer seemed like such a hostile person after all.

Posing for a picture in 1870, William "Boss" Tweed used political corruption to powerfully reign over New York City.

Born and raised in New York, Tweed quickly rose through the ranks of Democratic politics in the city in the mid-19th century. Much like today, New York was heavily slanted toward the Democratic Party, though what that means today compared to back then is drastically different. The party was held in place by Tammany Hall, the name given to the group of political bosses who ruled over the city through a variety of less than ethical measures. A lawyer by trade, Tweed became a U.S. congressman in 1852 before turning 30. He served only one term but became immersed in local Democratic politics and eventually he shot his way up the top of party's leadership, becoming the "Grand Sachem" or leader of the entire Tammany outfit.

It wasn't hard to see why Tweed rose so far so fast. He was an extremely affable man. Describing the scene when Tweed was called to testify before a congressional committee on alleged corruption, *Boss Tweed* biographer Kenneth Ackerman wrote that "Tweed lit up the room. Big and boisterous, he knew how to lavish congressmen with humor, look them in the eye, slap shoulders, shake hands, crack a joke, share a confidence, poke fun at his own girth."

Most importantly, though, Tweed knew how to maintain power over the city and how to extort money from the public. Those two attributes helped him maintain his grip over New York for years. The amount of corruption that took place under Tweed's guidance is so remarkable in its magnitude that it seems almost made up. In 1870 Tweed was the major driving force behind an effort to allow the city to retain more local control through a new charter instead of having operations overseen by forces from Albany, the state capital. Tweed was able to "convince" the legislature to go along with the plan through kickbacks and promises of having Republicans be part of the newly formed boards that would help oversee the city. Names known for their connection to Tammany sprang up in all sorts of new important positions. And of course, when the mayor of New York City needed a new commissioner of public works, he reached out to Tweed.

Tweed's move consolidated his power and brought in streams of new revenue for his pockets and those of the rest of the Tammany crew through an ingenious scheme. Since he and his friends essentially controlled the purse strings of the city, they simply tacked additional costs on to any new development projects. If a new building was going up, they'd add a certain percentage of the real cost to the bill—like their own finder's fee. And since they controlled the books and access to them, who was going to know?

Oddly, the decision to push through the new charter was an extremely popular move among New York City residents, who wanted more autonomy over their city. And the more power Tweed assembled, the easier it was for him to lavish the spoils of that power on the city's residents. Needing the people's support to maintain power, Tweed's factions never had a problem trading money for votes. They would host enormous parties, zeroing in on the city's immigrant communities all in the name of securing more support at the ballot box.

But the greatest scheme of them all involved the building of the New York County Courthouse. Originally chartered in 1858 at a cost of $250,000 (about $6 million today), the building ended up costing $12 million to complete. Nearly all the money went to pay off Tammany associates. Andrew Garvey, a Tammany devotee, was paid more than $2.8 million for two years worth of plastering work. Not only was that an enormous figure, but it turned out that most of the work he did was to fix the shoddy work he had originally done on the building. The amount of money listed for the purchasing of chairs would have equaled the purchase of 315,000 chairs—enough to make a line 17 miles long.

Boss Tweed's thievery was stunning in its largesse, but not all of the money stayed in his pockets or those of his associates. He was notoriously generous with what he spent—though one could argue it wasn't really his money, so what's the difference?—and had a deep affinity for New York City. As public works commissioner, he approved numerous projects that helped shape the city into what it is today. He had roads paved, sewer systems installed on various streets, and land graded for streets above Central Park. He was a proponent of building what would eventually be known as the Brooklyn Bridge and for making improvements in water travel. His actions and proposals helped make the city more traversable, which endeared him to local merchants looking for more business.

Tweed also insisted on providing services for the needy. While serving as a state legislator, he pushed to enlarge New York state's annual charity appropriation bill, which provided funding for hospitals, orphanages, etc. During Tweed's time as chairman of the Charitable and Religious Societies Committee, the number of charities benefiting from the fund jumped from 68 to 106.

These actions prompted many to see Tweed as something of a Robin Hood-type figure. Though no one had proved anything, the idea that there was something devious behind all of this was well known. But many chose to look the other way—either because they were directly benefiting from it or because they simply accepted corruption and would rather have at least some of the money come back to the people.

It is believed that Tweed stole anywhere from $20 to 40 million in his time with Tammany. And with all that money and all those favors, came power. Like Steinbrenner over the Yankees more than a century later, Tweed oversaw and ruled over every element of the Democratic Party in New York City. Anyone interested in public office had to deal with Tweed first and get his blessing, or they would face a long, difficult road ahead. But eventually that kind of power breeds anger and contempt. And as Tweed and his associates grew more reckless and careless, the media and elements within Tweed's own organization coalesced to take him down.

Nast was a talented artist with a deep seething hatred for everything which Tammany did and stood. Using his position as an illustrator for *Harper's Weekly*, Nast took direct aim at Tweed, publishing dozens of cartoons mocking the overweight leader as a corrupt charlatan. His drawings became famous, making Nast a celebrity and earning him a decent amount of wealth. So influential were Nast's drawings that Tammany eventually tried to bribe him to get him to stop. Nast turned down the offer.

William Tweed is depicted as having a money bag for a head in this 1871 political cartoon by Thomas Nast, the illustrator who routinely excoriated the powerful figure.

The drawings made Nast famous and actually brought more notoriety and fame to Tweed as well. But without any proof, the illustrations depicting Tweed's corruption were nothing more than entertaining satire of a public figure. The newspapers in New York by and large left the issue alone—either for their own benefit or for lack of evidence.

That changed, however, when a Tammany disciple turned on his leaders. Jimmy O'Brien, the county sheriff for New York City, had acquired ledgers from the city comptroller's office that showed the massive scale of corruption under Tweed. He at first used the information to try to blackmail Tammany. When that failed he brought the documents to *The New York Times*. Publication caused a sensation. That was soon coupled with additional evidence that popped up when a new comptroller outside the control of Tammany took office and discovered just how widespread the corruption was. Tweed was immediately arrested, but the proceedings against him lagged on for two more years. In that time he was actually reelected to his seat in the state legislature. After one hung jury trial, Tweed was finally convicted on more than 200 counts of corruption. He served time in jail and was released before being thrown into debtor's prison when he couldn't pay the bail money for a new suit brought against him by the state of New York.

Tweed eventually escaped from prison and made it all the way to Spain. But he was done in when Spanish officials, aided by the drawings of Nast, were able to identify and arrest him. Forced back to prison, Tweed was a broken man. Illness had greatly reduced his strength. He finally reached a point where, in exchange for getting out of prison, he would share all that he knew about the city's history of corruption.

By this point Tweed had become a figure of pity to many. "New Yorkers who earlier despised Tweed for his arrogance and greed now grudgingly grew to respect the 'old man'—for his terrible mistakes, his punishment, and his apparent atonement," Ackerman wrote. But the powers that be—including New York governor Samuel Tilden—who'd fallen out of favor with Tammany over the years, wanted nothing to do with the Boss anymore. They ignored Tweed's request and those of the public who asked for mercy. Instead, Tweed was left to deteriorate in prison where he died at the age of 55 in 1878. After his death even those who had been harshest to him suggested some form of leniency over his memory. *Harper's Weekly*, the publication that had done more than any other news outlet to bring Tweed down, wrote, "He was a hearty boon companion, a lover of his friends, and generous to 'the boys.' Should he, therefore, not have paid the lawful and not extravagant penalty of offenses that thin and morose men would have paid if they had committed?"

2

The Sky's the Limit

It is the most famous skyline on the planet. People travel from all across the world to see it. Couples getting married make sure it is in the background of their wedding photos. It can be seen from Long Island, Connecticut, and even in the hills that carry Route 287 through Riverdale and Pompton Lakes, New Jersey, some 30 miles east of the city. No matter what angle or direction you are looking from, the outline of New York City never disappoints. The southern tip is dominated by older skyscrapers that reflect the building boom of the early 20th century. They take up nearly all the space and absorb all the sunshine on the zigzag maze of 200-year-old streets. For 40 years the Twin Towers of the World Trade Center stood high above the rest of the buildings in the area. Now the new Freedom Tower at 1,776 feet juts out from the rest of the crowd. As you move north, the towering skyscrapers tail off, replaced by block after block of lower-level housing and bars. Hit midtown Manhattan, and the buildings climb skyward again. And this doesn't even include the high-rises of Brooklyn or the Bronx. Surrounding all of this are some of the most famous bridges ever constructed, including the George Washington, the Brooklyn, and the Verrazano.

Nearly 100 years ago, almost none of this existed. New York had a few high-rise buildings, but the skyline was mostly void of anything awe inspiring. In an extremely short period of time, that all changed. While cities also began experimenting with architectural wonders (Paris' Eiffel Tower debuted in 1889, the highest structure ever built at the time), New York drew in those with the biggest desire, the most daring, and the most money to invest, though many structures were built without enough thought given to who would occupy them. In addition to the large amount of wealth in the city, New York made sense for the tall-building boom because of its massive population located in such a small area. Amidst this growing landscape, up in the Bronx popped something no one had ever seen before.

The first true landmark structure to go up in New York City was the Brooklyn Bridge, which connects lower Manhattan to Brooklyn. Completed in 1883 the bridge—intended for foot traffic, horse drawn carriages, and cable cars—was a modern marvel of engineering. A walkway shot down the upper middle section of the bridge, allowing for pedestrians to cross the East River. On either side of the walkway ran specially designed cable cars, which, according to the National Register of Historic Places, were carrying more than 30 million passengers a year by 1888. The bridge also made use of caissons, essentially large boxes filled with compressed air that plunged beneath the surface of the river. Used to support the two towers of the bridge, that construction kept out water from the river and prevented the bridge from collapsing inward. The Brooklyn Bridge stood as the world's largest suspension bridge for 20 years.

The first landmark skyscraper in New York City was the Flatiron. The building's location on 5th Avenue between 22nd and 23rd Streets and Broadway resulted in its being built in the shape of a triangle. It became known as the Flatiron because its triangular design resembled that of a clothing iron. Completed in 1903 the building stood just more than 280 feet tall—not an astonishing height by today's standards but placing it among the tallest buildings in the country when it was finished. Crowds of people all dressed to the nines walked past the building. In the streets, trolleys crossed as did horse-drawn carriages. Flatiron's odd design has made it a

Located on 5th Avenue between 22nd and 23rd Streets and Broadway, the 280-foot tall Flatiron stood as one of the tallest buildings in the country at the beginning of the 20th century. (AP Images)

tourist attraction for more than 100 years, and the building is now considered a historical landmark.

At the time the Flatiron was finished, the tallest structure in New York was the Park Row Building located in lower Manhattan. Barely noticeable by today's standards, Park Row stood nearly 400 feet off the ground. In 1908 the Singer Building eclipsed Park Row as the tallest building in New York and became the tallest building in the world. The Singer Building featured a unique design that saw the space of the lower set of floors take up the equivalent of a normal office building. But then a tower shot up, encompassing the remaining 35 floors of the building. (It was sometimes referred to as the Singer Tower.) It topped out at just more than 600 feet above the streets of Manhattan.

The Singer Building, which was eventually demolished in the late 1960s, did not maintain its title for long. In 1909 the Metropolitan Life Insurance Company Tower took over as the city's (and the world's) tallest building, reaching 700 feet. The Tower, located not too far from the Flatiron, was similar in structure to the Singer Building in that a grand tower rose up above the lower set of floors. Near the upper floors, each side of the tower sported a massive clock that could be seen across the city. The Tower maintained its world's tallest status until 1913 when the Woolworth Building was completed in lower Manhattan. The world's new tallest building was born out of pure spite. Frank Woolworth, owner of the store chain, was angry over Metropolitan Life having denied him a loan years before. He got even by making a bigger building. Standing at nearly 800 feet, Woolworth also played off the tower design structure. But unlike the Singer Building or the Metropolitan Life Tower, the base of the Woolworth Building was much larger and ran up more floors. With its lime green top and gothic points, Woolworth jutted farther into the sky than any man-made structure ever had at that time. It got the skyscraper wars going, squabbles that would shape the city skyline. However, not all of this new, grand construction took place in Manhattan. Just across the northern tip of the island on the southeastern side of the Bronx, another new structure was soon to emerge.

Descendents of a 19th century failed Baltimore Orioles' experiment, the Yankees were first known as the Highlanders. This was due to the team playing its home games on top of one of the highest points in Manhattan (Hilltop Park). By 1913 the Yankees were sharing space with the New York Giants at the Polo Grounds, a horseshoe-shaped ballpark located on Coogan's Bluff on Manhattan's Upper West Side in Harlem. Since the Highlanders name was no longer apt, the organization took on the moniker of the Yankees (somewhat ironically given that New York was not the most pro-union area of the country during the Civil War). Two years later the club was sold to two successful businessmen, Colonel Jacob Ruppert and Captain Tillinghast L'Hommedieu Huston. The Polo Grounds-sharing agreement between the Yankees and Giants was amicable enough until Babe Ruth came along in 1920. Not overly successful, the Yankees had sort of been rambling along as a franchise until that point. Instead the Boston Red Sox dominated the American League. The trade that brought Ruth to New York changed all that. Ruth's power and status as the game's biggest star brought more than a million fans to the Polo Grounds to see the Yankees, the first time they had ever drawn over a million. Giants ownership was not pleased with their guest's newfound success. During Ruth's first season in New York, they quickly announced that the Yankees would not be welcome back to the Polo Grounds the following year. After cooler heads prevailed (somewhat), the Yankees were allowed to stay for another two seasons. But Ruppert and Huston knew it was time to go. They also knew that a new place to play would be financially beneficial for the team.

Ruppert didn't just want to build a ballpark. He wanted to make a statement: the Yankees were going to be the team to deal with in New York City. A club like that needed a grand home—not just a place to play but a building unlike anything anyone had seen before. Ruppert contracted with the Osborn Engineering Co. of Cleveland to build the stadium. Osborn was probably the premier builder of ballparks in that era, having designed the Polo Grounds and Braves Field in Boston. They got to work drawing up plans for the biggest, grandest structure ever imagined for a baseball team or any sports team for that matter. The original location for the park was on the Upper West Side of Manhattan. When that didn't pan out, the Yankees bought land in the Bronx from William Waldorf Astor. In May 1922 construction work began on the site. Less than a year later, it was completed.

The result was Yankee Stadium, the first multi-tiered stadium in baseball, which totally encompassed the field with stands. Everyone else played in an open ballpark with maybe one level of seating surrounding the diamond. The stadium was tailor-made for the team's left-handed star slugger, Ruth, as it was only 295 feet down the right-field line. (During that first year, it was actually only 257 feet down both lines.) The rest of the stadium, however, was not conducive to power hitters. Left-center field was 500 feet away, dead-center 487 feet, and right-center 423 feet. These distances would all be shortened in the next year but not by much, and left-center field continued to be one of the longest shots in baseball for decades. But dimensions only told part of the story. The stadium's tiered-level seating was a relatively new, unique aspect of the park. The frieze architecture that hung 16 feet down from the roof gave a certain majestic feel to the place—almost like the park was intended for royalty to play there. With the words "Yankee Stadium" prominently featured on the stadium's exterior, it seemed like a colosseum from the Roman Empire. It was everything that Yankees fans loved about the team and Yankee detractors hated: it was grand, grand, grand. Perhaps best of all, this new towering structure sat just across the East River from Harlem in full view of the Giants and the Polo Grounds.

On April 18, 1923, Yankee Stadium hosted its first baseball game. The parking lot overflowed with Model Ts as more than 70,000 people crammed into the new park. The attendance was roughly as much as the other Opening Day games in the American League drew combined. John Philip Sousa conducted the Seventh Regiment Band, which performed in the outfield before the game. Though they were not rivals yet, the Yankees fittingly hosted the Red Sox that day. Even more fitting, in the third inning, Ruth hit the stadium's first ever home run, a shot into the right-field seats.

The Yankees won 4–1. Just a week later, President Harding dropped by the stadium to take in a game. The Yankees would go on to win their first world championship in the inaugural year of their new park, though they clinched the title across the river...at the Polo Grounds.

Over the years Yankee Stadium would undergo many changes and take on a mythic status. New stands and sections were added here and there with second and third levels put into left-center field during the winter of 1927–28 and into right field in 1937. In 1932 the Yankees created the first ever memorial monument in honor of manager Miller Huggins, who died suddenly during the 1929 season. Eventually, they would add five more monuments: Ruth, Lou Gehrig, Joe DiMaggio, Mickey Mantle, and George Steinbrenner. (There is also a monument in memory of the victims of 9/11.) In addition to monuments, players were also honored with a plaque and/or having their jersey number retired. The Yankees were the first organization to retire uniform numbers. Seventeen players have had their number retired. (No. 8 was retired for two players, Bill Dickey and Yogi Berra.) The only two single-digit numbers remaining are No. 2 and 6, and the former certainly will be retired after Derek Jeter calls it quits. The Yankees have honored 28 individuals with plaques, including non-players like announcer Mel Allen, public address announcer Bob Sheppard, and general manager Ed Barrow.

Until the ballpark was remodeled, the monuments and plaques were all located in center field—within the field of play. After the remodeling, the monuments, plaques, and retired numbers were moved to an area behind the left-center field wall. It became known as Monument Park, a shrine unequaled in any stadium. For first-time visiting players, a trip to Monument Park was a must. When the park (originally closed to the public) became accessible, thousands lined up before the game to check it out.

As the years went on, the stature of the ballpark grew largely based on the talent on the field. Ruth, Gehrig, DiMaggio, and Mantle all played on the hallowed grounds of Yankee Stadium. Dozens of championships were won there. No-hitters and perfect games were pitched there. In addition the football Giants played

Mariano Rivera sits beside his retired number in Monument Park during a pregame ceremony at the new Yankee Stadium on September 22, 2013. (AP Images)

there as did various college football teams over the years. Knute Rockne's famous "Win one for the Gipper" speech was said at halftime of a Notre Dame-Army game held there. Max Schmeling and Joe Louis engaged in two of the most famous fights in boxing history in the middle of the stadium.

Visiting dignitaries were brought to the ballpark in the Bronx. Popes Benedict, John Paul II, and Paul VI held mass at the stadium. Shortly after being released from prison, Nelson Mandela addressed a crowd at the stadium. Two weeks after the 9/11 attacks, a public memorial was held there with former President Clinton and Oprah Winfrey in attendance.

Even somber moments were treated with pomp and circumstance and became the stuff of legend if they happened at Yankee Stadium. Having been diagnosed with a rare and fatal muscle degenerative disease, Gehrig stood before the stadium crowd on an emotional day on July 4, 1939. The Yankees retired his number that afternoon, and the "Iron Horse" stepped up to the microphone to say a few words. His declaration that "Today, I consider myself the luckiest man on the face of the Earth," has been heard by sports and non-sports fans alike. It has become a symbol of courage and strength in the face of adversity. When Mantle and Reggie Jackson had their numbers retired, they mimicked Gehrig's words. The speech became part of Hollywood lore as well thanks to Gary Cooper's portrayal of Gehrig in the 1942 film *The Pride of the Yankees*.

In 1948 Ruth succumbed to cancer at the age of 53. Instead of at a funeral home or church, his body rested in state at Yankee Stadium where nearly 100,000 people filed past to get one last look and pay their respects. For years young children thought that Ruth was actually buried in the stadium.

Thurman Munson was grumpy, surly, and didn't much enjoy the constant media attention he received in New York. But fans loved him for his hard-nosed play and all-out hustle. Munson became the first Yankees captain since Gehrig and won the 1976 American League MVP award. While injuries had begun to take their toll, Munson was still a valuable member of the team in 1979. Having acquired his pilot's license and not enjoying how playing in New York took him away from his family, Munson began flying back to his home in Ohio as often as he could during the season. Munson was home on the team's August 2, 1979, off day and decided to practice taking off and landing at the local airport. While attempting to land, he clipped a tree, and the plane crashed short of the runway. Munson initially survived despite a broken neck before dying of smoke inhalation when the plane burst into flames.

Munson's death was a shock to the baseball world. Rarely had an athlete still in the prime of his career been killed. The next day the Yankees played a home game against the Orioles. During a pregame ceremony, the catcher's position was left empty. Many of the thousands of people attending that night cried. Jackson could be seen violently sobbing in right field. A few days later, the team flew to Ohio for the funeral. Billy Martin, who'd loved Munson dearly, was nearly inconsolable. The team returned to New York that night for the final game of their series against the Orioles. It was an incredibly emotional night. The Yankees trailed 4–0 when Bobby Murcer, a close friend of Munson's who'd delivered a eulogy at the services that day and was the last Yankees player to see Munson alive, hit a three-run home run in the seventh inning to make it a 4–3 game. With two runners on in the ninth, Murcer again delivered, lining a single down the left-field line to win the game. Although the Yankees' season was lost by that point, that night was a touching and fitting memorial to the team's fallen captain.

In 1974 and '75, the city of New York agreed to refurbish Yankee Stadium. The place had grown old, and New York's newest team, the Mets, just had a fairly new, publicly financed stadium built for them. The Yankees wanted in on the action. A new stadium was not feasible, so fixing up the old one was the next best thing. While construction crews tore up and rebuilt the ballpark in the Bronx, the Yankees played their home games at Shea Stadium in Queens for two years.

The result of two years worth of toil (and over $100 million worth of cost overruns) was a place that was drastically different but still maintained the aura and history of the original ballpark. The frieze that lined the top of the upper deck was gone as was the top overhang. They were torn down, so that the pillars that obstructed fans' views could be removed. The outfield walls were brought in drastically, though left-center field still remained dauntingly far from home plate. The bullpens were moved to behind the left-center field wall, and the short fences in left and right field, which stood at just under four feet tall, were raised to eight feet and above. Seating was now banned in the center-field bleachers, an area that became known as "the Black" because of the color of the seats. Hitting a home run there would come to be seen as a rare accomplishment. The seats around the ballpark went from green to blue. The auxiliary scoreboard in right-center field was removed and replaced with an electronic scoreboard against the back wall of the stadium in left-center field.

Despite all the changes, the park still had a mythic feel that carried over from the old to the new. It would be hard to characterize it, but the stadium itself took on an almost human form. It was referred to as if it was the 26th member of the team. It was not just another place: it was *the* stadium. "It was like playing in a cathedral. It was like playing in Carnegie Hall," said former Yankees pitcher Al Downing. Whether it was the old park or the refurbished one, going there was a surreal experience described on countless occasions by sons and daughters retelling their first time there.

"When you're a kid…you hit that field, and it's surreal especially then because we had a black and white TV. You'd go, and all the colors are vivid," said actor Steve Schirripa, best known as Bobby Baccalieri from the HBO show *The Sopranos*. The story of someone's first experience at the stadium is almost always the same. "Walking through that tunnel, maybe it's like walking into the gates of heaven, I hope," said Paul Amoroso, superintendent of the Pompton Lakes New Jersey school district, who recalled attending his first game in 1976 with his father. "It was the colors that struck me more than anything. Really, I know it sounds cliché, but it was the blue seats, the green grass, and the perfectly manicured dirt. It just made the hair on my little neck stand up."

Ari Fleischer, former press secretary for president George W. Bush, is a lifelong Yankees fan with an impressive collection of memorabilia, though he has the somewhat unfortunate distinction of being born on October 13, 1960—right around the hour second baseman Bill Mazeroski's walk-off home run won the 1960 World Series for the Pittsburgh Pirates. "One of the biggest thrills of my life always was going to [Yankees] games, and that amazing feeling when you saw the green grass," Fleischer said. "And we would sit way upstairs in the cheap seats. You had to lean left to right to view around the pillars in the pre-76 stadium—always though, what a thrill."

The experience was just as thrilling for players as it was for fans. Jim Leyritz recalled the first time he went to the stadium as a player, shortly after he was called up in 1990. "I walked in and I saw Monument Park. I took it all in. Then I walked across the field,

I got to the mound, and I just stood on the mound," Leyritz said. "I look around and was like *you know what?* I know why this is so special."

By the turn of the millennium, Yankee Stadium had become similar to much of New York City: it was old. The style was quaint but outdated. Thousands of people were forced to walk through areas that would drive a claustrophobic to madness. And most of the place smelled like urine. In 1998 a 500-pound steel joist fell through the upper deck, crashing into the mezzanine. Luckily it occurred hours before the game, avoiding tragedy. The Yankees were forced to cancel two home games and play a third at Shea Stadium. (When the Yankees returned to Yankee Stadium, Steinbrenner—ever the showman—sat in the very seat that had been pulverized by the joist, showing the world that everything was fine.) Still Yankee Stadium was home. For all its shortcomings, it still made you feel good, still made your heart beat just a little faster when you walked through those tunnels. "The old Yankee Stadium—there was nothing like it," said Mitchell Modell, owner of Modell's Sporting Goods, "particularly in October when you went to a postseason game in the old Yankee Stadium, waiting in line to get into the bathrooms, the hot dogs, the smell of the beer, the briskness, the chillness in the air."

The old park made it 85 years before closing after the 2008 season. Ruth hit the first home run there. Jose Molina hit the last. The only similarity between the two players was their girth. In 2009 the Yankees moved across the street to a majestic, sparkling new ballpark. The new Yankee Stadium, the "House That George Built," had all the amenities of a 21st century park. There were more luxury boxes and concessions stands. Unlike the old park, where you couldn't see a thing once you left your seat, you see the field from every nook and cranny of the new park. The bathrooms were clean. It was a great, comfortable place to watch a game.

But it just wasn't the same place. Many would complain of the corporate feel of the new digs and that high priced tickets brought in wealthy folks who weren't true fans. It was not an unreasonable theory, considering that front row seats cost more than $1,000 a game. The design of the park, in which the field was visible from the concession stands, meant that the upper deck was farther away from the action. All this added up to a stadium that just didn't generate the same noise or feel of the old place. Given that the old place had nearly a century's worth of history in it, it's not entirely fair to compare the two. The Yankees did win the World Series in the first season at the new stadium, so they got off to a good start. Time will tell if they do as well as they did across the street.

———

Shortly after the original Yankee Stadium opened up in 1923, some aspiring minds began to realize that there was money and fame to be had in the construction of grand structures. Whoever could build the tallest building on Earth would be known worldwide. The eventual war to take over New York's skyline was born out of friendship. As outlined in Neal Bascomb's book *Higher*, William Van Alen and Craig Severance started out as friends and became partners in an architectural firm. But differences of opinion on just about all matters related to business caused them to dissolve the partnership and go their separate ways.

As fate would have it, two men interceded to bring Van Alen and Severance together again, but this time it was a bitter rivalry. In the late 1920s, developer George Ohrstrom set about designing the world's tallest building on a parcel of land located at 40 Wall Street in downtown Manhattan. The building would serve as the headquarters for the Bank of Manhattan Trust Company. At the same time, Walter Chrysler, owner of the car company, had his sites set on the very same goal, but his building would be constructed in midtown on the East Side. These two ambitious men set out to find architects to make their dreams become a reality. Ohrstrom settled on Severance; Chrysler chose Van Alen. What ensued was months of competition between the two old friends to see who could build higher and faster than the other. Though plans were kept secret from the public in order to hide who would end up with the taller building, the fight drew national attention from the media.

Construction on both buildings began in 1928. Each was originally designed with the intention of being taller than the Woolworth Building. Both buildings were put up with amazing speed, easily completing several floors a week. By the spring of 1930, the completion of both was not far off. The Chrysler Building at first seemed like it would win out. But Severance adjusted his designs by adding several floors to his building, ensuring that 40 Wall Street would just barely edge out Van Alen's design. It was all going to plan for Severance and Ohrstrom, who were set to take the prize with their 927-foot-tall building. Little did they know that Van Alen and Chrysler had an ace up their sleeves. They, too, had adjusted their own plans. Within the newly developing building, workers had been assembling a spire that would be perched atop the structure. Not only would the spire give the Chrysler Building its now signature look, but it would also ensure that it measured as the tallest building in the world.

By the time the spire became public and it was made clear that Van Alen would win, 40 Wall Street was too far along in the process for Severance to do anything about it. His building became the tallest in the world in April of 1930 and was completed in May. It topped out at 927 feet with a bright lime green crown atop the structure that helped it stick out even more from its neighbors in southern Manhattan. But on May 27, the Chrysler Building officially opened as the tallest building in the world. The spire and the antenna attached to the top of it added well over 100 feet to the height. This meant the building stood at almost 1,050 feet tall, 10 percent higher than its rival downtown.

Severance and others cried foul over the spire. They claimed that 40 Wall Street was actually the taller building because it contained the world's highest workable space. The spire and needle were just window dressing—and bad window dressing at that. They were unnecessary aesthetics that made their claims of being the tallest building in the world disingenuous. Few listened to their cries. Van Alen and Chrysler had won the race. But another building was taking shape in midtown.

John Jakob Raskob, a financier and businessman, decided he wanted to be the one to create the world's tallest building. Pushed vigorously by New York governor Al Smith, Raskob purchased the Waldorf-Astoria Hotel and surrounding properties on 5th Avenue and West 34th Street and then knocked them down. The plans for his building were never a secret. His skyscraper would eclipse 40 Wall Street and the Chrysler Building by hundreds of feet— in part because of the mooring mast on top of the building. The structure known as the Empire State Building was completed in just more than a year's time. Including the mooring mast (which was never actually put to use), it stood more than 1,400 feet tall, easily eclipsing its nearest rivals. Not only was it the tallest, but it was the most impressive from a structural standpoint. Designed in Art Deco style, the Empire State Building just popped out of the skyline. Its 86th floor observation deck provided an electric panoramic view of all New York City plus the surrounding areas of New Jersey, Connecticut, and New York state. Over the coming years, the upper floors of the building would be lit up in various colors, including Yankee blue and white, to pay tribute to local events and people.

For 40 years nothing would top the Empire State Building. Then two enormous steel towers went up side by side in lower Manhattan. Known as the Twin Towers, they were the world's tallest buildings from 1971 until 1973 when Chicago's Sears Tower (now called the Willis Tower) took the prize. But skyscrapers continued to rise across Manhattan, each one creating a new, unique piece of the New York City skyline.

Excluding the new towers going up at the World Trade Center site, at least eight buildings that have eclipsed 800 feet in height have gone up in the city since 1977. The Chrysler Building, which for years stood as either the second or third tallest in New York, was pushed into fourth in 2009 with the completion of the Bank of America Tower.

Even today, when it seems like there is nowhere else to build, skyscrapers are in the making. Plans for three high-rise condominiums, two of which will rise taller than the base of the

Empire State Building, have been announced. Construction is ongoing for 432 Park Avenue, a condo complex that is slated to be the tallest residential building in the Western Hemisphere at 1,396 feet. The Woolworth Building, which once stood as the tallest in the world for nearly two decades, will soon not even rank among the tallest 20 buildings in the city.

No matter how many buildings go up, though, the view of the skyline simply never gets old. As you leave the Lincoln Tunnel, you get that same rush of seeing the massive buildings sprawled out along the Hudson River. You can sit on a bench at South Street Seaport and glance northward as the towering structures provide a backdrop to the Brooklyn Bridge. No city in the world can offer these kinds of views.

3

The City That Never Sleeps

"I want to wake up in that city that doesn't sleep." So goes the line made famous by Frank Sinatra in his hit song, "New York, New York" (though Liza Minnelli actually recorded the song first). Certainly Sinatra knew as well as anyone that the description of New York City rang true. Born just across the Hudson River in Hoboken, New Jersey, Sinatra had his share of late nights in the Big Apple. He even got arrested once (granted it was just across the river in Bergen County, New Jersey,) for carrying on with a married woman. Yes, that was a crime at the time. But Sinatra's escapades are just one of a million tales of late night and early morning shenanigans in New York.

New York is truly unique in that it is one of the few places in the world that never really closes. In most major cities in the United States, you can enter the downtown area after hours on a weekday and find nary a soul around. But at every hour of the day in just about every part of the city in New York, you will see people out and about. New York teems with life. As a result it also has a noise problem. According to a Columbia University study released in 2010, "98 percent of Manhattan's public space exceeds healthy levels." Even places that are thought to be escapes from it all like public parks had unhealthy decibel levels. It could explain why

New Yorkers can be a tad ornery sometimes. When there are spikes in noise, "your blood pressure will increase even if you, yourself, don't recognize that that spike is happening," said Robyn Gershon, a Columbia professor.

In 2013 *The New York Times* reported on how "Silence has become a luxury in New York that only a scant few can truly afford." There were tales of people being kept awake all night because of airplanes, construction on the Brooklyn Bridge, or the construction of new buildings, which was at a five-year high. Even Madonna had been sued by her neighbors on Central Park West for playing music too loudly.

If you have an environment where people are active 24 hours a day, naturally there is bound to be some mischief. This is especially true in a city where there is a bar around every corner. Most American cities have their bars concentrated in one area. San Diego has the Gaslamp District; St. Louis has the waterfront area; Tampa has Ybor City, and so on. But New York's 302 square miles have no shortage of places to drink and have fun. The city has provided some of the most legendary late-night entertainment venues. There was, of course, the Copacabana, an infamous hangout for Yankees players of the '50s. There was also the Stork Club and its eventual replacement on the Upper East Side, Maxwell's Plum. But no spot might have been more famous than Studio 54, perhaps the most exclusive club in the city's history. Opening in April 1977, "there was no more thrilling nightlife than the dance on West 54th Street," wrote *New York Magazine's* Philip Noble.

Run by Steve Rubell and Ian Schrager, Studio 54 essentially had an anything goes policy. Drugs were consumed openly throughout the establishment, and sex acts under the shimmering disco balls were a somewhat common occurrence. Andy Warhol, Sylvester Stallone, Muhammad Ali, Reggie Jackson, Diana Ross, Richard Gere—the list of celebrities who stopped by seemed to grow everyday. Minnelli, Bianca Jagger, and Calvin Klein were regulars. People waited in lines a block long to get in, an almost impossible proposition if your name was not on the list. In one amusing instance, Rubell denied the president of Cyprus entry

Partygoers line up in hopes of getting into Studio 54, one of New York's hottest clubs at the time.

because he was mistaken for the president of Cypress Hill Cemetery in Brooklyn. When the real president of the cemetery found out, he was upset to learn he wouldn't have been admitted, even writing a letter to Rubell asking, "If I do come, would you let me in?"

The crowd at 54, while exclusive, was also eclectic. "It's bisexual," Rubell said during the height of 54's fame. "Very bisexual. And that's how we choose the crowd, too. In other words we want everybody to be fun and good looking. And have sex and do drugs in the balcony." Writer Truman Capote loved it, describing it as: "Boys with boys, girls with girls, girls with boys, blacks and whites, capitalists and Marxists, Chinese and everything else, all one big mix." Even Lillian Carter, the president's mother, enjoyed her visit there. "I don't know if I was in heaven or hell," she said, "but it was wonderful."

But Rubell and Schrager, through their constant public pronouncements about the wild goings on at 54, were essentially daring the authorities to come after them. And that is exactly what happened. They were both nailed for failing to pay their taxes and sent to prison. The original incarnation of Studio 54 closed in 1980.

The Studio 54 of excess is long since gone, but New Yorkers and those visiting the city certainly haven't lost their taste for a drink now and then. Although disco is dead and cocaine is not nearly as abundant as it was in the 1980s, the party not only lives on, but also more people are being invited. During the first decade of the millennium, alcohol-related hospitalizations in the city saw a 36 percent increase, reaching 8,840 such incidents in 2009. The ratio of alcohol-related emergency room visits among New Yorkers ages 21 to 64 doubled from 2003 to 2009. That latter year featured 70,000 cases.

The Yankees have been overshadowed for decades, in terms of drinking and late-night prowess, by the New York Mets. The 1986 Mets have become the stuff of legends: a blue collar team that partied hard, lived fast, and dominated on the field. And the Mets organization has no problem playing into that legend. You would be hard-pressed to find a story or video or special made about that '86 team that did not mention their drinking escapades. The Yankees, meanwhile, shun those kinds of stories. They are considered beneath the dignity of the sport's greatest franchise. That kind of philosophy, coupled with Yankees policies of short hair, postgame shirt and ties, and constant talk of tradition, may lead to a feeling that the Yankees are the most boring behind-the-scenes team ever.

The reality, however, is that bars, beers, and brawls are as much a Yankees tradition as Old Timer's Day. Throughout the decades the team has been filled with players who played just as hard off the field as they did on it. For some, drinking merely enhanced their already charming personality; for others, they drank to escape the pressure of playing in New York; and for others, drinking turned them into the meanest pricks you'd ever meet.

It seems only fitting that baseball's greatest player, Babe Ruth, was also its greatest partier. The Babe's adventures have taken on a mythic status with the amount of beer he consumed, growing larger with each story. In 1925 Ruth missed nearly half the season after experiencing flu-like symptoms early in the year. The press attributed his condition to poor eating habits and drinking too much soda. Others, however, think Ruth was either suffering from an undisclosed venereal disease or some form of alcohol poisoning. And keep in mind, Ruth did all of this partying at a time when alcohol was banned in the country. Ruth wasn't the only Yankee though who could down a few. Joe Page, who pitched with the team from 1944 to 1950, was known for his late-night adventures. Eventually the team hired a female private detective to track him. The detective ended up falling in love with him.

By the 1950s the perfect collection of drinkers mixed with practical jokers had come together in pinstripes. They included Mickey Mantle, Whitey Ford, Hank Bauer, and Billy Martin. Their late-night adventures became legendary. After the Yankees clinched the pennant in September of 1953, some of the team, including the aforementioned, went to the Latin Quarter nightclub to celebrate. When the $250-plus bar tab came due, Ford decided to sign the bill under the name of Yankees owner Dan Topping. The incident cost Ford and several others $500. The gang became so irksome to team management that general manager George Weiss began having private detectives shadow his ballplayers. The players easily spotted them and usually outwitted them.

Their manager, Casey Stengel, was no stranger to a drink and certainly did not attempt to curtail his players' late nights. His sternest measure against the antics of his players was to warn them never to go to the hotel bar because "that's where I do my drinking." To Stengel, you had the guys who were going to go out and the guys who weren't. Stengel figured: who was he to say which side was right or wrong? He was the perfect manager for this group.

In 1955 the team was sent on a goodwill tour across the Pacific, with stops in Hawaii, Wake Island, the Philippines, Guam, and Japan. While in Toyko one night, Martin and Mantle were in the hotel bar until three in the morning. They plotted a scheme whereby Martin called the room of every player, saying Mantle was getting beaten up in a fight, and they needed to get down to the bar immediately. "By the time Martin had called the troops, the entire team was in the bar laughing and drinking, some of the men in their undershorts, some in kimonos," wrote Pete Golenbock in *Dynasty*. "Stengel was in attendance wearing screaming red pajamas."

Things came to a head for the group, though, on what started as a harmless Wednesday evening on May 16, 1957. It was Martin's 29th birthday, and his friends, Ford and Mantle, had planned a party for him. Among those joining the celebration were Martin, Ford, and Mantle, along with Bauer, Yogi Berra, Johnny Kucks, and their wives. They all went out to dinner first at Danny's Hideaway in midtown Manhattan. Afterward they stopped at the Waldorf Astoria to watch a performance by singer Johnny Ray. Then they moved over to the famous Copacabana nightclub for an early hours performance by Sammy Davis Jr.

The nightclub sat their famous guests right at the front of the stage. A short time later, a nearby table made up of a bowling team made their presence known. One of them hurled a few racial obscenities at Davis. The Yankees responded immediately with Bauer telling the man to shut up. He didn't. In fact others from his table joined in to heckle the Yankees. Eventually, the two tables got up and approached one another. Workers at the Copacabana tried to prevent a brawl, but before anyone knew it, heckler Edwin Jones was lying unconscious on the floor of the bathroom. He'd suffered a broken nose and some head injuries. Those on the scene found Berra and Ford in the bathroom restraining Bauer. But Bauer would always maintain that he never hit the guy. Instead he claimed bouncers from the club had gotten to him first.

As the Yankees scrambled out of the club, *New York Post* columnist Leonard Lyons caught sight of them. With no Yankees left to talk to, he asked the remaining patrons what happened. Jones claimed that Bauer beat him up. And that was what got printed in the morning edition of the next day's *Post*. Yankees' upper management was enraged. They were furious about the bad publicity it would bring. Weiss had grown tired of Martin's antics and felt he was a negative influence on other players. He did not

(From left to right) Mickey Mantle, Billy Martin, Hank Bauer, and Hank Bauer's wife stand outside the New York City Criminal Courts building in 1957, following the grand jury's clearance of Bauer of assault charges at the Copacabana nightclub. (AP Images)

want to think that maybe Ford and Mantle were the negative influences. Even though a grand jury absolved all players involved of any wrongdoing, Weiss fined everyone who was there. And even though they all swore that Martin had nothing to do with what went down, Weiss used it as an excuse to finally get rid of him. Martin was traded to the Kansas City Athletics a few weeks after the melee.

Martin's trade did nothing to stop the antics of Ford and Mantle, who kept the party going for years. During a late-season 1963 game in Baltimore, Mantle rode the bench to recover from a vicious night of partying. Down 4–1 in the eighth, Mantle was sent up to pinch hit with a runner on. He homered into the left-field bleachers, making it a one-run game. The Yankees would go on to score two more that inning and win 5–4. Mantle's shot became known as the "hangover homer." Mike McCormick, the Orioles pitcher who gave up the shot, would hear for the rest of his career that "even the drunks can hit home runs off of you."

In Jane Leavy's biography of Mantle, *The Last Boy*, she includes a story from Detroit Tigers pitcher Mickey Lolich about when a Tigers trainer tried to keep Mantle and Ford from being of any use to the team for the next day's game. The trainer went out with both Ford and Mantle the night before an afternoon game. They stayed out until 2:30 AM at which point the trainer bought a bottle of vodka and brought it back to the hotel for all three to share. Mantle and Ford continued partying until 6:30 AM. It appeared the trainer's sabotage had worked. But it was all for naught. "The next day," Lolich said, "Whitey pitched nine innings of shutout ball, and Mantle hit two home runs."

Shortly after the Copa incident spelled the end of Martin, Ryne Duren made his way onto the scene. A pitcher with a blazing fastball, Duren had similarities to the movie character Ricky "Wild Thing" Vaughn from *Major League*. He had the glasses, the heat, and the ability to throw the ball 10 feet from home plate. Duren also drank *a lot*. And when he did, he was a bad person to be around. On a train ride in 1958, the Yankees celebrated clinching the pennant. Duren slapped a cigar out of the hand of coach Ralph Houk, who responded by punching Duren in the face. Duren, who died in 2011, eventually sobered up and became a vigorous advocate of helping other people do the same.

Eighteen years after the Copa incident, Martin returned to the Yankees as manager. The Bronx Zoo years were tumultuous ones for the team. Martin feuded with George Steinbrenner and Jackson constantly. Despite leading the team to two pennants and a championship, Martin was on thin ice halfway through the 1978 season. Then an alcohol-induced tirade led to his departure when he referred to Jackson as a "born liar" and Steinbrenner as a "convicted" liar. Less than a year after those remarks, Martin returned to manage the Yankees for a second time. After the 1979 season was over, Martin got into an altercation with a marshmallow salesman in Minnesota. Both men's accounts differ, but there was no denying the 20 stitches to the salesman's lip, and Steinbrenner fired Martin for the second of five times.

The 1980s saw a slew of late-night alcohol-fueled incidents. Though they occurred outside of New York City on consecutive nights in 1985, Yankees Dale Berra and Don Mattingly were both arrested for public urination outside the same Kansas City establishment. That same year saw the fourth return of Martin as manager. While Martin nearly took the team to the postseason in 1985, two incidents on back-to-back September nights in Baltimore sealed his fate. On the first night, Martin was having beers at the bar of the team hotel, the Cross Keys Inn. He bought a bottle of champagne for a recently married couple. But as the drinks flowed, the groom and Martin got into it. The groom accused Martin of saying his bride had a potbelly. Martin retorted, "I did not say she had a potbelly." Martin then pointed to another woman at the bar and clarified, "I said, 'she had a fat ass.'" The two went outside to sort things, but the groom did not follow suit, leaving Martin to fight another day.

Turns out that day *was* the very next night. Pitcher Ed Whitson was drowning his sorrows with a few drinks. Whitson had been a much hyped free-agent signing in the offseason, but he'd pitched poorly during the year. The fans were unmerciful in their treatment toward him, taunting him and leaving tacks under the tires of his car. Martin and Whitson had not gotten along all season, but as Martin went into the bar that night, he saw Whitson in an altercation with a fan from New York. Martin went over to try to help Whitson, telling him he didn't need the trouble. Whitson responded by turning on Martin, and the two engaged in shoving and fighting that eventually led out into the lobby. At that point Whitson kicked Martin in the groin. An infuriated Martin told Whitson he was going to kill him, and the fight actually spilled out onto the concrete in front of the hotel entrance. As the police were arriving, the scuffle was broken up, and both players were escorted back to their rooms in separate elevators. As fate would have it, Martin and Whitson ended up leaving their elevators at the same time on the same floor, and the fight continued.

Martin ended up with a broken arm and was let go after the season ended. Whitson performed so poorly in 1986 that he began only appearing on the road. He was traded to the San Diego Padres at midseason. Martin returned, however, for a fifth time in 1988. Things seemed to be going well. The team had a great April, jumping out in front of the pack, and he stayed out of trouble...until Martin got ejected from a Friday night game in Texas, eventually heading out to meet up with Mantle at a strip club in Dallas. Martin stayed after everyone had left and eventually got into a fight with someone in the men's room. Martin was beaten badly. He might nearly have gotten away with the incident, but due to a hotel fire alarm having gone off, all of the guests were outside when he got back. Martin's behavior grew worse from there as he kicked dirt on two different umpires during the course of a few weeks and threw dirt into the chest of another. Although the Yankees were in first place for most of the first two-and-a-half months of the season, Steinbrenner fired Martin a fifth and final time in late June.

In the spring of 1989, Rickey Henderson caused a stir when he said the Yankees missed the playoffs in '88 because the team drank too much. Henderson's comments did not go over well with his teammates. Many disagreed with both what he said and that he said it. When team officials indicated that some of the offenders were no longer with the team, it made matters worse, considering how many people the Yankees had parted ways with in the offseason. "I don't like the fact that people might think it was the reason they traded me," said pitcher Rick Rhoden, whom the team had dealt to the Houston Astros. "I don't think it's fair to me. I'm sure Jack Clark's not happy about it or anybody who's not there this year. I don't want people speculating that I have a drinking problem, which I don't."

Others had a different perspective. "I hated him for three of our months, but I'm not mad at Rickey because what he said made me think. When I started getting help, I thought, *I have to thank the guy. He might have saved my life*," pitcher Neil Allen told then-Yankees beat writer Michael Kay. Not long after Henderson's remarks, Allen gave up drinking, which he said had ruined his life. Henderson may have been proven correct when during airplane flights in the 1989 season a group of inebriated players began tearing apart the airplane seats, throwing food and playing cards, and harassing the flight attendants.

The late '80s and early '90s brought a reminder though of just how dangerous all that partying could be. On Christmas Day of 1989, Martin and a friend had stopped by a local bar for a few drinks. They eventually headed back to Martin's house. Just short of the driveway, the car crashed, killing Martin. He was only 61. Six years later, Mantle's years of drinking finally caught up with him. He underwent a liver transplant (controversial for how quickly he was able to find a donor) and was diagnosed with liver cancer. Shortly before his death, Mantle warned kids about living the way he had, telling them, "Don't be like me." On August 13, 1995, he died at the age of 63.

In the early and mid-1990s, the team mostly avoided headlines about partying. Then along came David Wells. Here is how Wells, in his own words, saw New York: "Here in Manhattan we've got sports bars, cigar bars, sushi bars, and titty bars, and music, and theater, and Letterman, and Howard Stern, and Ten's, and Papaya Kings, and Veruka, and the China Club, and 10 million *other* distractions that'll keep a boy smiling 'til dawn.'" The burly left-handed pitcher was known for his vocal personality, hard-living ways, and outstanding ability to throw strikes. On Sunday, May 17, 1998, against the Minnesota Twins at Yankee Stadium, Wells threw a perfect game. In his 2003 autobiography, Wells admitted he had pitched the game hungover. "As of this writing, 15 men in the history of organized baseball have ever thrown a perfect game. Only ONE of those men did it half-drunk, with bloodshot eyes, monster breath, and a raging, skull-rattling hangover," Wells wrote. "That would be me." When Wells was traded to the Toronto Blue Jays before the start of the '99 season, David Cone, not a stranger himself to the late-night scene, quipped, "There are going to be a lot of bars going out of business in New York." Wells returned to the Bronx in 2002 at the insistence of Steinbrenner. The Boss loved Wells, even though the two almost went at it in 1997 when Wells said the stadium needed more security to prevent fans from interfering with the play, and Steinbrenner told Wells to just worry about his pitching.

In September of 2002 after staying up all night at a bar, Wells went to grab a 5 AM breakfast at an Upper East Side diner. After ordering, Wells and another patron, Rocco Graziosa, exchanged words. According to Wells, he went over to Graziosa's table and told him enough was enough. At that point Graziosa allegedly stood up and sucker punched Wells in the face, knocking two teeth out. Wells placed a call to 9-1-1 in which he sounded disoriented and was slurring his words.

The Yankees were not pleased with the incident, especially Joe Torre, who claims in *The Yankee Years* that Wells later lied to him about where he had been that night and at what time. Naturally, the incident had no impact on Wells' performance as he went on to win his remaining three starts of the year, giving up only five runs in 22 innings. Graziosa was later convicted of assaulting Wells.

Derek Jeter never fit the label of a Martin, Mantle, or Wells-type partier. He'd avoided the negative headlines nearly his entire career. But even he wasn't immune to the allure of the city that never sleeps, at least according to Steinbrenner. "How much better would he be if he didn't have all his other activities?" The Boss told the *New York Daily News* in December of 2002. "I tell him this all the time. I say, 'Jetes, you can't be everything to everybody. You've got to focus on what's important. When I read in the paper that he's out until 3 AM in New York City, going to a birthday party, I won't lie. That doesn't sit well with me."

Steinbrenner's comments caused a media frenzy, not just because they came from The Boss, but because they were directed at someone who had basically never been attacked in all his time with New York. When Jeter responded by saying he wasn't going to change his lifestyle (which many people would have said wasn't filled with much partying anyway), the press got even more out of the story, with the *Daily News* running a headline that read, "PARTY ON."

Instead of letting the controversy get the better of them, though, Jeter and Steinbrenner deftly spun it into a positive when later that year they filmed a Visa commercial lampooning the whole incident. The Boss calls Jeter into his office to ask how Jeter can afford to spend so much time doing things other than playing baseball. Jeter holds up a Visa card. At the end the two join a conga line inside a nightclub.

4

The Times They
Are a Changin'

"Give me your tired, your poor, Your huddled masses yearning to breathe free…" So says a plaque located inside the pedestal of Statue of Liberty, one of the first sights many immigrants saw as they approached the final leg of their journey to America. For millions New York City became their destination. During the late 19th and early 20th centuries, nearly 17 million immigrants made their way through the city. While certain ethnicities came in greater numbers, no one area of the world failed to be represented by this new cast of Americans, including Germans, Russians, Chinese, Japanese, Polish, and Italians. Many of these groups settled into their own areas, and while many assimilated to certain American customs and attitudes, each retained their own ethnic pride and traditions.

Though some of these enclaves still exist in some form throughout the city, the landscape has significantly changed in that it is not nearly as ethnically defined as it once was. Once a vibrant bustling place home to thousands of Italian immigrants, Little Italy has now been reduced to a single city block made up mostly of shops and restaurants. The Yankees have changed and adapted in much the same way New York has over the years. The men in pinstripes have been a close reflection of the changing neighborhoods and social attitudes in the city that evolved throughout the 20th century. In this area the Yankees perhaps best explain New York.

In the early and middle part of the 20th century, the Yankees showcased much of the pride of the Italian American community. Italians had immigrated to the United States en masse from 1880–1920 with some 4.1 million taking the boat ride over. Approximately 340,000 remained in New York, and settled in all parts of the city—with the largest enclave being in East Harlem. The most famous section of the city to be inhabited by a large Italian community was named Little Italy. Located in southern Manhattan on Mulberry Street and stretching out in all directions, Little Italy was home to thousands of Italian immigrants in the early 20th century. Many maintained their own culture, language, and traditions, giving the area a genuine feel of being home or at least as genuine as possible.

Many of Little Italy's inhabitants found themselves rooting for the Yankees. In the 1920s and early '30s, it was Tony Lazzeri that helped draw Italians to the team. "Tony Lazzeri was the first great Yankee of Italian heritage," wrote Marty Appel in *Pinstripe Dynasty*. "He was, almost overnight, the second most popular player on the team [next to Ruth], and wherever the Yankees traveled, Italian American clubs would hold banquets in the rookie's honor."

In 1936 the greatest and most well known Italian American to ever don a baseball uniform popped up in the Bronx. The eighth of nine children of an Italian fisherman, Joe DiMaggio was straight out of central casting for a ballplayer. With his toothy grin and angular face, he wasn't especially good looking, but he looked good in a baseball uniform—like he was born to wear it. He strode the vast confines of center field at Yankee Stadium with grace and elegance. He even seemed classy when he swung and missed, which wasn't that often. (In 13 seasons he struck out just 369 times, an average of 34 a year. Mark Reynolds, whom the Yankees acquired in the 2013 season, once struck out 434 times over the course of two seasons.) Even his name, Joe DiMaggio, sounded perfect.

He was given nicknames like "Joltin' Joe" and the "Yankee Clipper." Les Brown and his orchestra recorded a song about him, "Joltin' Joe DiMaggio," in 1941. "He started baseball's famous streak that's got us all aglow," went the catchy tune. "He's just a man and not a freak—Joltin' Joe DiMaggio." Nearly three decades later, Paul Simon wrote about a country longing for heroes in a time of unrest when he penned the words, "Where have you gone, Joe DiMaggio? A nation turns its lonely eyes to you." "Mrs. Robinson" is the name of the classic song.

All the descriptors, though, still can't live up to his play on the field. In his first seven seasons, he never drove in fewer than 114 runs. He hit below .323 only once in that period. For his career, DiMaggio won three MVP awards, led the league in home runs and batting average twice, and was an All-Star in every single season in which he played. He hit below .300 only twice—the first season back after serving in the army and his last when he was hobbled by injuries. He played in 10 World Series, winning all but one of them. DiMaggio's 56-game hitting streak, accomplished in 1941, is considered one of baseball's most unbreakable records. It's even more remarkable when you consider that after his streak was snapped—thanks to two great plays by Cleveland Indians third baseman Ken Keltner—DiMaggio then began a 16-game hitting streak. DiMaggio ended up winning the MVP that season over Ted Williams, who hit .406 that year.

DiMaggio's career statistics don't do him justice. He finished far short of any of the benchmark achievements like 3,000 hits or 500 home runs. But he lost three years due to service during World War II, and his career was cut short at age 36 by injuries. So his statistics are actually all the more amazing when you consider he did them in just 13 seasons. For a 162-game schedule, DiMaggio averaged 34 home runs, 143 RBIs, and a .325 batting average during his career.

All of it—the statistics, the nicknames, the grace—was a source of pride to the Italian American community. They lavished him with praise and worshipped him as a hero. "A hulking driver named Peanuts would drive a Cadillac with JOE D-5 on the license plate to [DiMaggio's] Manhattan apartment and transport him to the worshipful Italian American community in Newark, N.J., where he got free haircuts, free meals, and priceless adulation for just being his silent self," wrote Jim Kaplan of the *Vineyard Gazette*. And like many of his heritage, he had to deal with the stereotypes of Italians that were prominent in the day. Early in his career, a reporter for *Life Magazine* described DiMaggio in this manner: "Instead of olive oil or smelly bear grease, he keeps his hair slick with water. He never reeks of garlic and prefers chicken chow mein to spaghetti."

But the insults only further endeared him to the community, who came to view DiMaggio as a shining example of what Italians could achieve. "Because of DiMaggio the Italian kids I knew were Yankee fans, almost all of them," wrote sportswriter Charles P. Pierce. "Their fathers and grandfathers had been Yankee fans, and they were Yankee fans." Moreover, DiMaggio's on-field

A three-time MVP, Joe DiMaggio was a hero to the burgeoning Italian American community in New York. (AP Images)

performance actually helped during a time when, thanks largely to the war in Europe, sentiment toward Italian Americans was not great. "DiMaggio's story was just so very important in terms of dispelling a lot of the myths and stereotypes about Italians," said David Kaplan, director of the Yogi Berra Museum in Montclair, New Jersey. DiMaggio helped make the path a little easier for future generations of Italian American players like Phil Rizzuto and Yogi Berra. (Berra grew up in a section of St. Louis derisively known as "Dago Hill.") Despite growing up right next to Ebbets Field, Joe Pepitone idolized DiMaggio, thanks largely to a shared Italian heritage.

DiMaggio was the first ballplayer to ever make more than $100,000 in a season, and his holdouts were legendary. Yet the money did not take away from his working class, everyman kind of status. "Joe DiMaggio was an inspiration to all the strugglers of his day," said former New York governor Mario Cuomo, who was both of Italian heritage and a pretty good ballplayer in his day. "He showed America would make a place for true excellence whatever its color, accent, or origin."

DiMaggio certainly wasn't perfect. He was extremely protective of his image and legacy—perhaps too much so. Shortly after his retirement, he insisted on being introduced as the "greatest living ballplayer," something that was not only overly arrogant but also simply not true. (Willie Mays anyone?) He was not overly friendly or trusting, rarely granting interviews. He could often be surly and maintained a very small circle of close friends. "DiMaggio took pride in avoiding controversy at all costs," wrote Pete Golenbock in his book *Dynasty*. "He knew instinctively when he was becoming involved in a conversation or a situation that would reflect negatively upon him, and his guard would always be up. He was suspicious of strangers, aloof, closemouthed, and standoffish. This was his best protection against a prying outside world."

Fortunately for him, DiMaggio came before the 24–7 fishbowl of the modern era. "Today they'd destroy or at least impair DiMaggio and [Ted] Williams and Joe Louis by telling stories about their tax returns and their temper tantrums…And the Drudge Report would come up with an old girlfriend, who said she went with all three of them," Cuomo said. Those shortcomings wouldn't have mattered to New York's Italians. DiMaggio was their hero, a shining example of what someone of their heritage could achieve in America. "Joe DiMaggio was grace, the fulfillment of the American Dream. That's why I keep his picture on my wall. And I'm going to keep it there even if Drudge does a report," Cuomo said.

As the 1940s became the 1950s, the Yankees also began to resemble the city in another way: race relations. Here the Yankees track record can't be described as anything but abysmal. They were one of the last teams in baseball to integrate, and their failure to sign black and Latino ballplayers would come back to haunt them in the 1960s and '70s.

It should not be shocking that the Yankees' race relations were horrific. This is a team that featured backup outfielder Jake Powell who said during a 1938 radio interview that one of the benefits of his offseason job as an Ohio police officer was "cracking niggers over the head." On Opening Day in 1945, several black men walked around Yankee Stadium carrying picket signs reading, "IF WE CAN PAY, WHY CAN'T WE PLAY?" and "IF WE CAN STOP BULLETS, WHY NOT BALLS?" Yankees owner Larry MacPhail met with them, heard them out, and then completely ignored them. MacPhail, like most other owners in baseball at the time, had no interest in integrating his team either through his own racism, not wanting to deal with the problems that would come with integration, or both. The team did sign a few black players in 1949, but complications with the deals and other factors resulted in the acquisitions not coming to fruition.

Years went by, and the Yankees still did not have a single black player. In that time they passed on Willie Mays. As noted by Appel, Bill McCorry, the scout who passed on Mays, once said, "I don't care what he did today or any other day. I got no use for him or any of them. I wouldn't want any of them on a club I was with. I wouldn't arrange a berth on the train for any of them." In 1951 Jackie Robinson publicly stated that he felt the Yankees were deliberately excluding black ballplayers from the club. When

Yankees general manager George Weiss said the Yankees were merely looking for a player that would live up to Yankees standards, Robinson responded by saying, "bullshit."

In 1955 the Yankees finally integrated. By that time 12 of the 16 major league teams had done so. The first black player on the team was Elston Howard. He could play catcher, outfield, and even a little infield. Howard went on to become a nine-time All-Star and won the 1963 AL MVP. Had it not been for his premature death in 1980 at the age of 51, he may well have become the Yankees' first black manager.

Although many of Howard's teammates easily welcomed him to the clubhouse, the transition wasn't necessarily smooth. The Yankees played several spring training games in the South, and local laws often prevented Howard from staying in the same hotels as the rest of his teammates. The Yankees were set to play a spring game in Birmingham, Alabama, but local ordinance forbid white players to play against black players. Rather than cancel the game and forfeit the thousands the team would make, something the Braves had done earlier, Weiss told Howard to stay home. Sometimes that home setting wasn't much better. When Howard attempted to live in Teaneck, New Jersey, his house was spray-painted with racial epithets.

The Yankees were also slow to move on Latin American players. "For the entire length of Roberto Clemente's career—1955 to 1972—the Bombers had only eight Latin ballplayers of any significance and no more than two at a time," wrote journalist Steve Wulf. "Even as late as '86, as the Hispanic population in New York City was exploding, the Yankees had no Latinos in the regular lineup and only one [Alfonso Pulido] on the pitching staff."

Ultimately, the Yankees paid a steep price for their failure to integrate. Their unwillingness to do so not only led other teams to snatch up some of the greatest talent to ever play the game, but it also shifted the balance of power from the Yankees and the American League to the National League. As Appel noted, "While National League teams had been signing African American players the caliber of Mays, Aaron, Banks, McCovey, Gibson, Frank Robinson, Billy Williams, Lou Brock, Ferguson Jenkins, and Willie Stargell and dark-skinned Latino stars like Clemente, Orlando Cepeda, Juan Marichal, Tony Perez, and more, the American League wasn't even close. The Yankees had let all those players get away." Al Downing, who pitched for the Yankees from 1961–1969 echoed Appel's comments. "Not that we weren't getting good players, but we weren't getting premier players," Downing said. "And when you look at what was going on in the National League, in the '60s especially, African American and Latino players were taking over the leagues."

Part of the reason the Yankees failed to integrate was the belief that black ballplayers would bring more black fans to the game, scaring away more affluent white fans. "I will never allow a black man to wear a Yankee uniform," an inebriated Weiss once said, according to Golenbock's *Dynasty*. "Box holders from Westchester don't want that sort of crowd. They would be offended to have to sit with niggers." While the Yankees slowly and finally embraced (some might say accepted) integration, the team certainly did not catch up with a speed that matched the changing Bronx neighborhood. In 1940 1.37 million of the 1.39 million people who lived in the Bronx were white. By 1970 that number shrank to 1.08 million out of 1.47 million, a drop of nearly 25 percent.

New York itself has never been a hotbed for civil rights. During the Civil War, the city was actually home to many who empathized with the Confederacy or who at least didn't think ending slavery was worth all the bloodshed. During the draft riots of 1863, white mobs specifically targeted blacks on the streets of the city, lynching nearly a dozen.

As more and more immigrants established themselves in the city, they came to see blacks as competitors for jobs and a threat to their livelihood. Race-related violence was not uncommon particularly in Harlem. When the civil rights movement gained momentum during the 1950s and '60s, racial turmoil continued to rock cities throughout the country. New York and the surrounding area was no exception. Two of the countries' worst race riots happened within a three-year span just five miles apart: one in New York City in 1964 and one in Newark, New Jersey, in 1967.

On July 16, 1964, 15-year-old James Powell of the Bronx was shot and killed by a white police officer in Harlem. The officer claimed that Powell had raised a knife at him while witnesses said no knife was there and Powell's raising of the arm was merely to fend off the impending gun fire. There were protests in the immediate aftermath of the incident, but it wasn't until after Powell's funeral that things turned violent. Groups of angry people—fed up over what they felt was constant abuse by the police force—began pelting officers with various objects. The rioting continued for nearly a week, costing approximately $1 million in damages and acting as the catalyst for other violent uprisings that happened throughout the country that year.

The largest city in New Jersey and visible from most tall buildings in New York, Newark had tensions that had been brewing for some time. Despite being home to a large black community, as noted by *The* (Newark) *Star-Ledger*, "Nearly every authority figure in the city was white—from police, whose reputation for brutality was notorious among the black community, to teachers, to City Hall bureaucrats." There always seemed to be plans in place to displace low-income black homeowners to make room for a new highway, building, or whatever was deemed more important than the homes of people living in that community. According to the Hughes Commission, the jobless rate among 16–19-year-old black men was nearly 38 percent, meaning almost a third were out of work.

Newark had avoided the kinds of violence that had broken out in many of the country's cities the last few years. But that changed on July 12, 1967. That evening two white police officers arrested a black cab driver, John W. Smith, for improperly passing them. Smith was eventually badly beaten in police custody with the cops claiming he'd resisted arrest. Smith survived, but rumors began circulating that a black cab driver had been beaten to death by the police. That was enough for many in the community, who showed up at the police precinct and began hurling objects at the building. The next night a handful of people actually charged the precinct itself, and that's when the looting began in the city's central ward. Stores were ransacked, TVs and other goods stolen, and windows were destroyed. Some store owners spray-painted "Soul" or "Soul Brother" on their windows, hoping that by indicating the store was owned by blacks, it would prevent looters.

The state police were called in and eventually so was the National Guard. The rioting spread from the central ward to downtown Newark. Chaos turned to violence. Believing that snipers were firing on them, officers would return the shots. For nearly a week, chunks of Newark resembled a war zone with trashed stores, garbage-strewn streets, fires, and random gun shots. The rioting and looting, one of the most extensive and deadly at the time, led to more than $10 million in damages (it would be about seven times that today) and left 26 people dead.

The riots were reflective of changing social attitudes in the country. The 1960s had commenced, and changes were about to alter the city (and country) forever. It's hard to pinpoint an exact moment when the '60s, as it has come to be known, actually started in the Big Apple. But February 7, 1964 is as good a date as any. On that day, four mop-top musicians from England set down at New York's John F. Kennedy airport. The Beatles had come to America.

Consisting of John Lennon, Paul McCartney, George Harrison, and Ringo Starr, the group had grown up in England, and the band started initially through mutual friendships between Lennon and McCartney. Eventually Harrison, playing the role of younger, annoying brother, joined in. The band went from the Quarrymen to The Beatles, swapping out members here and there with Ringo replacing Pete Best on drums. They went on tour in Europe, becoming especially popular in Germany. Eventually they caught the eye of Brian Epstein, who'd helped run his family's successful music retail store in Liverpool. Epstein saw something in them that others did not, became their manager, and through some clever marketing, was able to make the band a sensation in England in 1963.

Already hugely successful in England, Epstein's decision to bring them to the states brought their stardom to another level.

When they landed at JFK on that cold winter day, it was an international event. Thousands of teenagers braved the cold to stand on the runway waiting for them to land. The press conference afterward was a coup. The group answered questions with cheeky British humor, making clear that they were growing tired of the same old questions about their hair style and how long they felt the party would last for them. Some responses would have sounded standoffish coming from someone else, but the four of them easily charmed the hundreds of press that had gathered there.

Two days later they made their first appearance on *The Ed Sullivan Show*, the premier entertainment show of the era. An appearance on the show, broadcast out of a studio on Broadway between 53rd and 54th Streets in Manhattan, could be a career maker. Sullivan, himself, was no fan of the new genre. But he knew ratings gold when he saw it, and The Beatles didn't disappoint. Their appearance was one of the single most watched television events in history. They performed just five songs over two different sets, the first one featuring "All My Loving," "Till There Was You," and "She Loves You," and the second featuring "I Saw Her Standing There" and "I Want To Hold Your Hand." Their playing could barely be heard over the screaming of girls (and women) in the audience. It was clear: The Beatles were a hit in America.

A year and a half later, the Fab Four played on outdoor concert at the new home of the New York Mets, Shea Stadium. To play a venue that large, 56,000 seats, was nearly unheard of. Almost no one at the show actually heard their performance due to the incessant screaming of the crowd and the poor quality of the sound system. The Beatles performed for only 30 minutes that night. But their show remains a part of music lore. Years later Paul McCartney, one of two surviving members of the band, played the first concert at the Mets' new venue, Citi Field. The hysteria surrounding The Beatles, the emerging civil rights movement, and the violent racial strife signaled a changing era both in the nation and in New York. Soon enough the labor movement joined the shifting times.

On New Year's Day in 1966, the city's transit workers went on strike, resulting in a shutdown of the train system. Their contract had run out, and the new mayor, John Lindsay, had run as a candidate who would fight back against the emerging power of the unions. The day he was sworn into office, the strike began. The strike could not have come at a worse time, occurring in the middle of winter. It lasted 12 days before a settlement was reached. The unions attained a pay raise as well as other benefits but suffered a blow when their leader, Mike Quill, died of a heart attack before the month was over. The strike showed what the power of organized labor could do in the city and that they would have to be dealt with despite the politicians' tough talk. In the next few years, teachers would strike, the most famous of these occurring in 1968 and lasting months. The '70s saw strikes from policemen and newspapers. Working people were making their voices heard.

The '60s had already seen its share of turbulence, but there was one more group that had had enough. All they needed was a spark to ignite them. The gay community had to exist largely in the closet in 1969. An emerging gay advocacy community popped up in San Francisco, which had grown into a more tolerant area in the country. But nearly everywhere else, to be openly gay was to invite ridicule and even violence into your life. Countless individuals, fearing being disowned by their families, mocked by their friends, or attacked by strangers, felt no choice but to hide who they were.

New York City had a large gay community centered mostly in Greenwich Village, an area located south of 14th Street between the Hudson River and Broadway in lower Manhattan. The Village was a vibrant place with plenty of bars, quaint stores, and up and coming artists. But even within their own community, gay men and women had to remain largely out of sight and out of mind from the general public. Unlike most minority groups, they had no one lobbying for them in City Hall or up in Albany, New York, and there was certainly no organized effort to fight for the rights of gay men and women.

The New York City police, knowing they'd essentially be held unaccountable for their actions, severely harassed the community for years. Gay bars, because of the clientele, were not granted liquor licenses by the state of the New York. Without the license the bars couldn't legally serve patrons, so they had to run as illegal operations. The police were well aware of this catch-22 and used it to shake down and harass bars and their customers.

On June 27, 1969, the gay community finally decided it had had enough of the harassment. That night cops had raided a West Village bar on Christopher Street called the Stonewall Inn. As those arrested were being rounded up, one shouted to the crowd, "Why don't you guys do something?" So the crowd became rowdy and resistant. Over the next six days, a series of confrontations and rebellions occurred between police and locals. As described by Garance Franke-Ruta in *The Atlantic*, what eventually became known as the Stonewall Uprising included: fire hoses turned on people in the street, barricades thrown, Rockette-style kick lines conducted in front of the police, firebombs thrown into the bar, a gun tossed at the mob by a police officer, windows smashed, and parking meters uprooted. Along with gay cheerleaders chanting bawdy songs, protesters chanted: "Occupy—take over, take over," "Fag power," "Liberate the bar," "We're the pink panthers,"and "We Shall Overcome." Policemen became angry and frightened, and one was even hit in the head by a drag queen's purse.

Stonewall became a rallying cry for gay men and women across the country. It was the first instance of massive resistance by gays toward authority figures. It is widely viewed as the single most important moment in sparking what soon became the gay rights liberation movement. As the social mood changed and sex, drugs, and rock and roll took hold of the nation, the atmosphere of the Yankees clubhouse changed with it. The Yankees had their share of pranksters and partiers over the years. But drinks and jokes did not mean a liberal atmosphere. On the contrary the Yankees leaned more toward the conservative side in dress, in buzz cuts, in just about everything. Aside from their late-night escapades, the team didn't do anything outside of the social norms. That began to change, however, in 1963 with the emergence of three players: Pepitone, Phil Linz, and Jim Bouton. Each brought their own distinct personality and flavor to New York and changed the social construction of the clubhouse.

Pepitone was born and raised in Brooklyn, a true New Yorker through and through. In his senior year of high school, he was shot in the chest by a friend showing off a .38. He recovered, and it did not impact his playing career, which was fortunate given how much talent he had. He spent some time with the club in 1962 but was there to stay in '63. In his first four full seasons, Pepitone averaged 26 home runs and 84 RBIs. He became one of the few Yankees to ever hit a grand slam in the World Series with a shot in the 1964 series against the St. Louis Cardinals.

Pepitone was a talent on the field and what some might describe as a pretty boy off it. "Tall, swarthy, and handsome in a sinister way, Pepitone was a Yankee matinee idol, dressing in tight-fitting pegged pants and see-through shirts," Golenbock wrote in *Dynasty*. "The women—young, old, tall, short, fat, and thin—flocked to Yankee Stadium to watch him play—Joe loved to live and lived to love and he was not shy about getting his loving wherever and whenever he could get it."

Few players took greater care in their personal appearance than the Yankee first baseman. Pepitone etched his place in Yankee history when he introduced a new tool into the clubhouse: a hair dryer. It was a site to see: this young kid from Brooklyn blow-drying his hair in the clubhouse bathroom. At the time men just didn't do that, and players didn't know how to react. Mickey Mantle decided to have some fun. "I was dressed up to go to the Copacabana after a game, and Mantle put hair powder in my hair dryer, and the next thing I know, I couldn't go to the Copacabana anymore," said Pepitone with a laugh. But Joe would have his revenge. "The next day I put bubble bath in his Jacuzzi, so when he turned it on he turned into Mr. Bubbles." Pepitone, still a free spirit who loves to share a good story with a chuckle, also recalled how his first roommate, Moose Skowron, warned him that if Pepitone was not back in their room by 10 PM, he was locking the door on him. Sure enough, Pepitone came back one night at three in the morning, and Skowron would not let him in.

In an ironic twist, Pepitone, who took such good care of his hair, ended up having to wear a toupee as his career moved on. He lasted with the Yankees until 1969 when the team grew tired of his eccentricities. He spent the last few years of his career shuffling between the Houston Astros, Chicago Cubs, and Atlanta Braves. He wrote an autobiography, *Joe, You Coulda Made Us Proud*, with the title poking fun at the belief that his hard-living ways and questionable work ethic stunted his baseball potential. But even to this day, Pepitone is still a favorite at Old Timer's Day.

Linz was a quirky fella from Baltimore. A backup player, he never appeared in more than 112 games in a season with New York. He marched to a different beat. Oddly enough, though, the incident Linz is most remembered for is one in which he wasn't trying to pull a prank. In the midst of the 1964 season, the Yankees were leaving Comiskey Park on their way to the airport. They'd just lost their fourth game in a row, and the mood on the team bus was downcast to say the least. In the midst of the glumness, Linz pulled out a harmonica and sheet music for "Mary Had A Little Lamb." It was the only song Linz knew on the instrument, and he just barely knew it. As he began playing, manager Yogi Berra, sitting in the front of the bus, turned and said to knock it off. There are varying descriptions of what happened next, but according to some, when Linz asked what Berra had said, Mantle told him Berra had said to play it louder. Linz kept playing. An enraged Berra marched to the back of the bus to confront Linz, who tossed his instrument at Yogi. Berra swatted it away, deflecting it right into the knee of Pepitone. Ever the comedian, Pepitone fell to the ground in mock pain, screaming how much his knee hurt. Linz and Berra exchanged words before Berra returned to his seat. The incident has become part of Yankees legend, cementing Linz forever in the minds of fans. Unfortunately for Berra, Yankees management saw it only as an example of him losing control over the team and used it as part of their decision to let him go after the 1964 season.

A true intellectual, Bouton was different from many players. He read, he wrote, he articulated. "If you were on a bus, a team bus going to some…airport or something like that and you were reading a book, they called you the professor," Bouton said. Unlike many of his teammates, the pitcher wasn't disgusted or upset with the hippies and the anti-war protestors. He looked at things from their point of view. "These kids...are genuinely concerned about what's going on around them," Bouton said. "They're concerned about Vietnam, poor people, black people. They're concerned about the way things are and they're trying to change them."

Bouton was a talented player who won 21 games and posted an ERA of 2.53 in 1963. In three World Series starts for the Yankees between 1963 and '64, he was 2–1 with 1.48 ERA and a complete game. Arm troubles later derailed his career, but it wasn't Bouton's pitching arm that brought him everlasting fame. It was his writing hand. During the 1969 season, some teammates started to notice Bouton keeping a diary. They didn't think much of it. Turns out Bouton wasn't keeping a diary so much as making notes. He had agreed to write a no-holds-barred description of life during a baseball season. The book, *Ball Four*, published in 1970, detailed Bouton's previous year pitching for the Seattle Pilots and Astros, but it also went into intricate detail on his time with the Yankees. And it hit the majors like a thunderbolt.

Bouton talked about things no player had ever discussed publicly. He wrote about players "beaver shooting," which "can be anything from peering over the top of the dugout to look up dresses to hanging from the fire escape on the 20th floor of some hotel to look into a window." "I've known ballplayers who thought it was great fun to turn on a tape recorder under the bed while they were making it with their latest broad and play it back on the bus to the ballpark the next day," he wrote. Bouton described how players categorized groupies and what action was appropriate with whom. "It's not bad form to wine and dine an attractive stew...a stew can come under the heading of class stuff, or table pussy, in comparison with some of the other creatures who are camp-followers or celebrity-fuckers called Baseball Annies."

He mentioned players taking pills. "Greenies are pep pills—dextroamphetamine sulfate—and a lot of baseball players couldn't function without them," Bouton said. He ridiculed coaches, saying they were essentially useless. "The manager was usually...some former player who everybody liked. And then he chose a coaching staff made up of basically his drinking buddies," Bouton said. He talked about Pepitone's vanity, describing how he would carry around all sorts of hair products in a little blue bag. In one section he described how Whitey Ford used to scuff the ball, something that is forbidden by the rules of the game.

But many felt the worst aspect of the book was the way he described Mantle. Though Bouton did discuss several positive memories, he also painted a picture of the Mick that made him sound like nothing more than an alcoholic, woman-chasing, kid-hating partier. He talked about times when Mantle refused to give autographs to kids—shutting a bus window on them in one case—and how Mantle wouldn't sign autographs in the clubhouse before games, instead enlisting a clubhouse assistant, Pete Previte, to do it. "So there are thousands of baseballs around the country that have been signed not by Mickey Mantle, but by Pete Previte," Bouton wrote. Mantle was named as a beaver shooter and prankster extraordinaire. Because Mantle was idolized in New York, what Bouton said about him was considered blasphemy and resented by those who wanted to think of the Mick as a flawless hero.

It is hard to imagine now the idea that saying players were skirt-chasing partiers would be controversial. These guys weren't angels. They were young men with money, fame, and time to kill in America's biggest city. But back then most of that extracurricular activity stayed private. "They didn't have the access I had and they had been sort of pushing, you know, a milk and cookies Boy Scout kind of view of players," Bouton said. Reporters were aware of what went on but rarely said a word about it. The players certainly never discussed it. But entertainment standards were changing. Movies began featuring nudity and vulgarity. TV shows like *Laugh In*, *All in the Family*, and *The Smothers Brothers Comedy Hour* began making political statements through satire. And now Bouton had broken down the walls of the clubhouse, exposing the world to the male athlete culture.

Ball Four began a trend of autobiographies by active players that didn't pull any punches. In future years Yankees like Sparky Lyle, Graig Nettles, Don Baylor, Phil Niekro, Dave Winfield,

David Wells, and Joe Torre would all write detailed books on their time in New York. Bouton paid a price for his writing acumen. Teammates shunned him, and the Yankees cut off all ties with him for decades. Eventually Bouton was welcomed back, but *Ball Four* had made its permanent mark in Yankees history, and nothing was going to alter that.

One of the bigger social changes as the 1960s moved into the '70s involved the American family. Thanks to television shows like *Leave It To Beaver*, the typical American family became defined as a working husband, a stay-at-home mom, two kids, a dog, and a white picket fence. But the '60s changed all that. The emerging women's liberation movement advocated the working woman instead of the stay-at-home wife. Divorce was no longer considered taboo. Birth control became more acceptable and more available. And a new craze entered the lives of married couples: swinging.

Practicing an open relationship, couples would seek out other couples with whom to have intimate relationships. In some instances they would take it to the extreme and swap wives or husbands. Swinging (and swapping) was a fad, and on March 4, 1973, it landed smack dab in the middle of the Yankees clubhouse. On that day Yankees pitchers Fritz Peterson and Mike Kekich held separate press conferences to announce that they had been traded—to each other's families. The two friends were going to swap wives, kids, houses, *everything*. It has commonly been referred to as the biggest "trade" in Yankees history.

Peterson was an excellent left-handed starting pitcher for the Yankees during the late 1960s and early '70s. He won 20 games in 1970, and his 2.52 ERA was the lowest of any pitcher in the history of Yankee Stadium. Kekich was a reliever and sometimes starter who put up respectable numbers. His best season was 1972 when he won 10 games and had an ERA of 3.70. Peterson and Kekich became friends.

Peterson was always a bit of a free spirit. He once wrote a letter to former Yankee Moose Skowron on fake letterhead from the Baseball Hall of Fame, asking him to donate his pacemaker after he died. In the summer of '72, both Peterson and Kekich attended a party with their wives at the home of Yankees beat writer Maury Allen. "During the party we all had a couple of beers and were having a great time," Peterson recalled 40 years later to *The Palm Beach Post.* "When we were deciding to leave, we had driven two different cars and happened to park behind each other out in the street. I said to my wife, Marilyn, 'Why don't you ride with Mike to the diner in Fort Lee, New Jersey, and I'll take Susanne with me, and we'll meet there and then we'll go home from there.'"

A short time later, Kekich and Marilyn Peterson moved in together as did Peterson and Susanne Kekich. The arrangements were made permanent with each couples' two children staying with their mothers. The public and press did not know about it until the story broke in spring training. Both men initially did not think it was a big deal, but it became worldwide news. The Yankees treated the incident as a private matter, and new owner George Steinbrenner did not comment. Eventually, the friendship between Kekich and Peterson broke down due in part to the fact that the relationship between Kekich and Marilyn did not last long. Peterson and Susanne, however, flourished. They married shortly after the "trade" was made public and still remain together.

5

Instant Fame: Rags to Riches, New York Style

One of the many allures of New York City is the idea that anyone can fulfill the American Dream there. People can be born into poverty but through grit, hard work, and determination, they can achieve success. It's that allure that has brought millions of immigrants to the city over the centuries. The rags to riches story has been seen countless times in the Big Apple.

Lloyd Blankfein grew up the son of a postal worker in Brooklyn. He used to carry trays of soda as a concession vendor at Yankee Stadium. Working his way up through the system over several decades, Blankfein became the chairman of Goldman Sachs, one of the largest and most powerful investment banking firms in the world, in 2006. The guy who sold soft drinks has a net worth of more than $100 million.

Ursula Burns was raised by a single mother on the Lower East Side of Manhattan "when the gangs were there and the drug addicts were there," she later told *The New York Times*. Her mother made money by babysitting other kids and ironing clothes. After going to college, Burns joined Xerox as an intern in 1980. She quickly rose there and became the first African American female CEO of a Fortune 500 company. The woman, who was raised by a single mother in a bad neighborhood, has a corporate jet and earned over $1.1 million in salary, not including stock options, in 2012.

It's not just the money that comes from business, but also the fame that comes from the arts that lures people to New York. The city is the cultural and artistic epicenter of the world. Singers, writers, artists, actors, and dancers all come to make it big in New York City. Even those who have already achieved stardom gravitate to New York. John Lennon made the city his home for the last decade of his life, and some associate him more with New York than Liverpool.

Adam Sandler grew up the son of working class parents in Brooklyn, New York. Sandler's father, Stanley, was an electrical engineer, and his mother, Judy, was a nursery school teacher. His family is Jewish, descending from Russian immigrants on both sides. The Sandlers moved to New England when Sandler was young, and he spent his youth there, but he returned to New York City for college, attending New York University. It was working in New York, like so many other show business folks before him, where Sandler honed his talents as an entertainer. Eventually he became part of an emerging cast of new stars on *Saturday Night Live* in the early 1990s. He became a hit, especially with young viewers, particularly for his solo musical sketches during the Weekend Update segment. He parlayed his success on *SNL* into a movie career, which has produced a series of box-office winners. More than 25 years after fine-tuning his comedy at New York University, Sandler remains one of the wealthiest and most successful actors/comedians in the world.

The Yankees history is full of people who exemplify both aspects of making it in New York: those who come to achieve stardom and those who make their star burn even brighter. Babe Ruth was already among the game's stars before he came to New York. He had made a name for himself as both a great pitcher and baseball's premier hitter while playing for the Boston Red Sox. But it's with New York that the Babe established the single-season home run record, called his shot, and became the first athlete to score major product endorsements. Those kinds of opportunities were not coming to Ty Cobb in Detroit or Rogers Hornsby in St. Louis. Ruth was a guest conductor and made cameos in movies. His legend grew year after year thanks to tales like his having hit a home run for a boy in the hospital. Ruth did in fact write to 11-year-old Johnny Sylvester, who was sick in a New Jersey hospital after falling off a horse, saying he would hit a home run against the Cardinals in the 1926 World Series. Ruth actually went on to hit three that game, though the Yankees lost the series. (Ruth was thrown out trying to steal second base to end it.) The story took on a legendary status with false revisions, depicting Ruth at the bedside of a dying Johnny, promising him he would wallop a homer. (Ruth eventually did visit Sylvester, and Johnny went on to live another 64 years.)

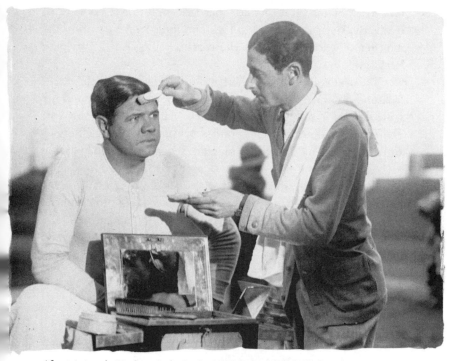

After joining the Yankees, Babe Ruth would become baseball's first glamorous superstar.

Decades later, Reggie Jackson would follow a similar path of fame. Jackson was a star outfielder with the Oakland A's dynasty teams of the mid-1970s. He'd hit one of the longest home runs in All-Star Game history, a shot that almost left Tiger Stadium completely. His flair for the dramatic and postseason performances were known years before he joined the Yankees. "I didn't come to New York to be a star," he said. "I brought my star with me." But the city brought Jackson's stardom to a new level. Reggie seemed made for New York. He drove flashy cars. He wore fur coats. He spoke about people not understanding "the magnitude of Reggie Jackson." This was great stuff for the big city. Jackson's persona was matched by his ability to come through in big situations. Nothing exemplified this better than his three home runs on three consecutive pitches in Game 6 of the 1977 World Series, earning him MVP honors. It wasn't just that Jackson hit three home runs. It was the way in which he did it—the three straight swings, the monster shot to center field, the curtain call. All of it was pure Reggie.

The next year featured the infamous Reggie candy bar incident. Jackson hit a three-run home run during the home opener and the same day the Yankees honored Mickey Mantle and Roger Maris. The Yankee Stadium crowd responded by chanting "Reggie, Reggie" and raining down hundreds of his own Reggie-brand candy bars.

After leaving New York and signing with the Angels, Reggie hit a home run in his first game back at Yankee Stadium. The fans loved it and began chanting "Steinbrenner sucks" in protest of the owner letting Jackson go. Did New York really escalate Jackson's fame? Consider this: Reggie played 21 seasons in the big leagues. Only five were spent in New York, but Reggie went into the Hall of Fame wearing a Yankees hat.

In the coming years, players like Roger Clemens, David Cone, Wade Boggs, and Alex Rodriguez—all of whom had made a name for themselves already—came to the Yankees and took on iconic status. Cone did it by pitching a perfect game and leading a staff that won four championships. Boggs, a great player for the Red Sox, did it by rejuvenating his career and riding a horse around

Yankee Stadium after the team won the '96 World Series. Boggs left Boston after a 1992 season in which he posted the worst batting average of his career, and the Red Sox front office was telling people he was done. "It was a continuation of my career—not the end of it. That was the good thing about it: that I didn't go over there and struggle," Boggs said. "And everybody knows…it's not Wade Boggs went to New York, and that's where he crashed and burned, but that my career got back on track, and I was able to throw up some numbers and the two Gold Gloves. That was the thing that was really lacking in my career."

Clemens achieved his iconic status by winning his 300th game, recording his 4,000[th] strikeout, and finally winning a world championship while wearing pinstripes (all pre-steroid allegations, of course). A-Rod earned fame—or rather notoriety—for nearly all the wrong reasons: the steroids, Kate Hudson, Cameron Diaz, questions about his ability to perform in postseason play. Still these issues would not have brought nearly the attention had A-Rod played in a small market.

The best stories, though, are the guys who aren't Hall of Famers or marquee players. There are countless examples of guys whose one shining moment in New York permanently earned them a place in baseball history. In New York it's relatively simple: if you are given space to perform on the big stage, you either rise or fall. And if you rise up, you become a big star in the Big Apple.

When second baseman Willie Randolph went down to injury during the 1978 World Series, the Yankees called on Brian Doyle to fill the void. Doyle grew up in Cave City, Kentucky, a town of less than 2,000 people in the southwestern part of the state. As a kid he loved Yankees players like Tom Tresh and Bobby Richardson. "The first day that I was called up, I went to every position on the field," Doyle said. "I stood there and named the Yankees that played there. It was…just so cool that one of my dreams was playing for the New York Yankees." Doyle had appeared in just 39 games in '78, his rookie year, mostly as a late-inning defensive replacement or pinch-hitter. He'd batted only .192 with no extra base hits or RBIs. In four seasons in the big leagues, Doyle never hit better than .192. He finished with a .161 career batting average and one home run.

But Doyle is forever remembered because of his performance as Randolph's replacement during that World Series. In six games he batted .438 with four runs scored and two RBIs, helping the Yankees win their second consecutive title. Doyle says his performance is brought up to him in some form or another nearly every day, and for a kid from Cave City, it means so much to him. "Maybe you can picture a nine-year-old kid in a plowed-over cornfield sitting on a cardboard second base, looking out into the outfield," Doyle said. "The outfield was a forest—just trees. And he is dreaming that it's Yankee Stadium, and people are going crazy for this nine-year-old kid. The nine-year-old kid gets up and runs and touches the cardboard third base and then slides into the cardboard home plate. There is a ditch by the gravel road there, and he jogs into the ditch, pretending it's the Yankee dugout. Roger Maris, Mickey Mantle, Yogi Berra, Elston Howard, Bobby Richardson, and Whitey Ford pat him on the backside and say, 'Nice going, kid.' Well, I stood at second base during the World Series and had tears going down my face."

The MVP of that '78 series was Bucky Dent. But no one remembers Dent for that. Instead, Dent is a household name for a deep fly ball he hit in Fenway Park one fall afternoon. Dent was a sure-handed shortstop known more for his defensive work than his offensive ability. In 1978, Dent's second year with the team, the Yankees struggled early on to gain any traction in the American League East. The Red Sox were off to a good start, the Yankees were riddled with injuries, and by mid-July New York was 14½ games out of first place. Billy Martin was soon fired and replaced by Bob Lemon. Then the Yankees took off. They climbed all the way back and even took over possession of first place with just one game left in the season. But the Yankees lost that game, and the Red Sox won, forcing a one-game playoff in Boston the next day.

On a beautiful early October day in Boston, the Red Sox and Yankees squared off for the AL East title. Boston took a 2–0 lead that stuck until the top of the seventh. With two outs and two runners on, Dent strode to the plate against Boston's Mike Torrez. There was some tension in the park, and Dent had hit only four home runs all year. In four full seasons before that, he'd hit only 18. So no one really thought Dent was a threat to give the Yankees the lead. That sentiment was even truer after Dent fouled a ball off his foot and tumbled to the ground in pain. He slowly recovered and—using a bat borrowed from Mickey Rivers since Dent broke his on the foul ball—stood back at the plate. Torrez delivered a fastball that Dent sent high and deep to left field. At first most people thought it would hit off the top of the wall. But the ball landed softly in the netting above the Green Monster. (There were no seats there at the time.) It got so quiet in Fenway that you could hear George Steinbrenner clapping from his seat beside the Yankees dugout.

Dent's home run put the Yankees ahead 3–2, a lead they would never relinquish. They won the game 5–4, went on to beat the Kansas City Royals in the AL Championship Series, and then knocked off the Los Angeles Dodgers for the title. Dent took home World Series MVP honors, hitting .417 with seven RBIs. But Dent will forever be remembered for his Boston home run, one of the biggest in baseball history. And in Boston he came to be known by a new, colorful name: Bucky "Fucking" Dent.

In 1990 the Yankees were among the worst teams in baseball and had one of the poorest seasons in team history. There was almost nothing to cheer about. With a record of 27–43, the team called up a tall, left-handed first baseman. It wasn't considered a headline-grabbing move. But within weeks Kevin Maas was making waves across baseball. He hit 10 home runs in his first 72 at-bats, the fastest any player had ever hit their first 10. He went on to set the record for fewest at-bats to hit 13 and 15 home runs.

Maas became an overnight celebrity. "I basically just tried to go to the park, keep my eye on the ball literally, and leave the park, and go home, and do it over and over again. I tried not to be influenced too much by it," Maas said. "At the same time, some opportunities came my way to do advertising or do a several-page spread in *GQ* magazine—okay, so I wasn't able to entirely shield myself from the fame—but some of that certainly was fun." He was so popular that at Yankee Stadium a group of women began sitting in the right-field seats. Every time Maas hit a home run, they would remove their "Maas-tops." The tradition did not last long before stadium personnel put a stop to it.

Maas could not maintain that level of power over his career. By 1992 he was a part-time player. He played his last games with the Minnesota Twins in 1995, having to give up a comeback attempt with the Yankees in 1996 due to injuries. But Maas is still a favorite for fans forced to watch that poor 1990 team. And even though Maas lives in California now, his time with the Yankees comes up "darn near every day. It's really remarkable."

Maas was a rookie on that 1990 team along with Jim Leyritz. Known derisively as "the King" because of his penchant for talking himself up constantly, Leyritz was a part-time catcher for most of his Yankees career. The result of his having once broken his leg, he sported an odd batting stance and twirled his bat after every pitch. No matter how poorly he might be doing, he always felt he should be playing. These were all little eccentricities that added to his allure.

But the legacy of Leyritz began in 1995. In Game 2 of the AL Division Series against the Seattle Mariners, Leyritz hit a two-run home run in the bottom of the 15th inning to win the game. It was the biggest home run in Yankees history since Dent's shot in Fenway. The following year the Yankees were down 2–1 to the Atlanta Braves in the World Series. In Game 4 they had fallen behind 6–0. In the eighth inning now trailing just 6–3, Leyritz came up with two runners on base. Braves pitcher Mark Wohlers hung a slider, and "the King" deposited it over the left-field wall, tying the game. The Yankees went on to win Game 4—as well as Games 5 and 6—to win the championship. Leyritz's home run is often credited as having turned the tide of the series.

Leyritz left the team after the '96 season, but he continued his postseason heroics with the San Diego Padres, hitting four home runs and driving in nine during their '98 playoff run. In 1999 he was traded back to New York midseason. There wasn't much of a role for him on the team, but come October he once again found a way to shine. With the Yankees on the verge of the sweep in Game 4 of the World Series, Leyritz pinch hit in the eighth inning and hit the last home run of the 20th century. As he crossed home plate, NBC announcer Bob Costas remarked, "You could send this guy to a resort in the spring and summer as long as he comes back for October."

Leyritz's post-baseball career was marred when he was arrested for driving under the influence and manslaughter charges after he hit another car while in Florida. The driver of the other car died as a result. Leyritz was eventually acquitted of manslaughter but not of the DUI. The accident certainly cast a pall over him, but many still remember Leyritz fondly for his uncanny ability to come through in the postseason.

Even during the dynasty years when nearly every player made a major contribution, some were able to distinguish themselves. Shane Spencer had toiled in the minor leagues for years. He caught his break in 1998 when the Yankees clinched a postseason berth by Labor Day. Able to relax a little, the team allowed some of their younger players time on the field. Spencer took full advantage, having one of the greatest months of any rookie in history. He hit eight home runs and drove in 21 runs in September. Three of those home runs were grand slams. During the final week of the season, Spencer hit six home runs and drove in 15.

Spencer's tear continued into the postseason. He homered in Game 2 of the ALDS against the Texas Rangers. Then in Game 3 in Texas, Spencer clubbed a three-run home run that put the game out of reach. "How do you explain Shane Spencer, and really, who wants to?" said Yankees radio announcer Michael Kay.

Spencer never came close to matching his '98 performance. He provided some key hits and defensive plays in the 2001 World Series, but by 2005 his career was over. Yankees rookies, however, who get off to a good start are often compared to Spencer.

Luis Sojo was also a member of that 1998 Yankees team. Sojo ended his career with a .261 batting average and spent parts of seven seasons with New York and hit only six home runs and 86

RBIs. But talk to any Yankees fan who watched him play, and they will tell you that Sojo was a hero and as solid a ballplayer as they come. He had a knack for delivering in big situations like in the 1996 World Series when he went 3-of-5 in what was mostly pinch-hitting and late-game defensive replacement duty. In a June 2001 game against the Red Sox, the Yankees had blown a lead in the top of the ninth inning, but Sojo, hitting all of .133, lined a single into right field to win the game.

The biggest Sojo hit, however, happened to be one of the biggest hits in Yankees history. Ahead of the New York Mets three games to one in the 2000 World Series, Game 5 was tied at two in the top of the ninth inning. The Yankees started a two-out rally with a walk to Jorge Posada and a hit by Scott Brosius. Up came Sojo. On the very first pitch from Al Leiter, Sojo sent a ball that seemed to bounce 87 times up the middle for a base hit. Posada scored as did Brosius on a throwing error. Sojo stood at third, sporting the biggest grin you will ever see. The Yankees ended up winning the game and the series on that hit. After retiring and even playing in the Old Timers Day game and managing in the minor leagues, he returned to play three games for the Yankees in 2003.

Midway through that 2003 season, the Yankees acquired Aaron Boone from the Cincinnati Reds. Boone had been a productive third baseman in Cincinnati, hitting .280 or better during four seasons. His half-year in New York, though, was underwhelming. He hit .254 with just six home runs. In the postseason he fared even worse, hitting just .200 in the first round against the Twins. As the Yankees duked it out with the Red Sox in the ALCS, Boone struggled mightily. With the series tied at three games apiece, Joe Torre sat the struggling Boone against Pedro Martinez in Game 7. Trailing 5–2 the Yankees scored three runs with one out in the eighth, tying the game. Boone entered the game as a pinch-runner that inning and stayed in to play third base. With the game knotted at five, Boone led off the bottom of the 11th inning against Tim Wakefield. Boone was only 2-of-16 in the series to that point with one RBI and six strikeouts. He was the unlikeliest of heroes. But before the series began, Randolph had told Boone that he was his sleeper pick to do something big. And before going to the plate, Torre had told Boone to just try to line Wakefield's knuckleball hard, and maybe he'd end up hitting a home run. On Wakefield's first pitch, a knuckleball that stayed flat over the plate, Boone crushed it over the left-field fence, sending the Yankees to the World Series. It was bedlam in the Bronx. Mariano Rivera ran out and collapsed on the pitching mound. The rest of the team ran screaming, fist pumping, and gesticulating wildly out of the dugout. In postgame interviews, Boone was clearly overwhelmed by the moment and in awe of what had just occurred.

Boone was the fifth player in baseball history to end a postseason series on a home run and just the second Yankee to do it. The fact that it came against the Red Sox after a grueling and sometimes violent series made it all the more special. Boone became synonymous with Bucky Dent in Boston, and his home run is often cited as the loudest many people had ever heard Yankee Stadium. Boone, though, never hit another home run at Yankee Stadium for the Yankees. While playing a game of pick-up basketball that offseason, he tore ligaments in his knee, ending his 2004 season on the spot. Because of the injury, the Yankees were forced to look for a new third baseman. And so, not only is Boone famous for his home run against the Red Sox, but he is also known for being the reason the Yankees went out and traded for A-Rod.

Aaron Small was a journeyman pitcher who spent the first seven seasons of his career playing for the Toronto Blue Jays, Florida Marlins, Oakland A's, Arizona Diamondbacks, and Braves. Desperate for pitching the Yankees picked up Small during the summer of 2005. Based on his career statistics, no one was expecting much. Small had never started more than three games in a season. In his last full year of pitching, he'd posted an ERA of 5.59. Instead of floundering, Small put in one of the most impressive two-and-a-half months of pitching in Yankees history. He went 10–0, including his first and only career shutout. During the stretch drive in September when the Yankees desperately needed wins, he won four consecutive starts. The Yankees won the division through a tiebreaker over the Red Sox, something that would not have been possible if not for Small's performance.

But Small never won another game again after 2005. In fact during the 2005 ALDS against the Angels, he actually lost a game in relief. Injuries hobbled him in 2006, eventually causing the Yankees to release him mid-year. He never pitched in the majors again. In 2008 Small found himself part of the last Old Timer's Day at Yankee Stadium just three years after his magical run, which forever gave him a place in Yankees lore.

Doyle, Dent, Maas, Leyritz, Spencer, Sojo, Boone, and Small will never receive Hall of Fame enshrinement, but each of them achieved lifelong fame by excelling on the big stage in New York. Even those players who are not necessarily positively remembered in New York still take joy in being remembered. Ken Phelps has had to deal with two decades of hearing about how he was the worst trade the Yankees ever made. (As Phelps correctly points out, he wasn't the worst Yankee—he did hit 17 home runs in about a full-season there.) The move actually took on national prominence thanks to the television show *Seinfeld*. Thinking George Costanza had died, Steinbrenner goes to Costanza's parents' house to inform them of what happened. Instead of being distraught over his son's apparent death, Mr. Costanza barks out, "What the hell did you trade Jay Buhner for? He had 30 home runs, over 100 RBIs last year! He's got a rocket for an arm…You don't know what the hell you're doing!"

For Phelps, that single line has brought him newfound fame. "That was quite an episode and, of course, that gets a lot of play," he said. "I still get calls whenever that is on. 'Hey, you were mentioned on *Seinfeld* again tonight.' I say that's great to be remembered for something."

Often in New York, it is all about the little moments. Those who come up big are rewarded with everlasting fame and adulation. They never have to buy drinks or wait for a table again. Todd Greene joined the team as a backup catcher in 2001. In his first game with the team, he hit a game-tying three-run home run against the Baltimore Orioles at Yankee Stadium. Greene's family came to visit two days later, and they headed out to a restaurant in Paramus, New Jersey. Someone working at the restaurant recognized him. "She came up and asked me, 'Are you that new Yankees catcher?'" Greene said. "I said, 'Yes ma'am, Todd Greene, nice to meet you.' She said, 'Well, Yankees don't wait here.'" Greene was a little uncomfortable with skipping ahead in line, but the manager insisted. Funny enough, Greene's first game homer would be his only one of the season, and it was his only season with the Yankees. But even if you hit only home run for the team in pinstripes—if it's in a big enough spot—it's enough to get you out of a 45-minute wait for a table.

6

The 1980s

I n the 1980s the Yankees and New York City had one thing in common: they were very unpleasant to be around. Both still maintained mythical status—New York as the epicenter of the world and the Yankees as baseball's most successful franchise. But the polish was wearing off both labels, and by the time the '90s came around, no one wanted to go to New York—the city or the team.

The city itself had been in decline for some time. Manufacturing jobs had departed in droves after the 1960s. Riots had left neighborhoods in tatters. Buildings started going up in flames in record numbers. Many of the fires were being deliberately set. Some landlords were either stuck with high vacancy rates due to white flight or were tired of housing deadbeat tenants. Others were set as a result of the ever escalating crime rates in the city. As building after building went up, which devalued the neighborhood, more people decided to torch their buildings and collect on the losses. The Son of Sam shootings in the summer of 1977 had terrified the entire city. A blackout that summer spurred looting on a scale never before seen in the city's history. New York's finances were in shambles. In order to cut costs, thousands of municipal employees were laid off, "creating a city in which almost nothing was maintained or repaired for a decade," said author Jonathan Soffer.

As pointed out by Neil Sullivan in his work, *A Diamond in the Bronx*, a substantial part of that borough, particularly the Grand Concourse, "had gone to the modern urban hell of drugs, gangs, arson, homelessness, abandoned children, violent crime, and other tragedies." The south Bronx had become so run-down that parts of it were used for a film about the bombing of Dresden, Germany, during World War II.

Once the pride and joy of the city, Times Square had turned into a squalid hellhole of sex shops, hookers, pimps, and drugs. In 1977 Show World, a gigantic "multi-story sex arcade complete with video booths, live sex acts, and private rooms where naked women sat behind thin sheets of Plexiglas," wrote Jonathan Mahler in *Ladies and Gentlemen, the Bronx Is Burning*, made it's debut right in the heart of Times Square. These kinds of shops didn't have to be hidden anymore, and thousands passed through its doors on a daily basis. At one point, according to Greg David's *Modern New York: The Life and Economics of a City*, police set up "barriers on Eighth Avenue to separate the theatergoers from the prostitutes."

Even the crowds at Yankee Stadium became more unruly and harder to deal with. Thousands stormed the field after Chris Chambliss' series-clinching American League Championship Series home run in 1976 against the Kansas City Royals. When the Yankees won the World Series the following year, the same scene ensued. Rather than celebrate on the field with their teammates, most of the players simply ran for their lives in an effort to get to the dugout and clubhouse as soon as possible. Even when they remained in the stands, fights broke out. In 1977 writer Roger Angell noted that he no longer felt safe bringing his family to a game at the stadium. This occurred after he watched a Yankees-Red Sox game in which "a group of fans in the upper deck showered their fellow spectators with beer, hurled darts and bottles onto the field, and engaged in a near riot with the stadium police. There was nothing fresh or surprising about this," Angell said. "It happened all the time this summer at Yankee Stadium."

Assistance from the federal government and changing economic policies under new mayor Ed Koch helped restore some sanity to the city's fiscal policy during the 1980s. There was even a spurt of economic development as a recession that had struck earlier in the decade came to an end. But many of the city's problems simply grew worse during the '80s, resulting in a place many saw as dirty, decaying, and dangerous.

Crime was an epidemic in New York. In every imaginable category, it was escalating at a frightening clip. Many problems that had festered in the 1970s—a poor national economy, dilapidated housing, lack of educational opportunities, racial and ethnic unrest—carried over and came to a boil in the new decade. But the biggest problem—the one that swept over the city with a plague-like fury—was crack cocaine.

Cocaine had become a popular drug during the '70s, becoming the status drug for the impoverished and the wealthy. It wasn't uncommon to see it at a club or swanky party. It was damn near required for entrance at Studio 54. But in the mid-1980s, a new form of the drug called crack cocaine began to appear. Unlike cocaine, a powder that was usually snorted, crack could be inhaled. And while cocaine was certainly a problem, crack became an epidemic for several reasons. First, it was cheaper than cocaine. Second, it was easier to resell on the street and therefore more available. Lastly, because it was inhaled instead of snorted, crack resulted in a much more potent and addictive high. It also allowed users to do more of it. "While heroin users or cocaine snorters may consume their drug two to three times per day, many crack abusers consumed crack five to 15 times per day," noted Dr. Eloise Dunlap and Dr. Bruce D. Johnson in their study on the crack epidemic.

According to Soffer, the first two years after crack emerged on the scene saw the murder rate increase by "more than 50 percent in 21 of New York's 75 police precincts—those where crack was taking root," Soffer said. "Murders increased in those areas, even though overall crime was up only 2 percent. In four of those precincts, the number of murders doubled in 1986."

Robert Stutman was special agent in charge of the city's DEA office in the mid-1980s. "Crack literally changed the entire face of the city," Stutman told PBS. "I know of no other drug—except maybe LSD in its heyday—that caused such a social change." The drug took hundreds of thousands with it, ruining families and the lives of individuals. The term "crack babies," referring to kids exposed to the drug through their pregnant mothers, entered popular lexicon. It was especially hard on poorer neighborhoods. People who used cocaine usually had an educational background to fall back on should they ever get clean. With crack, though, many of those who became addicted had little to no education, and if they ever were to become clean, they would essentially be starting from scratch with nothing to fall back on.

As more and more people got hooked, the side effects spread throughout the city. Subway cars became riddled with graffiti. Some of it was done by those who considered themselves artists. Some of it was done through "bombing," a process of spraying unreadable black scrawls everywhere possible. People were scared to ride subway cars for fear of being assaulted even in front of dozens of people. People were afraid to go jogging in Central Park. Jeff Pearlman, a sportswriter and author, noted that when playing for the St. Louis Cardinals on a road trip to New York, Keith Hernandez was with a coach staring out the window of their hotel. The coach pointed to Central Park and warned Hernandez, "Never, ever go there." When Diana Ross held a free concert there in the summer of 1983, there were more than 200 complaints regarding robberies and purse snatchings. People were afraid to walk almost anywhere in New York. Times Square had degenerated into a home for prostitutes and their pimps. Porn shops and adult movie theaters were everywhere. Despite the I (heart) New York campaign, the city's image suffered considerably. It became personified in movies like *Death Wish* and *Fort Apache, The Bronx*, where street punks dominated the landscape and everyday citizens were terrified to leave their homes. The 1981 film, *Wolfen*, was filmed in the South Bronx, largely because the area's decimated landscape was perfect for the setting of a film whose premise revolved around a series of murders caused by Native American wolf spirits. Even lighthearted comedies did the city no favors. In *Crocodile Dundee*, the main character is a fish out of water from Australia spending time in the Big Apple. He gets accosted on the street by a thug brandishing a knife. The only thing that saves the protagonist is that he has an even bigger knife on him (not exactly highlighting the safe streets of New York). In *Coming To America*, as two men from Africa emerge out of their cab on their first visit to the city, someone throws garbage out their window onto the street. The two men leave their luggage out on the corner as they check for room availability, and their bags are immediately stolen.

Public health also became a serious issue in the city as Autoimmune Deficiency Syndrome (AIDS) first started to appear in the late 1970s. By 1982, notes Soffer, more than half of all cases related to AIDS (a few hundred at the time) were based in New York. As the public became more aware of AIDS, panic ensued. Many didn't understand how the disease was spread, and the fact that it had initially struck largely in the gay community meant that many public officials were slow to react to it. In 1985 parents boycotted schools in two Queens districts where children who were HIV-positive (meaning they had the virus that causes AIDS) were allowed to attend. Gradually public officials fought back against this kind of hysteria, but the stigma around AIDS, which affected thousands of people in the city, took years to break down.

Homelessness became an increasing and more visible problem as the 1980s wore on. Somewhat ironically, part of the problem was the rebuilding of decaying or worn down neighborhoods. The early '80s saw a boom in wealthy residents who sunk money into low-cost housing, rebuilt the homes, and then sold them at huge profits. This made neighborhoods more upscale and helped revitalize certain areas, Central Park West and Park Slope in Brooklyn among them. But it also meant pricing out lower-income folks from the places where they had grown up and worked. After the fires of the 1970s, vacancy rates had shrunk to the point of almost being nonexistent. Combined with an economic recession as well as economic policies of the Reagan administration that saw cuts in federal funding, it led to thousands being left on the streets without a place to live. The crack epidemic only exacerbated the problem as low-income folks got hooked on the drug and were left essentially helpless to provide for themselves. In turn these new homeless were generally more violent than those already out on the streets, and many younger homeless folks attacked the older ones.

The crack epidemic only exacerbated the perception and reality of an unsafe city. Going into the 1980s, New Yorkers had already altered the way they acted and felt about where they lived. Ordinary citizens began carrying weapons, feeling a need to protect themselves even on the most routine of stops—whether it was going to work or simply grabbing groceries. A group of restaurant owners on 46th Street recruited the Guardian Angels, a group of volunteers who act as unarmed watchmen, to patrol their neighborhood. "They are not even fully operational yet, but you can feel the difference," Joe Allen, one of the restaurant owners, told *The New York Times*. "People are smiling again, old people are coming out of their homes without feeling in danger, and the tourists can cross Eighth Avenue without fear."

The tension came to a head on December 22, 1984, on the IRT No. 2 train. Bernhard Goetz, a 37-year-old electrical engineer, boarded the train and shortly thereafter was approached by four young black males. Goetz, who had begun carrying an illegal handgun after he was beaten in a mugging three years earlier, claimed he felt he was being accosted by the men. In response he drew his gun and fired, hitting all four of them. All were seriously injured, though each survived.

Nine days after the shooting, Goetz turned himself in to police. He was brought up on charges of attempted murder as well as other crimes. The shooting was national news, bringing unwanted attention to a city wracked with crime whose residents felt they now had to police the streets. "There is a broad sense of frustration and anger over the state of the criminal justice system, and right now people don't seem to care about the facts or whether or not Goetz used appropriate force," said Dave Walker at the time, co-host of *Take Two* on CNN. "They have found themselves a hero."

Many people had in fact found a hero in Goetz, dubbed the "Subway Vigilante" by the press. They were tired of feeling threatened simply through their own existence in the Big Apple and could only wish they had had an opportunity to fight back, too. Many individuals and groups came out in support of Goetz, who was eventually acquitted of murder. (He was found guilty of illegally possessing a handgun.) The Goetz incident was a preview of race relations in the city that were going from bad to worse. On December 20, 1986, two black men were at a pizzeria in Howard Beach, Queens, when a mob of white men beat them and chased them out with baseball bats. One of the men, fleeing for his life, ran onto the Shore Parkway, where he was struck and killed by a car.

In 1987, 15-year-old Tawana Brawley, a black woman, was found in a garbage bag in Dutchess County, about an hour north of the city. Brawley, who was covered in feces and had racial epithets written on her, claimed she had been raped be several white men, including a police officer and the Dutchess County assistant district attorney. The aftermath split along racial lines as many questioned the validity of her story. Others called media reporting of the case biased and unfair. In 1988 a grand jury ruled that Brawley had concocted the entire thing, a charge she refutes to this day. But the verdict only further widened the racial gap in the city.

Two years after the Brawley case, 28-year-old Trisha Meili was jogging through Central Park when she was viciously attacked, raped, and left for dead. She survived, but the severity of her injuries left her unable to remember exactly what happened. Most media outlets did not provide her name in subsequent stories, and she was often referred to just as the "Central Park Jogger." The incident sparked the *New York Post*'s headline "None of Us Is Safe." Five young black males were arrested for the crime. They all confessed or implicated one another in the attack, but shortly thereafter recanted, saying their confessions had been forced on them by the police. There was little evidence to directly link them to the crime, but each was found guilty. In 2002 a convicted serial rapist admitted that he and he alone had committed the crime, resulting in the original convictions being vacated by a court.

In 1991 a seven-year-old boy, who was black, was struck and killed by a car driven by a Hasidic Jew in Brooklyn's Crown Heights neighborhood. The accident brought boiling racial tensions in the neighborhood between the black and Jewish communities to a head. Three days of rioting ensued, resulting in the death of a Hasidic Jew, who was visiting from Australia. All of the crime, racial tension, riots, and disease created a stifling atmosphere of fear in the city. By 1993 *Esquire* was referring to New York as "the worst place on Earth," and nearly half of New Yorkers said they would move out of town the next day if possible.

As the city seemed to crumble all around them, the New York Yankees were also in a state of free fall. The championship teams of the 1970s were built on smart trades and wise free-agent signings. Yes, the Yankees threw money out there that other teams couldn't match, but they tended to spend wisely. Players like Reggie Jackson, Jim "Catfish" Hunter, and Rich "Goose" Gossage were vital cogs in the machine. There were some flops here and there, but for the most part, the deals made by the team worked out. Part of that was because Steinbrenner had smart baseball people around him and because The Boss, while constantly meddling, did allow his people to make important decisions. But that all began to change dramatically, and it started when the Yankees lost the 1981 World Series. They had led the Los Angeles Dodgers two games to none but lost the next four, culminating in the Dodgers celebrating on the field at Yankee Stadium. Not long after the last out was made, Steinbrenner issued a public apology to the fans of New York for his team's performance. That did not sit well with the players, who had tried their hardest and didn't see what it was they had to be sorry for. The Boss' apology wasn't his only bizarre behavior during the Fall Classic. Steinbrenner claimed that after Game 5 he got into a fight with two Dodgers fans in an elevator in Dodger Stadium. No one has ever come forward to say they were involved in the fight, leaving many to wonder if Steinbrenner simply made the whole thing up.

In 1981 Steinbrenner had more or less taken over the reins of being general manager from Cedric Tallis, a savvy baseball man who had trouble dealing with the constant phone calls and angry rants. For the next nine years, The Boss would not relinquish those reins. During the offseason that followed the loss to the Dodgers, Steinbrenner took the team in a completely new direction. The

Bronx Bombers were going to turn into the Bronx Burners, swapping out power for speed. Jackson was allowed to sign elsewhere, and in his place came guys like Dave Collins and Ken Griffey. "The team got to spring training, and he brought in his friend who had been in the 1940-something Olympics, Harrison Dillard," sportswriter Moss Klein said. "He was an Olympic hurdler. The idea was he was going to teach the Yankees how to run, like you can teach speed. Several days a week, they would have the players go in the back of the field with Harrison Dillard and just have races. It became a farce. Everyone was laughing about it."

The experiment was a spectacular failure. The team stole 69 bases all year only 22 more than they had stolen the previous, strike-shortened season. Bob Lemon lasted 14 games as manager before being fired. Gene Michael replaced him and didn't even last the rest of the year. The team used three managers en route to a 79–83 finish. The losing was only made worse by the erratic behavior of Steinbrenner, who drove his managers crazy, publicly blasted his players, and pushed for bad trades.

It was a vicious cycle. The Boss didn't feel his team was good enough to win, so he went out and got other ballplayers. But the players he got never worked out, making the team worse. But the worse the team got, the more he panicked and began searching for more players. On and on it went. He shipped out prospects Willie McGee and Fred McGriff for virtually nothing. He acquired aging slugger John Mayberry despite protests from his scouts, and Mayberry hit .209 during his year with the team. Steinbrenner traded for Butch Hobson, and Hobson hit .172. It was a pattern that would persist for the rest of the decade, and 1982 was just the start.

Moreover, when the team's performance failed to pick up, Steinbrenner began using petty tactics disguised as elixirs to punish his players. His favorite method was the mandatory team workout on scheduled off days. To Steinbrenner, you could never work hard enough, practice hard enough, try hard enough. There were no off days to him. A day off really meant a day to hone your skills in the batting cage or to take a few ground balls. To the players, though, his workouts were complete bullshit. They felt a day off would do far greater good than an hour of batting practice. "We are being punished. That's all," said Gossage after an early morning workout late in the '82 season. "A slap on the wrist for losing too many games, the workout doesn't accomplish anything. Even he [Steinbrenner] must realize that. But we're getting used to this shit."

In 1983 Billy Martin was brought back for a third tour of duty, and the team posted 91 wins, finishing third in a tough American League East Division. Martin was let go after the season, and staples like Gossage and Graig Nettles were sent packing after years of being disgruntled in New York. Yogi Berra took over the team in 1984, but a string of injuries and an incredible start by the Detroit Tigers ended the Yankees season by May. But Steinbrenner didn't care for excuses. He wanted results.

Around the All-Star break, Steinbrenner sat down Berra and his entire coaching staff for a meeting. But instead of discussing how to improve the team, it turned into a Steinbrenner session of berating. He belittled Berra and his staff for the team's performance, placing the blame squarely on them. Steinbrenner specifically kept referring to the team as "your team." The ranting went on for some time. Those in the meeting could see that Berra was starting to boil. The public persona of Berra was one of almost a class clown. He was the aloof goof, who came up with those funny Yogisms. Berra certainly was a nice person, well loved and respected. He rarely blew up or sought confrontation, but even someone like Berra had his limit and had it with Steinbrenner. "I don't want to hear anymore of this," Berra shouted at The Boss. "This is your fucking team—not my team. You put this fucking team together. You hire all these fucking players that nobody else wants and pay them more money than they should get." And then Berra threw a pack of cigarettes across the table Steinbrenner was seated at. It bounced off the table and hit Steinbrenner in the face. Berra then stormed out. Steinbrenner, perhaps shocked at how combative Berra had been, did not take any action against his manager. Not then anyway.

Led by a string of young talent called up from Triple A Columbus, Ohio, the Yankees posted baseball's best record in the second half. But even the winning couldn't prevent unhappiness. The race for the batting title between teammates Don Mattingly and Dave Winfield caused tension as the media and fans pitted the two against each other with most taking Mattingly's side. The story took on racial tones as well, highlighting what some players thought was a racial divide within the clubhouse. Winfield, a veteran who'd played hard and put up great numbers for New York, was even booed at Yankee Stadium. He was a proud man who had put up with a lot since signing with the Yankees, and his treatment by the fans especially hurt.

Things would only get worse for Winfield in 1985. The Yankees made a huge offseason trade, acquiring superstar Rickey Henderson from the Oakland A's. But Henderson got hurt in spring training as did Winfield and Mattingly. The squad that began the year was not the team Berra thought he would have, and they got off to a slow start. After losing a heartbreaking game in Chicago and falling to 6–10, the axe fell on Berra. He had been promised he'd last the entire season, but Steinbrenner thought he had lost control of the team and was too lax with the players. The Boss wanted a manager the players would kowtow to. Berra was informed of the decision by GM Clyde King, not Steinbrenner, another slight that resulted in Berra not going back to Yankee Stadium for 14 years.

Martin replaced Berra, assuming the reins for a fourth time. It was not a popular decision within the clubhouse. Don Baylor kicked over a trash can. Mattingly threw several objects in the shower. These guys loved Berra and couldn't believe he was being dismissed so callously. They also weren't thrilled with Billy IV—even if they liked him. They were getting tired of whatever sideshow he was certain to create down the road.

As players returned from injury, the team got hot, and Martin's managerial style seemed to do the trick. The Yankees were in contention all summer long with the Toronto Blue Jays for first place. But in September, Steinbrenner began making things hard for his team. After losing a game in Milwaukee (the team's only loss of the series), Steinbrenner infuriated the players when he singled out Winfield, Griffey, and Baylor as not coming through in the clutch. "They are letting us down. That's a fact," Steinbrenner said. He then asked where his Mr. October was before referring to Winfield as "Mr. May." As told in Bill Madden's *Steinbrenner*, just a few days later, he and Winfield got into a confrontation in the clubhouse when Steinbrenner entered and began passing out letters instructing his players to vote in favor of a new drug-testing program the commissioner was pushing. As the team's player representative with the union, Winfield immediately shot up and informed Steinbrenner he had no right to interfere in the process this way.

"Excuse me," Winfield said. "But what you're trying to do here is override the negotiation process. It's my responsibility as the player rep to pass out these letters."

"Not for long," Steinbrenner answered.

"Is that some sort of threat? Because you and I both know I'm not going anywhere next year but right here," Winfield retorted.

"We'll see about that," Steinbrenner said.

"Yeah, we'll see about that," Winfield responded.

The intense heat coming from Steinbrenner, which he always thought was a great motivator, only served to hurt the club. "After Steinbrenner ripped the team, we lost focus," wrote Baylor in his 1990 autobiography. The Yankees went into a tailspin, losing eight games in a row. During the losing streak, Martin seemed to collapse under the pressure. He sent Mike Pagliarulo up to the plate to bat right-handed, something the left-handed Pags had never done once in his career. He left reliever Brian Fisher in a game too long, seemingly out of spite, in a move that cost the Yankees the game. In a key situation one night, Martin accidentally called for a pitchout and didn't realize it. The move helped cost the Yankees the game. He got into altercations on two consecutive nights in Baltimore, one with a fan and one with pitcher Ed Whitson.

In the end the Yankees missed out on first place by two games. Martin was relieved of duty after the year and replaced by Lou Piniella, who lasted two full seasons, an astonishing accomplishment during the '80s. But Sweet Lou's time was not easy. Steinbrenner pestered him with incessant phone calls, meddled in team transactions, and leaked stories to the press that Piniella wanted to get rid of Henderson. Piniella did not return after 1987, paving the way for the fifth managerial stint by Martin. That fifth time seemed like a charm as the Yankees were in first place early in the '88 season. But during a road trip in Texas, Martin was beaten badly at a strip club in Dallas, forcing Steinbrenner to fire him a fifth and final time. Piniella took the reins the rest of the season, but the club's lack of pitching prevented it from taking first place.

The fact that the Yankees had no pitching in 1988 was not a coincidence or bad luck. It was the logical conclusion to a decade's worth of horrible transactions that were fueled by Steinbrenner's insatiable appetite to win and need to be involved in everything. That pattern that first emerged in 1982 remained in place every year during the rest of the '80s, and the team paid dearly for it. Sure, the Yankees were in contention for many of those years. In fact, no team in baseball won more games during the 1980s than the Yankees. But those wins did not translate into titles, even though they very easily could have if the Yankees had exhibited more patience and better judgment throughout the decade.

The internal turmoil was clearly bad for business. Between 1982 and 1988, the team had eight different managers, a pattern of instability that was bound to hurt the club. Each manager brings his own way of doing things and his own philosophy on the game. A change now and then is necessary, but to do so that many times disrupts the ebb and flow of the team, no matter how much the players make or how talented they are. And the constant back page headlines, whether it be another Martin incident or Winfield versus Steinbrenner didn't help either. And perhaps worst of all, the New York Mets were now a highly successful, well-rounded franchise that was outdrawing and outperforming the Yankees. That alone was enough to drive Steinbrenner crazy, and it caused him to do some truly ridiculous things.

The trades the Yankees made during the 1980s left many scratching their heads. In an effort to provide a quick fix for his team, Steinbrenner shipped out tons of talent with little return. The names sent away from New York read like an All-Star roster:

- McGee was traded to the St. Louis Cardinals for pitcher Bob Sykes, who had a career 23–26 record. Sykes never pitched another inning in the majors after the trade. McGee was the 1985 National League MVP, the 1985 and 1990 NL batting champion, and a four-time All-Star.

- McGriff was traded to the Blue Jays along with Mike Morgan and Dave Collins for Dale Murray and Tom Dodd. Murray won three games for the Yankees and retired before McGriff made his debut. Dodd never played a game for New York. McGriff hit 493 career home runs.

- Otis Nixon made his big league debut with the Yankees in September 1983 but was part of a deal that offseason that sent him to the Cleveland Indians in exchange for Toby Harrah and Rick Browne. Harrah hit .217 in his only season in New York, and Browne never played in the majors. Nixon, on the other hand, ended up with 620 career stolen bases.

- Greg Gagne was traded to the Minnesota Twins for Roy Smalley. He spent seven years as the Twins' starting shortstop during a time when the Yankees used six different players to fill that position. Smalley spent two and a half decent years in New York before being shipped off to the White Sox.

- In that White Sox deal, the Yankees acquired pitcher Doug Drabek, who made 21 starts as a rookie for the club in 1986. That offseason they shipped him out to the Pittsburgh Pirates along with Logan Easley and Brian Fisher for Rick Rhoden, Cecilio Guante, and Pat Clements. Rhoden led the Yankees in wins in 1987, but he'd already retired from baseball when Drabek won the 1990 NL Cy Young Award. Guante left the team in August of 1988, and Clements was sent packing a few months later. Rhoden, Guante, and Clements won 39 combined games for New York while Drabek averaged 15 wins a year for Pittsburgh.

- Jose Rijo made his debut with the 1984 Yankees, pitching mostly in relief. That offseason he was part of the blockbuster deal that brought Henderson to New York. Henderson had several great years with the Yankees, but he became disgruntled and a clubhouse problem, causing the team to ship him back to the Oakland A's in 1989. Rijo, meanwhile, won the 1990 World Series MVP and averaged 14 wins a year from 1990 to 1993 and never had an ERA above 2.70.

- Bob Tewksbury won nine games as a rookie starter in the Yankees 1986 rotation. But he pitched poorly in the early part of '87 and was traded to the Chicago Cubs for starter Steve Trout, who went 0–4 that year for the Yankees, walking 37 hitters in just over 46 innings. In one outing he walked five and had three wild pitches in less than four innings. Tewksbury averaged 13 wins a year between 1990 and 1994, finishing third in the NL Cy Young Award voting in 1992.

- Al Leiter, a New Jersey native, created a lot of excitement when he made his debut in 1987 and struck out the side in his first two innings. There were big plans for him to be a major part of the rotation. But with hints that he had serious arm troubles early in 1989, he was traded to the Blue Jays in exchange for Jesse Barfield, who led the Yankees in home runs in 1990 but retired from baseball after the '92 season. Leiter struggled for four seasons to recover from injuries. But he did recover and averaged nearly 14 wins a year from 1995 to 2003.

Imagine if by 1990 the Yankees had Drabek, Rijo, and Tewksbury in their starting rotation? And these trades don't even take into account what many believe to be the worst deal of the decade: Ken Phelps for Jay Buhner. Buhner was a big swinging outfielder with loads of potential, but Steinbrenner sent him to Seattle in the summer of '88 for Phelps, a power hitting left-handed batter. Phelps played the equivalent of one season in New York, hitting 17 home runs in fewer than 300 at-bats. He played his last game in 1990. Buhner, meanwhile, went on to hit 307 home runs for the Mariners, becoming a fan favorite in the Pacific Northwest

The Phelps-Buhner deal is not the worst one of the '80s, but it exemplifies everything that was wrong with the team. The Yankees needed pitching in 1988—not more offense, a fact Phelps himself readily admits. "When I joined the Yankees, they were really stacked with hitters. I was scratching my head, wondering how would I fit in," Phelps said. Then in 1989, they shipped away two of their biggest offensive weapons—Henderson and Jack Clark—for little in return. For John Sterling, who had just come on board as the Yankees radio play-by-play announcer in 1989, it was a stunning turn of events. "Mattingly was still very good in '89. Near the end he started to get back trouble. Rickey Henderson was traded away. Jack Clark was traded away. Dave Winfield came down with a bad back and didn't play at all. So from the team that I thought I was going to, they lost Henderson, Clark, and Winfield. All the sudden they didn't have a very good team," Sterling said.

The disgruntled Winfield followed Clark and Henderson out the door in 1990, meaning two future Hall of Famers were sent packing in one year's time. In return for Winfield, the Yankees got Mike Witt, a pitcher who in three injury-plagued years made 27 starts with the club, going 8–9. Winfield went on to average 25 home runs and 91 RBIs a year from 1990–92.

All the trades left the farm system nearly depleted of talent. Consider this: Randy Velarde and Lee Guetterman were the only players the Yankees acquired through any trade before 1989 that were with the team for the start of the '90s. The Yankees had almost literally gotten nothing in return for all their top prospects. They were forced to call on Hensley Meulens, Wade Taylor, Jeff Johnson, and a host of other players who never established themselves in the big leagues in order to fill the void.

Bad trades were coupled with bad free-agent signings. The Yankees poured dollar after dollar into poorly conceived contracts that almost always ended in the players being traded away while the Yankees continued to pay their contracts. Whitson, Dave

LaPoint, Andy Hawkins, and Pascual Perez were all decent players who benefited from one good year by signing overly large contracts that inflated the price for other free agents. All were traded away or released before their contracts expired (except Perez, who was suspended for violating baseball's drug policy and subsequently left the game for good).

The end result of all these bad deals and trades was a 1990 team that was the worst in the AL and one of the worst in team history. The Yankees finished 67–95 with only one pitcher winning more than nine games. An anemic offense finished last in runs scored, hits, batting average, and on-base percentage. The low point of it all came on July 1st in Chicago. Hawkins, who was almost released by the team earlier but was spared when Witt went on the DL, no-hit the White Sox. But due to three errors and two walks in the eighth inning, the Yankees still lost the game 4–0. It was the most lopsided no-hit loss in baseball history. Eleven days later, Melido Perez of Chicago, who was Pascaul's brother, no-hit the Yankees over six innings in a rain-shortened game.

After the disastrous decade of the 1980s, few would have figured that by the turn of the century, broadcaster Bob Costas would refer to the Yankees as the team of the decade.

7

The Fourth Estate

New York City is the media capital of the world with an eclectic mix of programs, political slants, and viewpoints. On 6th Avenue, between 47th and 48th Streets, sits the home of FoxNews studios, one of several 24-hour news networks. Right around the corner from Fox on 49th Street sits the studio headquarters of MSNBC in Rockefeller Plaza, another 24-hour news network. The two stations are polar opposites in terms of ideology. One offers a mix of ironclad conservative pundits, talk show hosts, and biased news media coverage while the other offers a mix of ironclad liberal pundits, talk show hosts, and biased news media coverage. And yet they sit just one-tenth of a mile from each other.

Also located in the Plaza is NBC News studios. Just a half a mile from Rockefeller, ABC's *Good Morning America*, the most popular morning news program in the country, does its broadcast from a studio overlooking Times Square. Less than a mile north of Times Square, David Letterman films his *Late Show* at the Ed Sullivan Theater. Two blocks west of Times Square, *The New York Times*, the newspaper of record, makes its headquarters in one of the tallest buildings in the world. About a half a mile northwest sits the studio of *The Daily Show*, a mock news program that in some ways has become a greater source of information for many than the actual news.

The most popular talk radio stations in America are based in New York City, including shows with Howard Stern and Rush Limbaugh. And sports talk radio, led by WFAN, exploded out of the Big Apple. All of these media outlets are within just a few blocks of each other in midtown Manhattan. In addition you have Steiner Studios, the largest soundstage outside of Hollywood, in Brooklyn. HBO, Showtime, and MTV all have their headquarters in the Big Apple.

The media not only engulfs New York, it engulfs all things New York, including the Yankees. Perhaps no organized sports team in the entire world receives the amount of media coverage, scrutiny, and spotlight as the Bronx Bombers. It stems not only from the size of the city they play in, but also the history of the team and the legacy of its players. While many sports teams are lucky to have two or three newspapers covering them daily, along with a radio station and TV, the Yankees have nearly a dozen print outlets that follow their every move. These include *The New York Times, New York Daily News, New York Post, Newsday, The* (Newark) *Star-Ledger, Bergen Record*, and *The Hartford Courant*.

How the team has been covered has shifted drastically over the years and not just because of changes in technology. In the 1940s and 1950s, sportswriters by and large stuck to the game on the field. They rarely, if ever, ventured into the players' private lives. The only instances they might do so was when a story simply could not be ignored, like the fight at the Copa, which was witnessed by dozens of people. Dick Young was perhaps the best representative of this bygone era of sports journalism, but it also featured Arthur Daly, Jimmy Cannon, and Red Smith. The '60s, though, brought a change in how the Yankees were covered. A new group of young and hungry writers emerged. They were known as "the chipmunks" for the manner in which they tried to go about the clubhouse finding stories. "It was fun to watch because the chipmunks were always about the gotcha," said former Yankees pitcher Al Downing. "Maury Allen, Len Shecter, Paul Zimmerman. You had Joe

Donnelly. These guys, they were all great writers, but they had to establish a reputation for themselves, so as a player, you sat back and watch this little repartee between these guys."

Competition began to get fierce with reporters having cordial relations with one another but also knowing that there would be hell to pay if they got scooped by another paper. "Things changed dramatically in the mid-seventies," wrote former Yankees public relations director Marty Appel in *Pinstripe Empire*. "While our daily press notes and occasional press releases once formed the day's news agenda, reporters were now stepping out on their own to discover what the news was."

As the '70s progressed, a new group of writers emerged, like Murray Chass, Moss Klein, and Bill Madden. All were outstanding writers who became some of the biggest and most important sources for all things Yankees during the George Steinbrenner years. They covered the games, the trades, the signings, the fights, and the firings all in minute detail that came from years of building relationships with both the players and the staff, people on the inside who tended to know everything that was going on. As a result coverage became much deeper and more extensive, bringing fans basically right into the clubhouse and, in some cases, the hotel bars.

The explosion in social media has produced even more coverage with blogs and Twitter providing outlets for fans to voice their opinion or frustration. Most major announcements, be they free-agent signings or injuries, are done through Twitter now. It was a different story in the late '70s and early '80s. "In those days," said former Yankees public relations director Rick Cerrone, "you could bury a story. You could announce something at 5 PM on a Friday, and it would just appear in the next day's paper. You could embargo something. You could put something out, so it would only get out the next morning. You can't do that today. If the Yankee PR director told a writer something, it's out to the world in five minutes."

There are numerous blogs dedicated to the Yankees such as Pinstripe Bible and River Avenue Blues. Of course, to be fair, there are many dedicated to hating the Yankees, too. And then there is the YES Network. Started in 2002, the Yankees Entertainment and

Sports Network is a behemoth not only in terms of the revenue it brings, but also because it saturates television with all things Yankees. There isn't just the Yankees game. There is also the pregame show a half hour earlier. And if that isn't enough, there is even a pre-pregame show where the Yankees' batting practice sessions are shown live. If approximately five hours of game-related coverage is not enough to satisfy a fan's appetite, don't fret, because YES offers hours and hours of additional non-game-related Yankees coverage. There is *Yankees on Deck*, a show catered toward children that shows Yankees providing tips on how to play the game as well as insights into their personal lives. You have *Yankees Magazine*, a half-hour show focusing on the previous week's games or, if it's the offseason, the latest trade and free-agent signings or rumors. And then there is *Yankeeography*, an award-winning hour-long program (though Steinbrenner's episode ran longer, of course) that showcases the lives of prominent Yankees. The show was so successful and so many players had been done that by 2013 the focus shifted from individual players to individual moments in Yankees history.

Dealing with all of this media can be daunting. Serving as the public relations director under Steinbrenner was a thankless task. Steinbrenner leaked stories on his own all the time without informing his PR men. He made phone calls at all hours of the day, wondering why certain stories had or had not been written. Tom Verducci noted in *The Yankee Years* that during the 1980s he earned the nickname "Mr. Tunes" among the team's beat writers because "getting outrageous quotes from him was as easy as dropping a quarter into a jukebox and making your selection." The Boss was obsessed with back page headlines—to the point where you almost had to question if it was more important to him than actually winning games. He frequently made big announcements in an attempt to thwart other important events like when he announced an hour before the start of Game 6 of the 1995 World Series that Buck Showalter would not return as manager. "Baseball interrupts George Steinbrenner's management seminar to present the sixth game of the 1995 World Series," *New York Newsday's* Joe Gergen sarcastically wrote about the timing of the announcement. "The

Indians and the Braves apologize for the intrusion and promise to relinquish the spotlight as quickly and quietly as possible. This is, after all, The Boss' favorite month of the year."

Steinbrenner used the media in a passive-aggressive way to let players and managers know he was displeased with them. If you read a story that went something like "a source close to the owner says George Steinbrenner is not happy with the way the team is performing, and manager Lou Piniella's job might be in jeopardy," odds were that the close source was Steinbrenner himself. "One of the reasons I didn't get along with him all the time was because he really tried to manipulate writers," Klein said. "If someone was critical of him, he would go to great lengths to cut that person off and give that story to a competing writer. He used that game with the *Daily News* and the *New York Post* cause he knew the competition they were in."

Those who have served as PR director have done so admirably, putting up with thankless tasks that would have driven lesser people crazy. Cerrone, the team's PR director from 1996–2006, actually grew up wanting that job. He recalled sitting in his high school guidance counselor's office, flunking out of high school. He was asked what he wanted to do when he became an adult. "That's easy," Cerrone said. "I am the public relations director for the New York Yankees." Cerrone took the long way to get there, working as both a PR person and a reporter for years before he finally landed the job in 1996. When Cerrone first inquired about the position with the Yankees, made available because of the holiday sacking of Rob Butcher, he was given a bit of warning. Arthur Richman, a Steinbrenner confident who Cerrone called initially about the job, said, "Are you out of your fucking mind?"

Cerrone wasn't deterred. But shortly after getting the job and meeting The Boss for the first time, he got an inkling of things to come. They first encountered each other in an elevator at the team's Tampa spring training complex. Cerrone made the first move, introducing himself. "Well, he lights up," Cerrone said. "'Oh, Rick, welcome aboard. Len Berman says great things about you.' Well, that honeymoon lasted about 24 hours because the next day I got called into his office, and he was going off on me about people eating in the press room."

The sheer size and magnitude of the media can be overwhelming for players. "It is surprising when you come from another city where you have four or five beat writers after the game every night. Then all of the sudden you come to New York, and on a given night, especially a playoff game, there could be hundreds of media," Paul O'Neill said. "Over the years newcomers and rookies were often taken aside by veteran players and given a rundown on how to deal with the press. "I remember when I got there, and Frank Howard was coaching there and he had a great line about New York. He said you were either eating filet mignon or you are starving, and there is nothing in the middle," said Ken Phelps, whom the Yankees acquired midseason from the Mariners in 1988. "In Seattle you had a couple beat writers, and that was about it. In New York you would come in the locker room the next day, and there would be 20 newspapers sitting there."

Yankees pitcher Dennis Rasmussen relied on his veterans for guidance. "When I got to New York, the best advice I got was in spring training from Phil Niekro and Ron Guidry. [It was] make sure that you give the media equal time. It is easy to talk about a good outing. It is tough to talk about a bad outing. But if you give them equal time, good or bad outing, they'll treat you more fairly in the media," Rasmussen said.

But even grizzled veterans can feel overwhelmed by it all. The revived Red Sox-Yankees rivalry of the late 1990s and early 2000s was great for fans, but the constant and overplayed media coverage left Joe Torre dreading those 18 or so games on the schedule. "It's the media coverage that can wear you out," said Torre in *The Yankees Years*. "It's one game on the schedule, and I know it's Boston. I know it's a team in your division. But I think the rivalry got out of hand as far as magnifying every single thing that went on in the game. It's absolutely exhausting."

Despite the pressure most players have handled it well. Derek Jeter is infamous for his dry, nearly useless quotes, allowing him to stay out of trouble. Don Mattingly endured a few controversial

The New York media swarms manager Joe Torre before a 2005 baseball game.

moments during his playing days but rarely did he ever say the wrong thing. Mariano Rivera established a great rapport with the press by always answering their questions, even after heartbreaking moments like the Game 7 loss to the Arizona Diamondbacks in the 2001 World Series. "I found it was a great place for me to cut my teeth because there was a real environment of being honest and frank," Showalter said. "And there was a real competitive nature between so many competing papers. It really weeded out people who weren't good at what they did."

Torre, even with his misgivings over the Red Sox games, also had a great relationship with the media and did a great job of trying to insulate his players from any sort of media-based innuendo or controversy. During his first season as manager, he directly confronted Michael Kay, then announcing games on the radio for the Yankees, in front of several players in the clubhouse.

Torre had not liked the tone of a question Kay had asked during the postgame the night before. He thought Kay was trying to stir up controversy where one didn't exist. "I don't need you to be a Rona Barrett around here," Torre yelled at Kay, referring to the gossip columnist. Torre later acknowledged that he used the incident to show his players that he could be tough with the press and would protect them from controversy whenever he could.

Others, however, have not had the same kind of success. News of the Yankees signing Reggie Jackson leaked out before he made his way to New York for the official press conference. As Jonathan Mahler details in *Ladies and Gentlemen, The Bronx Is Burning*, a staffer from the NBC news program *Grandstand* decided to call every single airline pretending to be Jackson confirming his reservation. That's how they found out when and where he was landing, and they had the camera rolling when he stepped onto the tarmac. In his first year in the Bronx, Jackson alienated many of his teammates when, in comments made to *Sport Magazine* that appeared shortly after he joined the Yankees, he called himself "the straw that stirs the drink" and then went on to take a shot at team captain Thurman Munson. This seemed to be a habit with Jackson, who the media loved because he was a great quote. But his fellow players loathed him because they thought he was pretty much full of shit. He spoke of himself in the third person. Reggie described his hitting as being "like a storm" and then went on to use a variety of storm-related metaphors before also mentioning that even when he struck out it was still storm-like. "Hurricanes ain't nothing but soft winds when Reggie starts missin' when he goes for the downs," he said. After undergoing a prolonged slump and attending a chapel service, he emerged, Bible in tow, to say, "I was reminded that when we lose and I strike out a billion people in China don't care." He spoke of the "magnitude" of Reggie Jackson. Who talked like that? Each comment drew further scorn from his teammates and more dollars for the papers selling the copy. "Just as nature fills a vacuum," wrote author Bob Marshall, "Reggie fills a spotlight."

Billy Martin had a love-hate relationship with the media. "If writers knew any goddamn thing, they would be managers," he said. He often felt the press treated him unfairly, but he also took a liking to certain reporters. "I always got along with him and found him to be a fascinating character," said Klein, who recalled how after their initial meeting in spring training in 1976, Martin provided him with a scoop by telling him that the Yankees were going to platoon shortstops to start the season. Still the media, through no fault of their own, became Martin's undoing several times. In 1978 Martin's comments that Steinbrenner and Jackson were made for each other because: "one's a born liar, and the other's convicted," made to Chass of *The New York Times* ultimately led to his dismissal from the team. During the 1985 season, Martin became so mad at the press after he felt comments he'd made were unfairly taken as a slight to Yogi Berra that he began carrying a tape recorder with him. Later that year Martin got into a fight with pitcher Ed Whitson, part of which took place in front of members of the media.

Randy Johnson got off to a rocky start with the New York media after being traded from the Diamondbacks to the Yankees before the 2005 season. Johnson was bringing an impressive, Hall of Fame career with him to the Bronx and was viewed as the Yankees' answer to the Red Sox's Curt Schilling. But Johnson, never considered the most outgoing person to begin with, created controversy on his first day in the city as a Yankee. In town for his physical, Johnson was confronted by a cameraman on the street. He swatted the guy away, shoving his camera in the process. Johnson would later lampoon the episode in a mea culpa appearance on Letterman, but it was a predictor of what would be two rocky years in New York for the big lefty.

The Yankees already had to deal with more media than any other team, but when they went international, the circus came to town. Hideki Irabu was perhaps Japan's most famous pitcher during the '90s. With a good fastball and filthy split-finger, he was highly coveted by the Yankees. The feeling was mutual because Irabu, though the San Diego Padres had purchased him from his Japanese team, only wanted to play for New York. The two teams reached a deal, and in the summer of 1997, Irabu made his way to the Bronx. He was one of the first Japanese star players to come to

America, and the press from his home country swarmed into New York City, joining an already overcrowded press contingent of local and national folks who wanted to see what the fuss was about. His first start came against the Detroit Tigers in Yankee Stadium, and it was a spectacle. The place was packed, and flashbulbs popped everywhere as Irabu fanned nine Tigers in a little more than six innings of work, picking up the win.

It was nearly all downhill from there. In six of his next eight appearances, Irabu gave up five runs or more. There were grumblings in the clubhouse over how big a fuss Steinbrenner had made about signing a guy who couldn't get big league hitters out while other guys with proven track records made less money. Worse still was Irabu himself. He was moody and never seemed comfortable either in New York or with the hoopla made about his career. He sparred with the Japanese media that covered him in the states and wasn't overly friendly with the locals either. Irabu rebounded somewhat in 1998 and for a time early in the season was probably the best pitcher in baseball. (As late as June 20 of that year, his ERA stood at 1.68 over 11 starts.) But he was never a good fit for the clubhouse nor did he live up to all the hype. "I really consider the Irabu situation probably my biggest failure," Cerrone said. "Maybe I am too hard on myself about it because you can't help someone that doesn't want to be helped. We did everything we could. It was just, it was never pleasant. He had such an antagonistic relationship with the Japanese media that it made it very difficult. They hated him, and he hated them." The Yankees traded him to the Montreal Expos after the 1999 season, and his career ended in 2002. Nine years later Irabu committed suicide.

The sour taste left by the Irabu episode may have led some to be skeptical when the Yankees signed Hideki Matsui away from the Yomiuri Giants. Matsui was one of the greatest power hitters Japan had ever known. He could have easily stayed in Japan and lived off his fame forever. But he wanted to give his skills a try in America. From the beginning it was clear that Matsui would be the complete opposite of Irabu. While he valued his privacy—when he got married in 2008, the media and his teammates were largely unaware—he interacted well with the media. The swarm of Japanese press that followed him to New York was even larger than that of the Irabu years because of both the growth in mass communications and social media and the scope of Matsui's fame. But Matsui treated his countrymen with respect and never lost his temper. He did right by the New York media, too, inviting them to dinner each spring and picking up the tab.

After seeing the throngs of media that attended Matsui's initial press conference, Cerrone grew concerned this would be an Irabu situation all over again. "Well, it's funny because if you asked me at any point, including today, what's the worst thing that happened with Matsui or with the Asian media because of Matsui, I would not be able to come up with a single thing. It was the most enjoyable experience that I really have ever had," Cerrone said.

Helping matters was that Matsui was the real deal. He drove in more than 100 runs in four of his first five seasons in New York. (A broken wrist in 2006 prevented him from likely doing it in five of five years) and was a .312 hitter in the postseason for New York. The combination of personality and big hitting made Matsui a hit with the fans and the media and helped them forget the Irabu years. So popular was Matsui that, even though he left the team after 2009 and spent three seasons elsewhere, in the summer of 2013 he signed a one-day contract with the team so he could retire as a Yankee.

Three years after Matsui left New York, Ichiro Suzuki brought the international media back to town when he was traded from the Mariners to the Yankees. Irabu and Matsui had both been stars in Japan, but Ichiro was on another level. In Japan he was like a baseball, rock, and movie star all rolled into one. His fame continued and perhaps even grew when he came to the United States. He won Rookie of the Year and MVP in the same season. He broke the all-time single-season hit record. He made ridiculous throws and catches that were replayed time and again on highlight reels. As he approached 4,000 career hits (including his Japanese and Major League Baseball career) more and more international media started following the team. The milestone was huge news back home.

Of course, the Yankees were also dealing with other issues at the time that gave the media plenty to write about. The suspension of Alex Rodriguez for his connection to steroids during the second half of the 2013 season was a media sensation that kept going throughout the season. The Yankees were in the midst of one of their worst years on the field since the early '90s. But the main focus was on A-Rod. He'd spent the entire first half of the season on the disabled list, and any talk of his returning was marred by constant rumors that he would be suspended for his association with a group that dealt performance-enhancing drugs. Each day a new rumor surfaced, and even though A-Rod wasn't with the team, those in uniform were still left to answer what might happen should he return. There was also tension between A-Rod and the Yankees front office, whom many felt simply wanted to be rid of the game's most expensive headache. When a suspension was finally handed down (it was the equivalent of a year and a half out of the game), A-Rod appealed, meaning he could play the rest of the 2013 season. When he did return, he was met with boos in every ballpark, including Yankee Stadium.

Rodriguez appeared to make the situation as difficult for himself as he could. He got into a public spat with the team over whether he was healthy enough to play, prompting general manager Brian Cashman to say, "Alex should just shut the fuck up." When rumors surfaced that Rodriguez and his associates may have thrown players under the bus in the steroids scandal, A-Rod flatly denied them before adding that "every day, expect a story like this—if not bigger." It was an attempt to say that rumors will fly until he was able to clear the air, but instead it just made people wonder what else he was hiding.

A-Rod, like Irabu and others before them, was an example of how the media can giveth and taketh away. Rodriguez seemed to have a unique ability for saying the wrong thing on any given day even when he tried to give sterile quotes. After winning the MVP award in 2005, he told reporters, "We can win three World Series, [and] with me it's never going to be over. My benchmark is so high that no matter what I do, it's never going to be enough." A simple "this award is nice, but we didn't win the championship" would have sufficed. A-Rod tried to show how determined he was to succeed but instead simply set the bar to a level he couldn't possibly be expected to (and never did) reach. After the Yankees lost the American League Division Series that same year to the Angels, a series in which A-Rod was 2-of-15 with no RBIs and, as the tying run in the top of the ninth inning of Game 5, hit into a double play, Rodriguez admitted he played "like a dog." But even that sounded hollow and like a fake, manufactured quote. And then there were the times when he just didn't say the right thing at all. In a Tom Verducci story for *Sports Illustrated* in 2006, Rodriguez questioned why so many people turned on him for the Yankees' postseason struggles and not others. "[Mike] Mussina doesn't get hammered at all," he said. "He's making a boatload of money. [Jason] Giambi's making [$20.4 million], which is fine and dandy, but it seems those guys get a pass. When people write [bad things] about me, I don't know if it's [because] I'm good-looking, I'm biracial, I make the most money, I play on the most popular team." Pointing out how much your teammates made (and which ones you think apparently suck as much as you) was not the most endearing thing to do.

He seemed to work hard at trying to make people think he didn't care what they thought, but it was obvious he cared way too much. To be fair the media was intrusive into aspects of Rodriguez's life that went unfairly (and probably unethically, too) beyond the bounds of journalism. In 2007 the *New York Post* ran photographs of Rodriguez with another woman while in Toronto. (A-Rod was married at the time.) The woman turned out to be an exotic dancer, and Rodriguez and his wife filed for divorce a year later. The media, particularly the tabloids, were also obsessed with whatever celebrity Rodriguez happened to be dating at the time and what paintings he may or may not have had in his apartment. And the tabloids seemed to go out of their way to use as unflattering a picture of A-Rod as possible.

Was Rodriguez treated unfairly? Depends on whom you ask and probably when you ask them the question. In 2009 when A-Rod was crushing everything in sight during the postseason, no one seemed to care much. But A-Rod is a case study in how the media in New York operates. So the question is not whether the media is fair or unfair—but whether players are ready to handle the storm. Most who have come through the Yankees organization have been able to. Several could not. But like it or not, the media is part of life in the big city.

8

The 1990s

In the early 1990s, New York City and the Yankees were both at a crossroads. The city was a haven for drugs, crime, filth, and racial strife. The Yankees were suffering from bad personnel decisions, player discontent, and poor public relations. Both institutions needed substantial changes or they would be condemned to years, maybe decades of irrelevance. A series of events, however, was about to unfold, some through careful planning and some through dumb luck that would bring both the city and the Yankees back from the dead.

One of the most fortuitous moments in the history of the New York Yankees came in July of 1990 when George Steinbrenner was banned from having any involvement with the team. For years The Boss had been behind a series of disastrous moves and managerial firings that wreaked havoc on the club. Baseball's most illustrious franchise had become a laughingstock. But Steinbrenner's banishment was the blessing the team desperately needed. In his place Gene Michael took over as general manager and as architect of the team's future. Some thought Michael would be a mere figurehead, a yes man who would do Steinbrenner's bidding from behind-the-scenes. But Michael was a serious baseball man with a keen eye for talent.

A below average player known for his phobia of just about anything that moved, Michael had been a shortstop with the team and then manager twice. As manager he had had his share of run-ins with Steinbrenner. When the team struggled late in the '81 season, Steinbrenner began pestering him with phone calls. It didn't matter that because of the midseason strike the Yankees had already clinched a postseason spot. Steinbrenner actually thought that was causing the Yankees to take it too easy and that Michael couldn't motivate them. One day, while the two were talking on the phone in Chicago, Michael had had enough. "I'm sick and tired of your threats, George," Michael told him, according to Bill Madden's book *Steinbrenner*. "I can't take this anymore. If you want to fire me, then get your fat ass out here to Chicago and just do it!" That alone wasn't enough to cost Michael his job, but when he later told the press about the conversation, that clinched it. Steinbrenner, using a tactic he would repeat in the years to come, let Michael hang by a thread for a while and then axed him. It gave Michael the distinction of having been fired after the Yankees had clinched a postseason berth.

In 1982 Michael was hired back to replace Bob Lemon just 14 games into the season. During the second game of a home doubleheader that summer, the Yankees were getting crushed 14–2 by the Chicago White Sox. Bob Sheppard announced that all fans in attendance would receive free tickets to a future game. Michael heard the announcement and figured he wouldn't last much longer. (He was right; he was fired that night.) But when he wasn't the manager, Michael was a trusted Steinbrenner confidant who was one of the few people who could tell off The Boss.

Years before Michael Lewis popularized the term Moneyball for Billy Beane's baseball philosophy, Michael was initiating the same kind of strategy to jump-start the Yankees. With Steinbrenner out of the picture, Michael was free to sign whomever he wanted. Instead of going for the biggest names on the market, Michael signed players like Mike Stanley, a catcher with a great on-base percentage and plate discipline, and Jimmy Key, a pitcher who constantly posted at least 13 wins or more a season and had pinpoint control. But Michael needed more than just new players. He needed someone who could properly guide them toward both a winning attitude and a winning team. He found that man right within his own organization.

Buck Showalter had never played for or been associated with a different organization other than the Yankees during his professional baseball career. He'd been a first baseman in their minor league system before retiring in 1983. He immediately became a coach for the Yankees' Single A Team in Fort Lauderdale, Florida, moving up to manager of the Oneonta, New York, team in 1985. Showalter managed five years in the minors, and his teams finished in first place in four of those years. This experience allowed Showalter to familiarize himself with young prospects in the system, something that would come in handy later. "I was fortunate enough to have Buck Showalter as my first coach," Jim Leyritz said. "Buck was probably the biggest Yankee advocate at the time. He really instilled that in all the kids that he coached throughout the minor leagues, that it was something special to be a Yankee."

Showalter joined the Yankees in 1990 as a coach, lasting through 1991 until he was part of a purge that included manager Stump Merrill. Michael at first wanted to replace Stump with a proven manager such as Hal Lanier or Doug Rader. But the brass told him he should consider Showalter. Having just been fired by the team and not realizing they were even interested in him taking over as manager, Showalter was nearly speechless when Michael called to offer the position. On October 20, 1991, Showalter was named manager. The 35-year-old was the youngest manager in the game and the youngest for the Yankees in 77 years.

Michael and Showalter agreed that they had to rid the team of many of the negative influences that permeated the clubhouse. Too many players were focused on themselves and not on the team. That was unacceptable to Showalter, a man who'd come up through the team's system and considered being a Yankee an honor and a privilege—not a right. Showalter was going to create a place where the team always came first. And he was going to instill the team's image of old. The Yankees were going to look classy, they were going to be dressed well after the game and on the planes, and their clubhouse was going to look better. It wasn't just about performance on the field; it was about the image you created off it. The Yankees were going to be all class, all the time.

In addition you weren't going to find another manager who studied longer and harder than Showalter. "[He was] somebody that covered all his bases, that did his homework, did his research," Stanley said. "There weren't many things that caught him off guard. People even now talk about what kind of brilliant mind that he had, and that is just hours and hours and hours of being at the field and studying matchups and mannerisms."

Showalter devoured videotapes and statistics. He spent every waking moment thinking of ways to win the next day's game. "He was the most prepared manager that I had ever played for," Paul O'Neill said. "Every little detail was taken care of before a game started. He was part of turning that organization around and a big part of it." In time Showalter's micromanaging style would wear some people down. But it was exactly what the Yankees needed at first.

Utilizing the new team concept, most of the players who were the biggest problems were cast away within two years of the Yankees' dreadful 1990 performance. In their place came guys like Spike Owen, Steve Farr, and Mike Gallego, grind-it-out guys for whom losing was not acceptable. Then in November of 1992, Michael executed one of the biggest trades in team history when he acquired outfielder O'Neill from the Cincinnati Reds in exchange for Roberto Kelly. Kelly spent just a year and a half in Cincinnati while O'Neill went on to win a batting title in New York, hit over .300 six times, and drive in more than 100 runs four times. "The resurgence of like-personalities was a complete 180 makeover that the Yankees were making a conscious effort to do," Wade Boggs said. "They brought in myself, Jimmy Key, Paul O'Neill. They got rid of a ton of guys and just sort of revamped basically their whole lineup."

With Steinbrenner gone there was no urge to ship away young prospects for aged talent. Even in 1993 after The Boss returned, Michael refused to sacrifice the future for any big names, even though the Yankees were chasing the Toronto Blue Jays for first place. Michael was correct in his belief that the team just wasn't good enough yet to stay in competition and he wasn't going to make it worse with an ill-advised trade. Because of that players like Leyritz, Sterling Hitchcock, Scott Kamieniecki, Derek Jeter, Mariano Rivera, Jorge Posada, and Andy Pettitte were allowed to grow within the system and eventually make major contributions at the big league level. Each of them would have almost certainly been traded away under the old Steinbrenner way of doing things.

The combination of Steinbrenner's absence, Michael's moves, and Showalter's managerial style altered the landscape of the team and organization in ways that are still felt 20 years later. The more immediate impact was a new powerhouse in the American League. In 1990 the Yankees finished last in the AL in batting average, hits, runs scored, and on-base percentage. By 1993 they were first in hits, first in batting average, and second in on-base percentage. The next year they were the best team in the American League. "Our '94 team is probably the best Yankee team I ever played on," Boggs said. "We were really taking names and just blowing people out of the water."

But the strike derailed any playoff hopes. The following season they became the first ever AL wild-card, clinching a postseason berth on the last day of the year. It was the first time the Yankees had gone to the playoffs in 14 years, their longest drought since first winning the World Series in 1923. They lost a heartbreaking, five-game series to the Seattle Mariners, even though they held a 2–0 lead, were up 5–0 in Game 4, and led 4–2 in the eighth inning of Game 5 before taking the lead in extra innings.

The next year was important not just for getting the playoff monkey off the team's back, but also because it showed the Yankees could retain homegrown talent and be successful. Bernie Williams broke out in 1995 and set a major league mark when he homered from both sides of the plate in Game 3 of the AL Division Series. The Yankees could never have made the postseason if not for the pitching contributions of Kamienicki and Hitchcock or the timely hitting and defensive play of people like Randy Velarde and Pat Kelly.

In addition to the homegrown talent that contributed to that squad, 1995 was also significant because it saw the arrival of four minor leaguers who would have a significant impact on the team for nearly two decades: Jeter, Rivera, Pettitte, and Posada—also known as the "Core Four." Each of them made their major league debut that season, though in the end, only Pettitte would make a significant contribution during the regular season while Rivera would emerge as a pitcher to be feared during the postseason. Pettitte made the club out of spring training and was critical all season long as the team's starting rotation was decimated by injuries. He went 12–9 that year, making 26 starts and finishing third in Rookie of the Year voting.

Rivera made his debut that season on May 23rd as a starter against the California Angels in Anaheim. He got clobbered, but he picked up his first major league win in his next start. Then he got clobbered again…and again. After four major league starts, Rivera's ERA stood at 10.20. He was sent down to the minors. Then something happened. No one has any idea what, though Rivera, an extremely religious man, chalks it up to the man in the sky. All of the sudden, Rivera's pitches began moving, and his fastball gained speed. It happened totally out of the blue. The Yankees brought him up to face the White Sox on July 4th in Chicago: he struck out 11 in eight innings, giving up only two hits. The rest of his season was just okay. He made his last major league start on September 5th and got hammered. From that point on, Rivera never appeared in another major league game as anything but a relief pitcher. In the ALDS against the Mariners, he struck out eight in five-plus innings and picked up the win in Game 2. Entering the eighth inning of Game 5 with the bases loaded, two out, and the score tied, Rivera struck out Mike Blowers on three straight pitches. Michael, watching the performance, turned to no one in particular and said, "I think we found something here."

Six days after Rivera made his debut, while they were playing the Mariners in Seattle, Derek Sanderson Jeter made his first start at shortstop for the Yankees. The next night he collected the first of what would eventually become the most hits by a Yankees player.

The 1990s would feature not only a revival of New York City, but also the launch of the "Core Four"—(from left to right) Jorge Posada, Mariano Rivera, Derek Jeter, and Andy Pettitte—as Yankees.

Jeter played for two straight weeks before being sent down to the minors. He was called up in September but only got into two more games. He was the only member of the Core Four not to be on the postseason roster that year, but Showlater had him in uniform and on the bench anyway during the ALDS. He knew how special Jeter was going to be and he wanted him to see up close what playoff baseball in New York was going to be like. Even though he was just a rookie and not even playing, Jeter was usually the first person out of the dugout to greet a teammate during the series.

Posada got into one game in 1995. He was a defensive replacement at catcher in the ninth inning of a Yankees blowout against the Mariners. He didn't even get to hit, and yet when the postseason came around, Showalter wanted to carry three catchers, so Posada actually made the roster. And even though Posada never even batted during a major league, Showalter inserted him as a pinch-runner in the bottom of the 12th inning of Game 2 with the Yankees down a run. Posada eventually scored to tie the game. It was his only appearance in the series.

The Core Four would go on to win five world championships together while appearing in a total of seven World Series. Only once in the 13 seasons, in which all four were on the club, did the Yankees fail to make the playoffs. It was truly a remarkable run— perhaps unparalleled in baseball history. To have two teammates play together for that period of time might be considered an accomplishment. But to have four do it, and with so much success, was unheard of. Technically, Pettitte was the first to hang them up, retiring after the 2010 season. But he returned to baseball in 2012. Posada retired after 2011, and Rivera announced that 2013 would be his last year. Pettitte also hung up his spikes after 2013. It was the beginning of the end of an amazing era in Yankees history.

As a result of the loss to Seattle, Steinbrenner did not bring back Showalter to manage for the '96 season. It was an extremely controversial move at the time, but the lessons and the pride Showalter instilled carried over to the next version of Yankees. That version was led by Brooklyn native Joe Torre, who had been a highly successful ballplayer mostly with the St. Louis Cardinals. But his managerial record of 894–1,003 left something to be desired. At that point Torre was perhaps best known as having played and managed the most games without ever reaching the World Series. His hiring was so explosive that Steinbrenner actually asked Showalter to come back, saying he would make Torre club president instead. Showalter, who had already committed to being manager of the expansion Arizona Diamondbacks, refused.

The manager wasn't the only change. After the playoff loss in '95, Steinbrenner completely revamped the entire organization from top to bottom. Gone was Gene Michael, who was pushed out as general manager and moved over to scouting. Gone was most of the scouting department. Gone was the public relations director.

Gone were most of the players on the field with 60 percent of the team changing from October 1995 to October 1996. Most of these moves were universally panned. Joe Girardi, a light-hitting catcher from Colorado, was brought in to replace fan favorite Mike Stanley, one of the greatest offensive catchers in team history. Randy Velarde, another fan favorite, was allowed to sign elsewhere. Don Mattingly retired. And on and on it went.

Few could have guessed how successful Torre's hiring would be. Torre was a calming clubhouse presence who willingly provided a buffer between his players and The Boss. Instead of trying to avoid Steinbrenner, Torre would proactively reach out to him, especially when times were bad, to defuse any potential problems before they exploded. Torre also brought over a National League style of baseball that focused on the hit-and-run and double stealing. He set the tone early when on the first day of spring training in '96, he told his assembled team that he didn't just want to win one championship. "I want to win three of them in a row," Torre recalled in *The Yankee Years*. "I want to establish something here that's special. I don't want to sacrifice principles and players to do it one time. I want to establish a foundation to be the kind of ballclub that is going to be able to repeat." It was a great, reassuring way to introduce himself to a bunch of players who, for the most part, had had no dealings with Torre before.

"I mean he was the perfect guy at the time to go through the World Series and to win," O'Neill said. "He understood people and things off the field. He understood that things off the field affected players more than any manager I ever played for. You just had respect for Joe Torre. He kind of belonged in New York because he grew up in New York."

Nearly all of the moves made worked out in the end. People could complain about the Yankees buying championships all they want, but unlike the '80s, the Yankees spent wisely on free agents and made smart trades during the '90s. Each piece they picked up seemed to fit perfectly whether it be Girardi, Tino Martinez, Tim Raines, Jeff Nelson, Mariano Duncan, Doc Gooden, or Darryl Strawberry. In later years Chad Curtis, Scott Brosius, Jason

Grimsley, Luis Sojo, and Jose Vizciano would each play enormous roles in the team's success. And throughout nearly all of it, the principles used by Michael and Showalter to bring the club back to glory stayed in place—even if the names changed. It was about grinding out at-bats, building up pitch counts, getting to bullpens early, and drawing walks.

All these changes during the course of the decade, both in attitude and personnel, created a dynasty nearly equal to that of the Yankee teams of the 1930s and 1950s. From 1996 to 2001, the Yankees won four championships with only a bottom of the ninth inning Game 7 rally by the Diamondbacks keeping it from being five. In an eight-year period, they won six pennants and from 1995 to 2012 and missed the postseason only once.

It wasn't just that they won but how they won. The Yankees were the very definition of a team. On none of those championship squads did a single player hit more than 30 home runs. The 1998 team may go down as the greatest in baseball history, winning 114 games during the regular season and, playoffs included, finishing the year 125–50. Six players that year had at least 10 home runs and 10 stolen bases while 10 players hit double figures in home runs. Six different pitchers won 10 games or more. The 2000 team won just 87 games—fewer than eight other teams and less than the 1993 Yankees, who missed the postseason. But during the playoffs that year, they used timely hitting and big pitching to eek their way to a title.

The Yankees' postseason performance during this period was almost incomprehensible. As noted in *The Yankee Years*, they played .805 ball during the playoffs from 1998 to 2000, going 33–8. They allowed zero, one, or two runs in 32 of those 41 games and were 15–3 in playoff games decided by one or two runs. In three World Series during that time, they were 12–1 with their only loss coming in Game 3 of the 2000 Subway Series. That loss actually snapped a baseball-record string of 14 consecutive World Series wins, dating back to 1996.

Their dominance, however, certainly did not mean a lack of drama. With the exception of the 1999 postseason, in which they lost only one game, the Yankees were in serious peril of being eliminated during each of their championship runs. During the ALDS against the Texas Rangers in 1996, the Yankees trailed at least once in every single ballgame. They lost the opener 6–2 and then trailed 4–1 in Game 2 after three innings. A base hit by Cecil Fielder in the eighth tied things up, and the Yankees won it in the 12th on an error by third baseman Dean Palmer off a Charlie Hayes sacrifice bunt. In Game 3 they trailed 2–1, heading into the top of the ninth. But base hits by Jeter and Raines, coupled with a Williams sacrifice fly and a two-out hit by Duncan, put the Yankees ahead for good 3–2. They were down 4–0 after three innings in Game 4 but clawed back to take the lead in the seventh inning. They won the game 6–4. For the series the bullpen was 3–0 and gave up only one earned run.

In the AL Championship Series opener against the Baltimore Orioles, the Yankees trailed 4–3 in the eighth when Jeter hit a long fly ball to right field. As outfielder Tony Tarasco attempted to settle underneath it, 12-year-old Jeffrey Maier reached over the outfield wall and deflected the ball into the stands. Right field umpire Richie Garcia controversially ruled it a home run, tying the game. In the bottom of the 11th, Williams homered to end it. After dropping Game 2, the Yankees trailed 2–1 in the eighth inning of Game 3 when two-out hits by Jeter, Williams, Martinez, and Fielder gave them a 5–2 lead that they never relinquished. Key, who went eight innings that night, was the first Yankees starter to win a game that postseason. The Yankees went on to win the series 4–1, moving on to face the Atlanta Braves in the World Series.

The first two games played at Yankee Stadium were a mess. New York dropped the opener 12–1, its worst World Series defeat at the time. The next night Greg Maddux shut them down 4–0. Things were not looking good, but the series changed in Atlanta. The Yankees won a tense Game 3 in which they came close to squandering the lead in the sixth inning, but David Cone pitched out of a bases-loaded jam. They won 5–2. Game 4 saw the greatest comeback in team postseason history. The Yankees fell behind 6–0 after five innings, scored three in the six to cut the lead in half, and then had two runners on with one out in the eighth inning for Leyritz. Atlanta pitcher Mark Wohlers left a slider over the plate that Leyritz deposited over the wall in left field, tying the game. It was one of the biggest home runs in World Series history. In the 10th a bases-loaded walk by Boggs and an Atlanta error gave the Yankees an 8–6 lead. The Yankees never trailed again in the series. They won 1–0 as John Wetteland prevented a runner on third from scoring with less than two outs in the ninth inning in Game 5. In Game 6 with his team ahead 3–2 and the go-ahead run on base, Wetteland got Mark Lemke to pop up, giving New York the title. During that entire run, the Yankees went 8–0 on the road with the bullpen winning four of those games.

In 1998 the Yankees trailed Cleveland 2–1 in the best-of-seven ALCS before Orlando Hernandez saved the season with seven shutout innings in Game 4. David Wells won the next day, and the Yankees clinched the pennant at home in Game 6. In the opening game of the World Series against the San Diego Padres, Wells gave up three home runs to put the team in a 5–2 hole. But in the seventh, Chuck Knoblauch hit a three-run home run to tie the game and with two outs, Tino Martinez crushed a Mark Langston fastball into the upper deck for a go-ahead grand slam. The Yankees took the first two games, and the series shifted to San Diego. There the Yankees trailed 3–2 in the eighth inning of Game 3 when Brosius came up with two on against closer Trevor Hoffman, the best closer in the National League. Baseball's career leader in saves at one point, he tried to get a fastball by Brosius. The Yankees third baseman lined it over the wall in center field, putting the Yankees ahead 5–3. New York went on to sweep the Padres with Brosius winning the World Series MVP.

The 2000 Yankees were certainly no guarantee to win it all. They had stumbled badly in September, finishing the year 3–15, including losing their last seven games by a combined score of 68–15. They won 87 games that year, the lowest total of the Torre er. The playoffs looked like they'd be no different as the Yankees lost the first game in Oakland against an upstart A's team. They rebounded to win the next two games but were crushed in a

Game 4 loss, forcing them to fly cross-country back to Oakland. Finally showing the spark that had been the calling card of previous teams, the Yankees jumped out to a 6–0 lead in Game 5 and eventually held on to win 7–5.

In the ALCS against the Mariners, they trailed late in both Games 2 and 6, but big hits by David Justice, including a three-run home run in Game 6 that gave them the lead for good, helped them win the series. On came the New York Mets. It was the first Subway Series in 44 years, and for many fans, the past three championships did not matter if the Yankees failed to beat their crosstown rivals. Game 1 at Yankee Stadium was classic with the Yankees trailing 3–2 heading into the ninth. With one out O'Neill worked a now legendary walk against Mets closer Armando Benitez. Two base hits and a sacrifice fly later, the game was tied. In extra innings the Yankees wasted several chances before finally winning it in the 12th.

The next day brought some fireworks after Roger Clemens threw a piece of shattered bat in the direction of Mets catcher Mike Piazza, who earlier in the year had suffered a concussion courtesy of a Clemens fastball. The Yankees won that night, lost Game 3, and then took Game 4. They trailed in Game 5 when Jeter hit his second home run of the series to tie it up. In the top of the ninth, Sojo's base hit gave the Yankees the lead, and Rivera finished off the three-peat in the ninth. It was the last championship the Yankees would win under Torre and it brought to an end one of the most remarkable five-year runs in baseball history: five playoff appearances, four titles, and an overall record of 46–15 in the playoffs, including a staggering 25–7 on the road.

Just as the Yankees were taking back their status as the game's greatest franchise, New York City was taking back its status as the world's greatest city. Much as the suspension of Steinbrenner altered the course of Yankee history, the election of Rudolph William Giuliani as mayor was a game changer for New York. There can certainly be a debate on how much if any credit he deserves for what transpired. But no one can question that New York became a different and much improved place under his watch. Love him or hate him, Giuliani was in many ways just what New York City needed after the turmoil of the '80s.

Having narrowly lost the mayoral race in 1989, Giuliani came out swinging in a 1993 rematch against incumbent mayor David Dinkins. He blasted Dinkins for the city's high crime rate and poor economy. Neither of these were Dinkins' fault. He'd inherited these problems from the Koch administration, and a national recession had occurred halfway through his term. But Dinkins had trouble communicating with the public and often appeared indecisive. Giuliani was forceful, blunt, and understood the importance of good public relations from his days as U.S. Attorney.

The campaign also took on a harsh racial tone. Dinkins had overseen racial strife in the last years of his administration, particularly in the Crown Heights section of Brooklyn. It was there in the summer of 1991 that seven-year-old Gavin Cato, who was black, was struck and killed by a car driven by a Hasidic Jew. The accident exasperated tensions in the neighborhood between black residents and the small Jewish population. With rumors swirling that an ambulance driven by members of the faith had left the boy to die, rioting erupted. In the aftermath, a 29-year-old Hasidic Jew traveling from Australia was killed.

Giuliani used the riots against Dinkins in the election, claiming he allowed the rioters to go on unrestrained. He also chided Dinkins for creating racial tension, saying the mayor was too willing to retreat "into black victimization" in order to deal with the issues he faced. Dinkins' campaign did not hold back either. His campaign manager compared Giuliani to former Ku Klux Klan leader David Duke.

In the end Giuliani eked out a slim victory over Dinkins. The mayor had actually retained much of the support he'd received four years earlier, but Giuliani was able to boost his numbers in white ethnic strongholds in Brooklyn, Queens, and Staten Island. Moreover, Giuliani skillfully exploited the crime issue. Almost four in 10 voters chose crime as one of the two most important issues, and two-thirds of those voters chose Giuliani. More than half of all voters said the city had become less safe under Dinkins, and 75 percent of them voted for Giuliani.

Giuliani made no secret that crime reduction was going to be a major concern of his administration. What kind of crime, though, was a little uncertain. During the campaign he'd made a point of attacking the city's squeegee men and panhandlers as well as the large amounts of trash that littered the streets. It was quality of life crimes that infected the city and allowed for other more serious crimes to flourish. These smaller, petty crimes were a drag on the entire city both for the obvious direct impact and the indirect impact of keeping people away from New York.

Somewhat ironically, it turned out that crime fell in New York not because of going after these small crimes, but because the bigger, more serious crimes were targeted. Much has been made of the "broken windows" theory, the idea that if you allow small crimes like vandalism and larceny to occur without consequence, quality of life declines, and crime goes up in the neighborhood. This idea, which fit into Giuliani's squeegee men attack, has often been credited with having turned around the tide of crime that rocked the city in the '80s and early '90s. There is certainly no doubt that Giuliani initiated a crackdown on these kinds of crimes, pushing these people off the streets or at least out of the more popular New York neighborhoods where tourists flocked. He declared war on such things as air pollution, littering, jaywalking, even riding bicycles where they weren't permitted. Times Square and 42nd Street, areas that had become synonymous with hookers and porn shops, were cleaned out and cleaned up.

Although there were those who felt Giuliani took this fight too far, sometimes impinging upon people's rights, few could deny that the streets were becoming cleaner and there was less of a chance of getting hassled by the dreaded squeegee men. But the truth behind New York's amazing drop in crime is better explained by two simple things: more cops on the street and better targeting of certain crimes.

Giuliani selected William Bratton as police commissioner in 1994, and Bratton set about changing how the department dealt with crime. They initiated the CompStat system of tracking crimes. Through CompStat the police were able to get a better feel for where certain crimes were occurring and deduce any visible patterns. Of course, it helped that the city was able to hire thousands of new police officers during the decade, the result of new taxes and a growing economy. With more officers on the beat, the city was able to place more of them in hot spots, areas with the highest concentration of violent crimes. Franklin Zimring, a University of California, Berkeley criminal justice professor wrote, "Police increased narcotics unit manpower by 137 percent and dedicated their efforts to destroying open-air drug markets." This helped deter crime in the long and short run. Criminals are most likely not going to commit a crime with an officer in plain view or just around the corner. Moreover, if a criminal does not act one day, it does not mean they will simply save that crime for another day. They may just give up on the idea.

There were other possible reasons for the drop in crime. The national economy was improving as the mid-1990s hit. The crack epidemic had come to an end. But regardless of where the credit belongs, the results were striking. According to Greg David in his book, *Modern New York: The Life and Economics of a City*, violent and property crime in New York fell by nearly 26 percent from 1993 to 1995, far greater than the national trend of 3 percent. Malcolm Gladwell noted in the *New Yorker* that by 1996, "New York's violent crime rate ranked 136th among major American cities—on a par with Boise, Idaho." In 2000 there were 673 murders in all of New York compared with 2,251 that had occurred in 1990. The number of rapes fell by half in that same time period, and violent crime overall dropped by 43.5 percent.

James Q. Wilson, a former UCLA and Harvard professor who is credited with developing the broken windows theory of crime reduction, gave credit to Bratton for much of what happened, but not necessarily for implementing Wilson's theory. "The biggest change in policing in this country that's occurred is usually associated with Bill Bratton," said Wilson a year before he died. "And that's a correct association. He made a huge difference. But people misstate what the change was. They say he adopted the broken windows theory. Well, I'm not sure he did, and if he did, I'm not sure it made much difference to the crime rate. What he really did—his fundamental contribution—was to persuade the police that your job is not to make arrests. Your job is to prevent crime."

The numbers didn't regress after the turn of the century. Instead they got better. The murder rate in 2007 was the lowest it had been since 1963. New York remained the safest big city in the country.

While crime was falling, the national economy rebounded, taking the city along with it. Giuliani, who made sure he was there when Steinbrenner was presented the championship trophy, remarked that the Yankees winning the 1996 World Series was "a metaphor for a city that is undergoing a great renaissance." In 1996 New York added 44,500 jobs, its best performance since the early 1980s. The unemployment rate in the city, which reached 11.9 percent in January of 1993 dropped to 6.4 percent by March of 1999. New jobs in both New York and the rest of country coupled with an explosion in the dot.com industry sent the stock market soaring, and those involved in Wall Street made money hand over fist.

By the 21st century, the character and public persona of New York City had drastically changed even before the events of 9/11 unified a nation around the Big Apple. Instead of a haven for criminals and dangerous streets, New York became one of the safest cities in the country. The cleaning up of Times Square and the surrounding area allowed mass media and corporations to come in. The Gap opened up a store there followed shortly thereafter by the Disney Corporation, Madame Tussauds wax museum, and a new movie theater. (To be fair these deals happened during the Dinkins administration but did not come to fruition until the mid-1990s.) As these new megastores came about, the Giuliani administration stepped up its efforts to rid the area of the porn shops and sex stores, for which Times Square had become synonymous. They did so through a series of zoning ordinances that drew the ire of civil liberties groups. As the area became more sanitized, literally and figuratively, more brand name stores followed suit, revitalizing midtown Manhattan and bringing in millions of tourists each year. Instead of worrying about their kids bumping into a prostitute, parents could get pictures of their children standing next to the latest Disney musical character to hit Broadway. By 2009 New York City was the "No. 1 tourist destination in the country," drawing in more people than Disney World, according to David. It was a long ways removed from the days where Charles Bronson exacted vigilante justice on the streets of New York.

Giuliani took credit for much of this transition and was still popular even after a messy and very public divorce. After he left office, crime rates continued to fall at nearly unheard of levels. The economy, hurt badly by the 9/11 attacks, rebounded and was able to stave off the ill effects of the recession of 2008 better than most cities. Like the Yankees the city's rehabilitation from the '80s and early '90s had an impact that lasted long after the new millennium.

9

Wall Street

The sun was shining over Kauffman Stadium, a quaint ballpark located about eight miles outside of downtown Kansas City. Situated next to Arrowhead Stadium, Kauffman was simple yet elegant. In the outfield, water fountains shot into the air while a huge scoreboard adorned with a Royals crown stood beyond the center-field fence. In the 1970s and most of the 1980s, the hometown Royals had been among the cream of the crop in the American League. In a 10-year period, they won six division titles and took home their first championship in 1985. They repeatedly clashed in the playoffs against the New York Yankees during the late 1970s. Now on this warm April 30th night in 1999, they hadn't made the postseason since '85. Their owner and the stadium's namesake had died in 1993, and they had never really recovered. The economics of baseball were leaving this small-market team behind while big-city teams motored ahead. The Royals simply couldn't compete in the current climate, or at least that's what many of their fans felt. They were angry and they were looking for change.

On this night the Yankees were in town. Their leadoff hitter, Chuck Knoblauch, strode to the plate on this beautiful spring evening, the first in a four-game series. The second baseman earned

$6 million a year more than the entire starting lineup of the Royals that night. Bernie Williams, the Yankees center fielder, earned $9.5 million that year—almost double the Royals' starting lineup. As Knoblauch awaited the first pitch from Royals starting pitcher Jay Witasick, thousands of fans seated in the left-field grandstand turned their backs to the action. Royals fans were staging a protest. They were fed up with the growing inequality of the game, an inequality that allowed the Yankees to pay their team nearly three times what Kansas City could afford to pay theirs. Whenever the Yankees batted, the fans refused to watch. And when the Royals were up, fans would wave fake dollar bills in front of the Yankee players in the field. "We are not there to bash the Yankees," said Kevin Kietzman, then the sports director for KCTE radio, which had organized the protest. "These people are passionate about baseball. They want to protect baseball."

Kietzman's claim, however, was unconvincing. Of course, they were there to bash the Yankees. Who better to showcase greed and all that was wrong with the way baseball's economics worked than the Yankees? They were the poster children for wanton, reckless, win-at-all costs spending. Hell, even the large-market teams complained about the Yankees payroll. Royals fans, who had seen their team go winless against the Yankees in 1998, won the battle on this night, watching their home team pound New York 13–6. But when the season ended, the Yankees had "bought" another championship, and the Royals were home watching it. To most fans the Yankees had become baseball's version of Wall Street: the corporate titans who screwed over working people and rigged the game so they always came out on top. Their owner, George Steinbrenner, was Rockefeller, Carnegie, and Vanderbilt all wrapped into one. The owner, the team, and the fans, who were complicit in allowing their championships to be bought while other teams scratched and scrapped just to get to .500, were easy to hate. And in a sense, that night in Kansas City was a reflection—perhaps even the start of what a decade later would be an occupy movement situated in the heart of New York City's downtown to protest corporate greed and excess. Only this time it wasn't the Yankees.

The Yankees had just come off perhaps the greatest season in baseball history. They'd finished the 1998 regular season 114–48, setting what was a single-season American League record for wins at the time. Six different pitchers won 10 or more games. Six players had double-digit home runs and stolen bases. They'd clinched a postseason berth by August 29, the earliest any team had done so in modern baseball history. The Boston Red Sox comfortably won the AL wild-card that year and still finished 22 games behind New York in the standings. In the playoffs the Yankees easily dispatched the Texas Rangers in a first-round sweep. They survived a brief scare against the Cleveland Indians to take the AL pennant in six games. Then in the World Series, they twice overcame late-game deficits of three runs, sweeping the San Diego Padres and finishing the year a combined 125–50.

The 1998 Yankees were arguably the greatest team ever assembled, and as the team headed into spring training in 1999, there was little reason to believe New York would not again dominate the American League. Their entire starting rotation and starting lineup were returning, healthy and intact. There was nothing else the team could possibly need to solidify it. Then on February 18, it happened: the Yankees acquired the game's best pitcher, Roger Clemens. Clemens had signed with the Toronto Blue Jays two years earlier after a falling out with the Red Sox, a team for whom he'd pitched 13 seasons. In Boston "the Rocket" won 192 games, three Cy Youngs, and led the league in strikeouts three times. He'd set a record for most strikeouts in a nine-inning game with 20, a feat he accomplished on two different occasions. But after a subpar '96 season, the Red Sox had wished Clemens well in the twilight of his career. In Toronto a rejuvenated Clemens simply dominated, leading the American League in wins and strikeouts in 1997 and '98. He won the Cy Young Award both years. His $8 million a year salary would have made him untouchable for any team the Blue Jays could think of trading him to—except the New York Yankees. And for a growing number of teams and their fans, that was starting to become a major problem. The Yankees simply, and many would say unfairly, had too much money.

By the late '90s, criticizing the Yankees' spending habits became as time-honored a tradition as the seventh-inning stretch. For most Yankee haters, it was simply a part of the game. Going back to the time Jacob Ruppert and Cap Huston purchased the team, the Yankees had spent lavishly on players. Babe Ruth earned $80,000 a year, more than President Hoover, prompting Ruth's famous quip, "I had a better year than he did." But earning that much was unheard of at the time for an athlete. After Ruth, DiMaggio and Mantle followed suit, signing astronomical contracts that made them rich beyond their dreams. And it wasn't just star players that they spent on either. The Yankees lured in hundreds of young prospects through the power of offering substantially higher signing bonuses than most teams. Over the years the Yankees wasted thousands (a substantial amount at the time) on kids who never made an impact at the major league level, and all just because they could.

As championships continued throughout the 1930s, 1940s, and 1950s, the success brought in more money, allowing the team to remain on top. "The Yankees traditionally dominate baseball by sheer economic might," wrote Jim Murray in a 1950 article for *Life* magazine. As titles piled up, resentment began to build around the league. The Yankees were viewed by many as corporate "like rooting for U.S. Steel," comedian Joe E. Lewis remarked. Replace the pinstripe uniform with a pinstripe suit, and there was really no difference to many. Even the fans were seen as elitists. Brooklyn Dodgers fans were working-class stiffs out to enjoy a game. Yankees fans were suit-wearing Manhattanites out to socialize at a baseball event. The Yankees represented the wealthy elite—Wall Street. The Yankees in some ways certainly earned the corporate designation. As early as the 1930s, they were doing things other teams didn't because they could afford to. Most teams traveled in a single train car. The Yankees traveled in two and always toward the back so they could maintain privacy. Manager Joe McCarthy required players to wear jackets when dining out, and everyone was expected to arrive on time. McCarthy even banned card playing. McCarthy once gave a player $100 for a new overcoat because he didn't think the one the player was wearing was good enough for the Yankees. "Young man," he told him, "I want you to dress like a Yankee."

The Yankees were viewed as the white-collar organization. "Back in the '50s and '60s, we played more than half our games in the daytime. So a lot of businessmen would come right from work, from downtown in limousines and corporate cars. That is where that image came from of the Yankees being a corporate-type thing," said former Yankees pitcher Al Downing. The corporate status was ironic given that most of players on the team were country boys who grew up relatively poor in working-class families. But for many fans, that reality didn't matter.

By 1939 the other teams in the league had grown so leery of the Yankees' success that Washington Senators owner Clark Griffith proposed a resolution banning any team from trading or selling a player to the defending championship club. Clearly aimed at New York, it was a desperate move that the other American League owners actually ended up approving, though it didn't last long. Despite the feeling of inequality, the playing field was still fairly level at the time. Team revenue was almost entirely attendance driven, and while the Yankees played in the most populous area of the country, their attendance figures were certainly not blowing other teams out of the water. And because players were shackled to their teams for life due to the reserve clause (unless a team gave them their release), there were no bidding wars among teams for a player's services. Clubs offered their players whatever they saw fit, and a player's only recourse was to hold out for more money. He either didn't play or he gave in and accepted a lower salary.

The age of free agency and the development of television to broadcast games changed all of that. In late 1974 an arbitrator ruled that the Oakland A's had violated the terms of their contract with pitcher Jim "Catfish" Hunter. The contract was now null and void, meaning Hunter was a free agent. It opened the floodgates. Just a year later, the same arbitrator ruled that pitchers Andy Messersmith and Dave McNally were free agents, too, after they went an entire year without signing a contract. The ruling killed the reserve clause once and forever. Players were now going to be free agents with clubs outbidding one another for their services.

Having bought the team in 1973, Steinbrenner made it known immediately that he would go after all the top-line free agents and pay any price to get them. First was Hunter in 1975 at five years and $3.35 million. (Though Steinbrenner was suspended at the time of the signing, there is little doubt he was involved.) Then in 1976 Don Gullett signed for six years and $2 million, and Reggie Jackson signed for five years and nearly $3 million. Then in 1977 it was Rich "Goose" Gossage for $2.8 million and six years. In 1980 Steinbrenner's 10-year, $23 million offer to Dave Winfield (complete with a cost of living adjustment that would be the source of great tension between the two) was the largest contract in history to that time. Before the start of the 1977 AL Championship Series matchup between the Royals and the Yankees, no wonder Kansas City manager Whitey Herzog said, "All of baseball wants us to win. Not that they love us…they just hate the Yankees and their check writing."

It wasn't just that Steinbrenner was buying up all the best talent either. He was also paying top dollar for mediocre and questionable talent. He signed outfielder Steve Kemp to a five-year contract for more than $5 million for what turned out to be two injury-plagued seasons that resulted in a total of 19 home runs and 90 RBIs before he was traded away. He signed pitcher Ed Whitson to a five-year, $4.4 million deal for what turned into a season and a half of absolute horror for both the pitcher and the team. Whitson's performance was so poor and his treatment from the fans so merciless that he eventually only would pitch on the road. Late in the 1985 season, he broke manager Billy Martin's arm in a bar room fight. Steinbrenner paid pitcher Dave LaPoint $1.6 million for 13 wins over two years and Pascual Perez $3.5 million for three wins over two years before he was suspended an entire season for drug use.

Other owners and their fans might laugh seeing these large contracts backfire, but they also knew that these deals were just as bad for their clubs, too. If Andy Hawkins was making more than a million dollars a year to post an ERA of 5.37, how much were small-market teams going to have to shell out to a premier pitcher like Greg Maddux or Jack Morris? "If another team seemed to overpay for a player, it was seen as the 'Yankee factor,'" wrote Marty Appel in *Pinstripe Empire*. "If they didn't, the Yankees would. And every agent wanted his player to be coveted by the Yankees, driving up the value." Things became so bad that during the mid-1980s, the owners conspired together to hold down salaries by refusing to sign long-term contracts or shell out big dollars to the best free agents. For two offseasons the owners managed to keep things on track. Only Steinbrenner, of course, dared defy them when he offered catcher Carlton Fisk a deal. But even Steinbrenner backed down when Chicago White Sox chairman Jerry Reinsdorf asked him to rescind the offer. Eventually, collusion, as it was called, became public with dire consequences for the game.

Collusion added to an already poisonous relationship between the owners and players. It was the final straw that officially removed any trust between the two sides. Combining that with escalating salaries and a growing revenue gap between big and small-market teams, things finally came to a head in 1994. Years of pent-up hostility between players and management resulted in the owners enforcing a new agreement on their employees that included a salary cap, something the players union would not accept. A strike date was set for August 12th. Things had become so poisonous that the two sides didn't even meet to hash out an agreement despite the looming deadline. As a result the players went on strike. It had short-term consequences in that it ended up canceling what was shaping up as one of the greatest seasons in baseball history. And it had long-term economic consequences that were crushing for certain teams.

An injunction against the owners allowed baseball to resume in April of 1995. Ironically, the strike only made the gap between big and small-market teams worse. The Montreal Expos had been the best team in baseball. But due to lagging revenues after the strike was resolved, they were forced to shed several star players. As a result of that and anger over the work stoppage, fans simply never returned, and the team was forced to relocate to Washington in

2005. The small-market Royals were continually parting with top talent because of a shrinking fan base.

Between 1995 and 1998, nine teams were forced to reduce their payroll, including small-market teams like the A's, Expos, Cincinnati Reds, Pittsburgh Pirates, and Florida Marlins. (In 1997 the Marlins had splurged on free agents but promptly traded away nearly every single high priced player after winning the World Series.) Toronto, after scooping up Clemens in 1997, could not afford to make other improvements to the team and trimmed $11 million in payroll the following year. In 1998 the Yankees won the World Series with a $74 million payroll—second in baseball behind the Orioles. It was the last time the Yankees have not had the highest payroll in baseball.

By 1999 fans were starting to become angry. Attendance had returned in droves in the last two years thanks to a barrage of home runs. (Regardless of how the home runs were hit and with what substances they were augmented by, there is no denying fans came back for them.) But for many their teams still could not compete with the Yankees payroll muscle. The situation was becoming worse when a report commissioned by Major League Baseball made clear that revenue disparity was killing competition. According to the report, "large and growing revenue disparities exist and are causing problems of chronic competitive imbalance. Year after year too many clubs know in spring training that they have no realistic prospect of reaching postseason play." Among the figures cited by the panel was that by 1999 the top seven payroll teams in baseball averaged more than double the revenues of the bottom 14 teams. It noted that none of those 14 teams won a single playoff game during the last half of the decade. Although the Yankees weren't directly blamed, they were clearly the main culprit. The Yankees were the 20th century equivalent of a trust, and baseball needed a trust-busting law.

The Yankees went on to win the 1999 World Series (though Clemens endured one of his worst seasons on the mound) and repeated as champions in 2000. In 2001 they came within two outs of winning a fourth consecutive title. In the seven years following the '94 strike, the Yankees won four titles, five pennants, and never missed the postseason. When many of their key players retired or left after the 2001 season, they simply went out and landed baseball's most prominent free agent, first baseman Jason Giambi, with a seven-year, $120 million contract. And perhaps worst of all for the rest of baseball, the team launched the Yankees Entertainment and Sports Network, known as YES, in the spring of 2002. Although it would incorporate various sports programming as the years went on, the channel was devoted almost entirely to all things Yankees. In addition to the games, the network featured multitudes of other Yankees programming. Prior to the establishment of YES, the Yankees already had led the field in terms of TV revenue thanks to their groundbreaking deal in the 1980s with the MSG network. But YES took them to a different level, providing a whole new revenue stream for them. By 2010 reports claimed the network earned $435.2 million in revenues.

In 2002 when the collective bargaining agreement between the players and owners came to an end, management decided they'd had enough of the Yankees' spending ways. A revenue sharing formula was put into place. Although there have been some variations over the years, essentially all major league teams place a certain percentage of their revenues in one big pot, and the money is then distributed equally among all teams. In addition a luxury tax was placed on any team whose payroll rose above a certain number. The cap was placed so high, however, that the tax almost always applied only to the Yankees—and sometimes the Red Sox. In classic fashion Steinbrenner did not take the luxury tax news well. "This thing is aimed at the Yankees," he told the *New York Daily News*, before attacking commissioner Bud Selig. "I am a Bud Selig man. I consider him a good friend. He's a master at building people together. But while I'm loyal to Bud Selig, the biggest beneficiary in this whole plan are the Milwaukee Brewers. That doesn't seem quite right. I don't know how he sleeps at night sometimes." Around this same time, MLB.com, a website for fans of the game to buy tickets, get game packages, and check the latest news on their teams, was launched. By 2007 the website was bringing in nearly $400 million in revenue, which was divided equally among the teams.

The new luxury tax system did not stop the Yankees from paying top dollar. In 2003 they brought over Japanese superstar outfielder Hideki Matsui followed by Cuban sensation pitcher Jose Contreras. The new signings prompted the satirical newspaper *The Onion* to write a story headlined, "Yankees Ensure 2003 Pennant By Signing Every Player In Baseball." The Yankees engaged in a very public dispute with the Red Sox over the services of Contreras, a pitcher with a devastating split-fingered fastball. With Contreras staying at a Nicaraguan hotel, the Red Sox rented out every room in the place to ensure no one could get close to the pitcher. Red Sox general manager Theo Epstein made his pitch and was certain they had Contreras signed. Instead representatives from the Yankees showed up overnight and offered a deal that would pay nearly a million more a year. Contreras couldn't turn it down. The Red Sox were not pleased. "The Evil Empire extends its tentacles even into Latin America," said Boston CEO Larry Lucchino in a phrase that would become repeated throughout the following years. George Steinbrenner, of course, gave as good as he got. "I've learned this about Lucchino: he's baseball's foremost chameleon of all time. He changes colors depending on where he's he standing," The Boss told the media. "He talks out of both sides of his mouth. He has trouble talking out of the front of it."

Then on Valentine's Day of 2004 came the mother of all Yankee big-money deals: the team traded for Alex Rodriguez. A-Rod was baseball's best all-around player. The shortstop had signed a ridiculous $252 million, 10-year contract in the 2000–01 offseason to play for the Rangers. (It was ridiculous because the Rangers far overbid everyone for A-Rod's services.) When the contract became an albatross on the team, Texas sought to trade him, even though he led the league in home runs in each of his three years there and won the 2003 AL MVP. (Rodriguez would later admit to using steroids during this time.) A deal with the Red Sox fell apart, and that's when the Yankees moved in.

The trade sent shockwaves throughout baseball. Though the Rangers would still pay a large part of A-Rod's salary, really only the Yankees (and maybe the Red Sox and New York Mets) could have afforded to make this deal. And as if to pour salt on the rest of baseball's wound, the Yankees already had an All-Star shortstop in Derek Jeter. They were simply going to move Rodriguez to third base, a position that became vacant when Aaron Boone injured his knee during a pickup basketball game. Actor Ben Affleck, a die-hard Boston Red Sox fan, had a near meltdown upon hearing the news. Attending the Daytona 500, he was unaware of the deal until asked by a member of the media for his reaction. "Affleck's head fell, his smile disappeared," wrote ESPN.com's Wayne Drehs. "You know, George Steinbrenner is the center of evil in the universe," Affleck said. "Eventually, they might be able to just buy everybody."

The Yankees payroll went from $152 to $182 million, an increase larger than Tampa Bay's total payroll. In 2005 the Yankees signed several free agents to lucrative contracts, including a four-year, $40 million contract to Carl Pavano, a pitcher who'd won more than 12 games in a season only once. The Yankees became the first team ever with a payroll over $200 million that year. In 2007 they paid Roger Clemens nearly $28 million to play just 60 percent of the season for them. In 2008, thanks largely to reformulating his deal after A-Rod opted out of his contract, the team reached a high-water payroll mark of $209 million—more than the Tampa Bay Rays, Pirates, A's, and Marlins combined. A-Rod, at $28 million a year, earned more than the entire Marlins team, who collectively were paid $21.8 million. The top three highest paid players in baseball were all on the Yankees: A-Rod, Giambi, and Jeter with Giambi making more than the Marlins, and Jeter falling only a few $100,000 short.

The Yankees signed high priced pitchers CC Sabathia and A.J. Burnett and first baseman Mark Teixeira in 2009. All three made major contributions to a team that went 103–59 and won the World Series. Many fans, however, wrote off the victory as nothing more than a purchased championship, a hollow victory brought about by a ridiculous amount of television revenue and a new stadium. Three years later the Yankees refused to make any additions to their team that would push their payroll above $189 million. Progress, some would say.

From 2003 to 2012, 12 different teams appeared in the World Series. Among them were first-time appearances by the Rangers and Rays. The Detroit Tigers, who hadn't made the postseason since 1987, won the AL pennant twice. The White Sox, who hadn't won a title since 1917, took home the 2005 championship. In that 10-year span, the small-market A's made the postseason three times, the Rays three times, the Reds twice, and the Minnesota Twins five times. Twenty-six of the 30 major league teams made it to the postseason. By 2007 the average revenue differential between the top seven richest teams and the seven poorest had fallen from 118 percent in 1999 to 67 percent. Many agreed that the growing success of so many teams was due to the revenue sharing and luxury tax system.

Almost 12-and-a-half years after fans in Kansas City let out their frustrations on the Yankees, a different group of people selected a different target to highlight the issue of growing income inequality. Like the Royals fans' protest, this display had grown out of years of frustration over the wealthy acquiring more wealth while others were left to struggle simply to make ends meet. Their calling card had not been fake dollar bills, and they hadn't been drawn in by a radio station. Instead they'd been put on notice by a clever ad campaign designed by and appearing in the magazine *AdBusters*. "On September 17 we want to see 20,000 people flood into lower Manhattan, set up tents, kitchens, peaceful barricades, and occupy Wall Street for months," declared the magazine. They also designed an eye-catching poster that featured a ballerina atop the famous Wall Street bull.

As September 17th approached, no one was sure what to expect. But eventually, thousands of people from all walks of life showed up in lower Manhattan's Zuccotti Park—not far from the financial

Police arrest a participant in the Occupy Wall Street movement, which protested economic inequality, on November 15, 2011. (AP Images)

center of the country. These folks were tired of the increasing wealth gap between the haves and have-nots. They were tired of seeing CEOs bring home millions in bonuses after accepting taxpayer-funded bailouts. They were tired of the game being rigged against them. And just like that, the Occupy Wall Street movement, eerily similar to protests that had been made against the Yankees for so long, was born.

Downtown New York City differs from the rest of the city. It was developed earlier, so its streets seem a little more narrow and its outline more slipshod. It feels a little more like the mishmash of uncollaborated city streets that reside in Boston than the nice, neat grid outline of midtown and upper Manhattan. Tucked away under the constant shadow of the skyscrapers that engulfed it during the 20th century sits the New York Stock Exchange. Not far away stands Federal Hall. George Washington was sworn in as the first president of the United States there in 1789. Nearby sits Trinity Church, the final resting place of Alexander Hamilton, the country's first secretary of the treasury and the leading developer of the country's financial system. The Museum of American Finance isn't far away. Connecting all of these locations is a seven-tenths-of-a-mile-long roadway called Wall Street. The street itself, however, is merely an afterthought to many. Its name has taken on a larger, more deeper meaning, coming to symbolize the financial system of the country and usually not in a positive way.

For many Wall Street has come to mean greed, excess, and spend-free attitudes. They are the haves, and almost everyone else is the have-nots. Yankee Stadium and Wall Street are separated by about 10 miles, but they might as well occupy the same building to a lot of people. In theory a successful, thriving Wall Street means a successful, thriving economy for the country. Similarly, if the Yankees do well, it generally means better things for Major League Baseball as a whole. (New York consistently ranks among the highest draws on the road.) But just like the Yankees, resentment against Wall Street ran high when their success was perceived as grossly unfair to the rest of the people in the game. And just as fans in Kansas City had finally had enough of the Yankees, people around the country would reach a breaking point with Wall Street.

The origins of Wall Street occurred in the 1790s when a group of traders met under a buttonwood tree on the street to trade securities. They eventually formed a more structured mechanism for trading, the roots of which became the New York Stock Exchange—perhaps the most famous element of Wall Street. During the 19th century, downtown Manhattan became a much more businesses-oriented area as people began moving toward midtown and uptown. As more and more businesses came to the area, the strength and influence of the exchange grew enormously. By the early 20th century, financial giants like J.P. Morgan had their headquarters there. The market crash of 1929, however, altered the landscape for decades. Thousands were left out of work, and the riches they'd accumulated in stocks were wiped away in an instant. As the Great Depression ensued, Wall Street lost its cachet with only the wealthiest of the wealthy being able to maintain the lifestyles to which they'd become accustomed.

As the U.S. economy recovered in the ensuing decades, Wall Street rose to the top again. Several factors helped it gain new prominence in the 1980s. The first was the election of Ronald Reagan as president. He represented a new kind of capitalism in America: a do-it-yourself attitude that shunned government in nearly all forms and stressed individual achievement. It fit perfectly into a decade that saw baby boomers grow out of the sex, drugs, and rock and roll culture and start focusing on career building and money accumulation. With its traders and fortunes earned and fortunes lost, Wall Street seemed to fit the mold of the '80s perfectly. And everyone seemed to want in on it especially when bonuses skyrocketed to new heights in 1986. Forty percent of that year's graduating class at Yale University applied for positions at a single investment bank. "The next year, Harvard's principles of economics course enrolled 1,000 students in 40 sections, triple the figure from 10 years earlier," according to Greg David's *Modern New York: The Life and Economics of a City*.

The attitude of the financial community was summed up for many in the 1987 Oliver Stone film *Wall Street*. In the movie a young stockbroker played by Charlie Sheen resorts to underhanded and criminal behavior in order to impress his idol, Gordon Gecko (played by Michael Douglas in an Oscar-winning performance) and earn riches for both of them. Gecko, the ultimate capitalist, might as well have just been called Steinbrenner. The "greed is good" mentality began to wear somewhat thin, however, during the late 1980s and early '90s especially after the stock market suffered a near historic plunge in October of 1987. But the late 1990s brought economic prosperity unheard of in American history, and New York City benefited greatly.

Shortages of qualified workers began appearing in 1997, and companies began increasing pay despite an unemployment rate of greater than 9 percent. Restaurants were among the first to feel the pressure, and the Oyster Bar in Grand Central raised the salary of assistant managers above $30,000—up a third in just two years. Fast food places were swept up in the competition. Waiters at the city's best restaurants like the steak house Smith & Wollensky took home $100,000, including their lucrative tips. Placement firms reported administrative assistants had cracked the $50,000 barrier, and accounting and other professional service firms began emulating the tech companies with signing bonuses, though these were in cash not stock options. Unemployment was low, stock prices were high, and retirement funds were secure. As long as times were good, who cared if some Wall Street CEOs and bigwigs were swimming in money?

But the era of detente between Wall Street and the middle class and working poor would last only as long as those good times rolled. And by 2008 the financial party was over. In March the investment bank Bear Stearns, one of the largest in the nation, was acquired by J.P.Morgan Chase in order to avoid imminent collapse. Six months later Lehman Brothers, an investment bank larger than Stearns, filed for bankruptcy. The insurance company AIG needed $185 billion in government funds or it would collapse, and mortgage companies Fannie Mae and Freddie Mac were in such complete disarray that the government took them over.

The bankruptcies and near collapses had ripple effects that caused panic. The Dow Jones dropped by over one-third. As a result of all this economic chaos, people who'd worked hard all their lives saw their pension plans and retirement savings disintegrate almost overnight. In a 22-month period, unemployment skyrocketed from 5 percent to 10 percent. The housing market collapsed as millions of people who'd been suckered into taking on mortgages they couldn't possibly afford fell into foreclosure.

As major corporations continued to collapse, the United States government got involved. The Bush administration sprung into action with the Troubled Asset Relief Program (TARP), which injected billions of dollars into the economy. Of these hundreds of billions, a sizable piece went to the country's largest financial institutions, and this was in addition to money already provided to prevent firms from collapse. The tab for all of this was picked up by the American people with the hope that the money would be repaid down the line after the firms had stabilized (which is indeed what happened). In February of 2009 with the economy still sputtering, newly inaugurated president Barack Obama instituted a stimulus package worth nearly $790 billion dollars. The package included a variety of spending measures meant to jump-start the economy.

But when results were slow to come, people began wondering where exactly almost $1.5 trillion of their money had gone. Nearly all of the big companies that had failed were located in New York City, so the country's anger was directed squarely at the southern tip of Manhattan that played host to many of these institutions. A collection of labor unions set up shop in front of the New York Stock Exchange after TARP was passed. "We want our tax dollars used to provide a hand up for the millions of working people who live on Main Street and not a handout to a privileged band of overpaid executives," said AFL-CIO president John Sweeney.

Anger grew to outrage when the American public began learning about the bonuses Wall Street was ringing up. Despite all the turmoil and collapses in 2008, financial companies in New York paid out an estimated $18.4 billion in bonus money. In 2009 it got worse (or better depending on your point of view) as the average Wall Street bonus jumped 25 percent to $123,850. That figure was nearly four times the median annual American salary. "For most Americans these huge bonuses are a bitter pill," said New York state comptroller Thomas DiNapoli. And many folks were angered to learn that the very same mortgage companies that had sold them on mortgages they couldn't afford had actually taken out policies predicting that they would fall into foreclosure.

Enough was enough. For millions of Americans, they could no longer stomach the thought that while they had been playing by the rules for years those who cheated not only ended up on top, but they also got away with it. Instead of being punished for what many perceived as creating the very actions that tanked the economy, they were being rewarded with taxpayer-funded bailouts and big bonuses. None of them were even sniffing a hint of being sent to jail for their crimes. Moreover, the widening income gap had become untenable. According to David, "by 2007, the top 1 percent of households in [New York] city accounted for 44 percent of the income in New York, more than triple the 17 percent in 1987. The bottom 90 percent accounted for 34 percent compared with 59 percent two decades earlier."

Out of this anger and with a little assist from *AdBusters*, "Occupy Wall Street" was born. Hundreds of protestors soon turned to thousands, residing in the city's financial district. The movement birthed a slogan, "We Are the 99 percent," that caught on with many even those who didn't necessarily empathize with the demonstrators. The slogan was a reference to the richest 1 percent of Americans, who earned 23 percent of the total income in the country. Eventually, celebrities began to drop by, and the country's leading politicians were forced to acknowledge the movement. Occupy movements began popping up in different cities across the country. The movement suffered from a series of problems: lack of money, no central organizing figure, and an unclear message at times. But no one could question the constant attention it was drawing to the issue of income inequality in America.

But unlike the outcries and protests made against the Yankees, it is questionable how much the Occupy movement achieved in the end. After several months it effectively shut down. Whereas Major League Baseball made changes to limit—or at least attempt to limit—the impact the Yankees wealth could have on the quality of the game, many would argue that little has been done to change the impact that Wall Street can have on the quality of life for average Americans. Either way, be it fair or unfair, the Yankees and Wall Street both remain synonymous with corporate greed and in a sense downright evil. Unless you are, of course, a Yankees fan or someone who works on Wall Street.

PR Stunts

There are few better places on Earth to hold a publicity stunt than New York City. With nearly nine million people and most of the world's major media outlets, even the most mundane of stunts will draw some kind of attention. Over the years business people, actors, politicians, and the New York Yankees have all done their best to exploit the use of a good stunt. Some results were better than others. It is no coincidence, though, that public relations stunts play well in New York, a city known for its eccentric personalities, gaudiness, and overall over-the-top manner.

Everything in the city seems to be a little bit flashier, a little bit bigger. For all the hubbub and excitement over Times Square, in reality all the flashing lights and neon signs just add up to one big billboard for corporate America. Yet millions of people flock there to see what it's all about. And it's not just Times Square; it's everywhere in New York. It's the shops on Madison Avenue, the world famous Christmas displays in the Macy's windows, and the most famous Christmas tree in the world standing in front of the most famous ice skating rink in the world in Rockefeller Plaza. The Theater District is overflowing with advertisements, billboards, and marquees.

Most of what we see on the streets of New York is really just a creative cry for attention. But it works. That's why for decades before—and decades after—the city will continue to play host to publicity stunts big and small. And it all started when the greatest and most successful PR stunt ever happened right on the streets of Manhattan. It worked out so well that few people alive today realize that one of the country's favorite holiday traditions started out as a publicity gimmick to boost product sales. That event is the Macy's Thanksgiving Day Parade.

It all began in 1924 when Macy's employees decided to both celebrate the Christmas season and bring attention to their store by dressing as clowns, knights, and cowboys while marching six miles down the streets of New York from Harlem to Herald's Square. Animals from the Central Park Zoo were included. The event drew 250,000 people and was so successful that Macy's decided to hold the parade annually, though it evolved into a Thanksgiving theme. In 1927 Macy's upped the PR ante when it introduced the first official parade balloon, Felix the Cat. In the next few years, new balloons were introduced. But rather than deflate them after the parade was over, Macy's decided to simply release them into air. Thinking they would end up in all parts of the country, they even included a return address in the balloons, so that when people found them they could turn them in for $100. It was good and clever publicity in theory, but in reality the balloons became hazards. One even ended up wrapped around the wing of a plane. Eventually the release idea was scrapped. But there is no doubt about the success of the original idea. The parade is now attended by more than three million people every Thanksgiving morning and watched by 50 million more on television.

Almost 50 years after Macy's began one of the world's most famous holiday traditions in the streets of the city, spectators were forced to gaze skyward. Exactly 110 stories above them, Philippe Petit was walking on a tightrope he'd suspended between the two towers of the World Trade Center. The two recently completed buildings were the second tallest structures in the world at the time, but Petit was strolling in between them as if he were walking across the beach on a beautiful summer's day. He made the trek back and forth several times as thousands of people looked on from down below.

Petit was not the only one to use the towers as a means of attaining worldwide, daredevil fame. On a late spring morning in 1977, George Willig, a 27-year-old resident of Queens, stood in front of the South Tower of the World Trade Center. With a little assistance from a contraption he designed himself, Willig then began to climb the exterior of the building. In three hours time, he ascended all 1,350 feet of the tower without any sort of rope to secure him. He'd used only his climbing device and his hands and legs. Willig became an instant celebrity. (Even the officers who arrested him at the top of the tower asked him for his autograph.) Shortly after the stunt, he met with Mayor Beame, who fined Willig $1.10, one penny for each floor of the tower.

No one in New York City was immune to the act. As mayor, Fiorello LaGuardia would show up at every major fire in the city sure to have his picture taken. When a strike shut down delivery of newspapers, LaGuardia took to the radio to read the comics section to the city's children, a stunt so popular it remains his most well-known act as mayor. Sometimes the stunts were done to stop politicians. In the early '80s, Mayor Koch was pushing for a plan that would have overhauled Times Square, including the demolition of the Times Tower itself. The plan met with stern opposition from locals, especially the Broadway crowd, who felt the area would lose its character if the plan went into place. In the fall of 1984, Hugh Hardy and the Municipal Arts Society were able to arrange it so that on one night every single light in Times Square was turned off except for one sign. The sign read: "Hey Mr. Mayor! It's Dark Out Here! Help Keep the Bright Lights in Times Square." The redevelopment plan was eventually scrapped.

With the development of 24-hour media and expanding news networks, stunts became more frequent and publicized. In 1998 eccentric millionaire Richard Branson drove a tank into Times Square to promote the launch of his new soft drink, Virgin Cola. Two years later magician David Blaine enclosed himself in ice while suspended above Times Square. Blaine stayed inside the six-ton block of ice for almost 62 hours, and the entire drama played out live in front of thousands of people who passed by below.

In June of 2005, the beverage company Snapple engaged in a massive publicity stunt when it tried to set the world record for the largest frozen popsicle. They mixed a giant concoction of their kiwi-strawberry flavored Snapple on Ice in a factory in Edison, New Jersey, then had it shipped by frozen truck to Union Square in the city. But because it was the first day of summer, the huge popsicle, weighing in at 35,000 pounds, began to melt. As a result pink liquid began to ooze down East 17th Street. The event organizers needed to get the popsicle upright in order to officially break the Guinness record. But fearing that the inner core had possibly melted and the whole thing would collapse if they tried to move it, it was never attempted. The record was not broken, though Snapple snagged itself some free press despite the major embarrassment.

But not all stunts in the big city go well or joyfully wrong. In April of 2009, the defense department caused panic throughout the city when it flew two jets at low levels across Lower Manhattan for a photo shoot. Only seven and a half years after the 9/11 attacks, the incident sparked hundreds of phone calls to emergency management and led to numerous office evacuations. "Poor judgment would have been a nice way to put it," said New York City Mayor Bloomberg.

But all of these stunts and the people behind them couldn't hold a candle to George Steinbrenner when it came to cheap, cheesy gimmicks to garner media attention. For The Boss anything he could do to take attention away from the New York Mets was good. To Steinbrenner there was no such thing as bad press. Winning the back pages of the *New York Daily News* and *New York Post* were almost as important as winning ballgames. Newly signed free agents were always paraded in front of the media, and Yankee Stadium was the background scene for many motion pictures.

Steinbrenner's biggest stunts were always grand. In the middle of the 1978 season, Billy Martin resigned as manager rather than endure being fired for insulting public comments he made toward Steinbrenner. In what was to be a repeated pattern over the years, Steinbrenner immediately regretted letting Martin go. He was worried that another American League team would snatch up Martin, who could exact his revenge on the field somewhere down the line. So just five days after Martin stepped down, Steinbrenner snuck him into Yankee Stadium during the team's Old Timer's Day festivities. The ceremony normally concluded with the introduction of Joe DiMaggio, but after the Yankee Clipper was announced, Bob Sheppard had one more thing to take care of. "Ladies and gentlemen, your attention please," said Sheppard in that familiar tone. "The Yankees announce today that Bob Lemon has agreed to a contract to continue as manager of the Yankees through the 1978 and 1979 seasons." This announcement was met with boos by fans still bitter over the departure of Martin. "Your attention, please. Your attention please," repeated Sheppard over the boos. "In 1980 Bob Lemon will become the general manager of the Yankees…and the Yankees would like to announce at the same moment that the manager for the 1980 season, and hopefully for many years after that, will be No. 1, Bill Martin." Just then Martin emerged from the dugout wearing his Yankee uniform. He waved and soaked up adulation from the crowd for seven minutes.

It was a bombshell announcement. Almost no one knew about it, including members of the team, and DiMaggio, who was upset over being upstaged. Amazingly, no one had seen Martin enter the stadium that day, and Steinbrenner had warned Martin that should anyone find out ahead of time and leak it to the press, the deal was off. Martin kept his mouth shut. In the meantime many people were upset, including those players who'd had enough of Martin's antics, but no one could deny that it made great theater. By 1979, of course, Steinbrenner had had enough of Lemon and fired him, putting Martin in a year ahead of schedule. He fired Martin shortly after the season ended, so Martin never actually did manage the club in 1980.

Twenty-nine years later on a beautiful Sunday afternoon at Yankee Stadium, a similar stunt awaited Yankees fans. The start of the 2007 season had not gone well for the Yankees. Their pitching staff was decimated by injuries, and they finished the first month of the year 9–14. They needed a shot of energy to help keep the season alive. And so during the seventh-inning stretch of a game against the Seattle Mariners, the camera panned to a familiar face standing up in the owner's box. Dressed in a suit, holding a microphone, and looking directly out at the crowd, Roger Clemens had an announcement for the 52,000-plus fans in attendance. "Well, they came and got me out of Texas, and I can tell you it's a privilege to be back. I'll be talking to y'all soon," Clemens announced. It was a major coup. Clemens had the most wins of any active pitcher. He'd just completed three incredible seasons with the Houston Astros after pitching five years with the Yankees. In desperate need for pitching, the Yankees offered Clemens $28 million for the year, even though he would miss the first two months of the season.

Ultimately, the move did not work out for New York. Clemens was nowhere near the pitcher he'd been with the Astros, and his final major league start in Game 3 of the American League Division Series against the Cleveland Indians was cut short due to injury. Clemens' legacy has since been severely hurt due to accusations of steroid use and other personal issues. But at the time, no one could deny the entertainment factor of the Yankees' seventh-inning stretch announcement.

Stadium theatrics weren't confined to just players either. Steinbrenner loved having a bald eagle named Challenger swoop in from the upper deck and land on his handler's hand before games. He also had no issue pimping himself out to create a media stir. He starred with Martin in a famous Miller Lite commercial. The two argued over whether it tasted great or was less filling before Steinbrenner fires him on camera. (A few weeks later, Martin was fired for real.) He did a Visa commercial with Derek Jeter, in which the pair mock comments Steinbrenner had made to the media about Jeter partying too much. On more than one occasion, The Boss took control of an orchestra, once helping conduct the New York Pops. In 1990 he hosted *Saturday Night Live* and even poked fun at himself by playing a convenience store manager who just can't bring himself to fire an employee.

And no one appreciated a good magazine cover photo op more than The Boss. In 1985 he sported a fake mustache and top hat so he could look like former Yankees owner Jacob Ruppert for *The Sporting News* cover. When he returned after his exile from

Always embracing a PR stunt, George Steinbrenner (right) jokingly spars with manager Billy Martin during a 1983 press conference, poking fun at their famous Miller Lite commercial. (AP Images)

baseball in 1993, he donned a full Napoleon Bonaparte outfit complete with a hat, sword, and even his hand tucked in between the buttons of his shirt, to appear on the cover of *Sports Illustrated*. Ten years later he again appeared on the cover surrounded by his entire starting rotation (minus David Wells, who refused to appear after a spat with The Boss and *Sports Illustrated* over his book) with the headline: "You Can Never Have Too Much Pitching (Just Ask George)."

The Boss wasn't the first, or only, person associated with the Yankees who appreciated a gimmick or good stunt. In 1929 Ruppert introduced the concept of uniform numbers to baseball. (Numbers on jerseys had been mostly confined to football, though the Indians had experimented with the idea a bit.) It was done in part because Yankee Stadium was so big that people had trouble telling who was who on the field. It also promoted purchasing scorecards as people were better able to keep track of who did what. When the Yankees won the pennant in 1947, general manager Larry MacPhail silenced everyone at the postgame celebration. MacPhail felt largely responsible for the team's success and wanted to make sure everyone felt that way, too. He had accomplished his goal of making the Yankees a winner, so what was left for him to do? In order to draw attention away from his own team and onto himself, he announced, "I am stepping down. I am resigning at the end of the season."

In 1972 the Yankees began playing theme music every time reliever Sparky Lyle entered the game. Driven to the mound by a bullpen car, Lyle would emerge to the sounds of "Pomp and Circumstance." Lyle asked that the practice be stopped the following season, but it started a trend of closers emerging to theme songs, something that has become commonplace. Mariano Rivera became famous—or infamous if you were the batter who had to face him—for entering to the tune of Metallica's "Enter Sandman."

Steinbrenner also wasn't the only person associated with the Yankees who understood the benefit of showing your lighter side. Martin co-hosted *Saturday Night Live* in 1986, appearing in a skit where he is fired by Lorne Michaels for being drunk. Martin then sets fire to the set at the end of the show. Jeter also played the role of *SNL* host with former Yankees pitchers Wells and David Cone joining in a guest appearance. Yankees fan Larry David incorporated many members of the team onto *Seinfeld* over the years, including manager Buck Showalter and players Jeter, Bernie Williams, and Danny Tartabull. In one episode Kramer informs Yankee outfielder Paul O'Neill that he promised a boy in the hospital O'Neill would hit two home runs for him. O'Neill responds in disgust, saying hitting home runs is hard, and even Babe Ruth wasn't stupid enough to promise hitting two.

In addition to *SNL*, Jeter has appeared in numerous television commercials and has done spots in a couple of films, including appearing as himself in *Anger Management* and *The Other Guys*. In

The Other Guys, Mark Wahlberg, playing a cop, recalls in a group therapy session how he shot Jeter as he was walking down a subway tunnel, mistakenly thinking Jeter's bat was a lethal weapon. "You dick!" Jeter screams at him. One of the other cops shouts, "You should have shot A-Rod."

And, of course, who could forget Don Mattingly's appearance as himself on *The Simpsons*? In the episode Mr. Burns hires several major league players to act as ringers on his company softball team so he can win a $1 million bet. In the end Mattingly is thrown off the team for not getting his haircut (poking fun of a 1991 incident when Mattingly was benched for having his hair too long). As Mattingly leaves the dugout after being dismissed by Mr. Burns, he mumbles, "I still like him better than Steinbrenner." Coincidentally, nearly all of the players who appeared on the team, including Wade Boggs, Darryl Strawberry, Jose Canseco, and Clemens, ended up playing for the Yankees at some point.

9/11

O n Tuesday, September 11, 2001, in New York City, the sun shone through a near cloudless sky as millions of New Yorkers went through their daily routines. Some walked the streets or took the subway to work. Others made sure to stop and vote as it was Primary Day in the city's mayoral race. The Yankees were scheduled to play that night at home. Then at 8:46 AM, the entire city and the entire country were altered forever. American Airlines Flight 11, which 45 minutes earlier had been hijacked by members of the al-Qaeda terrorist organization, flew right over Manhattan, directly south, then crashed into the North Tower of the World Trade Center. Seventeen minutes later, as New Yorkers were still grasping the magnitude of what had happened, another plane, American Airlines Flight 175, crashed into the South Tower.

Confusion, shock, and fear reverberated through southern Manhattan. Thousands of people began evacuating the area while hundreds of firefighters and police officers descended on and into the towers. The two structures, each well over 1,000 feet tall, were now towering infernos. Thousands remained on the streets below, looking up in horror. Unbeknownst to many of them, another hijacked plane had crashed into the Pentagon in northern Virginia, and another, because of the heroism of passengers, avoided buildings and crashed in a field in Shanksville, Pennsylvania.

At 9:59 AM the South Tower, still filled with firefighters, police, and others trying to get out, collapsed. Chaos ensued. Thousands scrambled to avoid being hit with falling debris and a massive dust cloud that soon engulfed all of lower Manhattan. The North Tower fell 29 minutes later, causing Mayor Giuliani, his staff, and the press in tow to run for cover. In just 102 minutes, the two tallest buildings in the city had fallen. Including those on the two planes, 2,753 lives were lost in the tower attacks.

9/11 was like nothing that had ever happened before in America. Some would compare it to the attacks on Pearl Harbor 60 years earlier. Others would say it reminded them of when President Kennedy was shot. But 9/11 was different. Mass communication and 24-hour media brought the events directly to people as they happened. Millions were watching as the towers fell, so even those who were 3,000 miles away felt like they were standing right there as events unfolded. In the hours and days that followed, cameras panned over a landscape of twisted steel that was still smoldering from the millions of gallons of jet fuel contained in both planes. It was a constant reminder of the horrific events that occurred.

Stories of heroism—of lives saved and lost—slowly began to emerge. There was Port Authority construction manager Frank De Martini, who led a group through the upper floors of the towers to rescue people closest to the impact zones. With De Martini was Pablo Ortiz, Pete Negron, and Carlos DaCosta. Each of them had two children at home and each of them selflessly searched several floors, finding and helping survivors before heading farther up to see who else they could assist. They were last seen on the upper 80th floor of the South Tower. There were countless stories like theirs of people, who without much thought for their own well-being, ascended the towers in an effort to help as many people as possible. They were cops, firefighters, Port Authority employees, and World Trade Center workers.

Each new tale brought tears of joy or sadness or both. In the days following, people weren't sure what to do or how to feel. Was it okay to go back to work? To try and laugh? To just go for a walk outside? The country, New Yorkers in particular, needed a break—a distraction to take them away from the constant pangs of hurt and sadness that clung to the city. They needed something that could make them smile if only for a few hours. For many that need would be met by the New York Yankees.

Since the team was home when the attacks occurred, many Yankees saw and felt the devastation up close. Like everyone else they wanted to help, but they didn't know how. Turns out simply being visible was a great way to make people feel better. Several players made trips to Jacob Javits Center, which was being used as an emergency staging ground; St. Vincent's Hospital; and the New York Armory, the place where people were doing DNA testing to help find and identify missing loved ones. "The most emotional part was the Armory," said Joe Torre in *The Yankee Years*. "That was the toughest one because we walked in. I didn't even want to go in, but then I remember that [Yankees president] Randy Levine sent somebody in or he might have gone in just to see what the mood was. And the people who were in there wanted us to go in there." After walking in, Bernie Williams encountered a grieving family, a wife still looking for her husband. "I don't know what to say," Williams said. "All I know is, I think you need a hug." In the coming weeks, many members of the team would visit firehouses throughout the city. Derek Jeter called Brielle Saracini, whose father, Victor, had been the captain of American Airlines Flight 175. Brielle was a huge fan of both the Yankees and Jeter. He invited her and her family out to the stadium. In the documentary *Nine Innings From Ground Zero*, Brielle's mother recalled how it was the first time in weeks she'd seen her daughter happy. "When 9/11 happened it made you realize that baseball is just a game that you were very fortunate to play," Paul O'Neill said. "But then I remember going to Ground Zero and meetings kids and fans. I was almost embarrassed to be part of it because we were asked to go down there. But when it was all said and done, to see kids smile and to see how important it was that we continued to win, you understand that it meant a lot to a lot of people."

A week after the attacks, baseball resumed with the Yankees playing in Chicago. Before the game Torre held a meeting with his players. He informed them that like everyone else they had a job to do, and they were going to be called on to provide some temporary relief from all the grief that had occurred. "It gives people an option to watch something else or pay attention to something else," Jeter told sportswriter/author Buster Olney.

The game provided its share of emotional moments as fans at Comiskey Park gave New York a warm welcome. In the stands someone unfurled a sign reading, "Chicago loves New York." Another read, "We are all Yankees." The Yankees wore the hats of the New York Fire and Police Departments. Many cried during the singing of the national anthem. "It's inevitable that the Yankees will be viewed as representatives of a devastated and resilient city," Olney wrote.

The Yankees split their six games on the road, which was enough to leave them with a chance to clinch the division title at their first post-9/11 home game. In some ways the event was anti-climactic as the New York Mets had already played (and won) an extremely emotional first game back the week before. Still there was plenty of emotion left to go around the Bronx that night. Police officers, firefighters, and emergency workers stood along the foul lines with Tampa Bay Devil Rays and Yankees players mixed in between them. Branford Marsalis played taps followed by the Harlem Boys Choir singing "We Shall Overcome." Michael Bolton then followed by leading the crowd in a rendition of "Lean on Me." A large American flag that covered a good portion of the outfield was unveiled. Roger Clemens took the mound that night. Earlier in the day Clemens had visited Fire Station 22 on the Upper East Side of Manhattan, where he saw that the firefighters didn't want to dwell on what happened. "We spent probably three minutes on it, and collectively they said, 'Let's talk about baseball.'" Now on the mound, he was joined by four emergency workers who threw out the ceremonial first pitch.

There were hugs. There were tears. But there was a sense of community and of uniting in the face of adversity even over something as trivial as a game. "A lot of people like to go to church to feel together with the city, with different people," Richard G. Cirino, a schoolteacher who attended the game, told *The New York Times*. "I get the same feeling here at Yankee Stadium and I expect that feeling today."

Though they lost the game, the Yankees clinched the division that night when the Boston Red Sox lost to the Baltimore Orioles. For the seventh consecutive year, they were headed to the playoffs. This time, however, it would be different. They were the three-time defending world champions, but they would be playing for more than a title. They would be playing for the pride, grit, and determination of an entire city. Though the NFL and NHL seasons had just gotten underway and the Giants and Devils were both defending conference champions, it was the Yankees who were the city's focus. It was the Yankees who were going to provide New Yorkers with hope with a sense of normalcy amongst all the sadness and destruction. For many people who hadn't laughed or smiled in weeks, the Yankees' playoff run was going to be their inspiration and their conduit for a return to better times. "[For] the people, who have been down there going through the 12-hour days and looking for something to lift them up and maybe feel good for even a brief period of time, we're going to be one of those outlets they can look to for a little motivation and to take their minds off of what everybody's been going through," Mike Mussina told Olney. When asked what winning games meant after the attack, George Steinbrenner separated his fingers about an inch, "It's this much," he said. "It's that much barely. But that much can be made bigger because if it makes everybody come together and feel better, then it becomes a bigger thing."

"All the players were asking at some level, 'What are we doing? Is baseball really that important? Should we be playing again?'" Scott Brosius said. "But when we got back and started playing again, we realized how important playing was to the healing process, especially in New York."

All of that hope and anticipation nearly ended before it started. Facing the Oakland A's at home in the Division Series, the Yankees looked flat. Oakland's young pitching staff overpowered them as the team managed to score just three runs in the first two games, losing both. They headed out to Oakland with history squarely against them. No team had ever won a five-game series after losing the first two games at home. The Yankees needed a jolt, something that would spring them back to life. In Game 3 they got it. Protecting a 1–0 lead with two outs in the bottom of the seventh inning, Yankees pitcher Mike Mussina allowed a two-out single to Jeremy Giambi. Terrence Long then sent a shot down the right-field line and into the corner. Right fielder Shane Spencer missed both cutoff men with his throw, sending the ball hurtling into no man's land past first base. Giambi came charging around third base, destined to score. Suddenly Jeter appeared—seemingly out of thin air—halfway down the first-base line. He quickly gloved the ball and then in one motion, turned, and dished a shovel pass to catcher Jorge Posada, who spun and tagged Giambi on the right calf just before Giambi stepped on home plate. It saved the game as the Yankees went on to win 1–0. Yankees general manager Brian Cashman compared Jeter to Superman. Tom Verducci seemed to concur, writing in *The Yankees Years* that "Jeter made a play that only could have been made by a player with supreme alertness, the mental computing power to quickly crunch the advanced baseball calculus needed to process the trajectory and speed of Spencer's throw and the speed and location of a runner behind his back, and the athletic and improvisational skills to actually find a way to get the ball home on time and on target while running in a direction opposite to the plate."

The Yankees won 9–2 in Game 4, setting up a decisive Game 5 in New York. Yankee Stadium was roaring, shaking with an anticipation and excitement not seen since the 1996 World Series. It was a cathartic event filled with American flags, chants of "USA, USA," and 56,642 people looking for both a comeback from the Yankees and a comeback for their city. The A's jumped out to an early 2–0 lead, but New York would not back down. In the bottom of the second, Alfonso Soriano lined a based-loaded single into left, tying the game. The reaction from the crowd was so intense that Brosius, who'd moved up to second base on the hit, could actually feel the ground moving beneath him. In the bottom of the third, an error, a hit-by-pitch, a walk, and another error gave the Yankees a 3–2 lead. They tacked on another run to make it 4–2. The A's scored a run to make it close, but David Justice lined a home run down the line in right field in the bottom of the sixth, making it a 5–3 game.

In the top of the eighth inning, Jeter again stole the show. With one out and a runner on first, Long popped a ball up along the left-field line in foul territory. Scrambling to his right, Jeter reached over and gloved the ball before falling into one of the photographer wells. The Yankees got out of the inning without any damage. In the ninth Mariano Rivera closed the game with a strikeout of Eric Byrnes, sending the crowd into a frenzy. It was the first time the Yankees had ever clinched a division series at home in the wild-card era, fitting that it occurred in a year when the city and the fans needed so badly to see the accomplishment firsthand. A beaming Rudy Giuliani, donning his Yankees cap with a mini-American flag embroidered on the side, walked the field with Torre afterward. Torre later remarked that as the final outs of the game ticked away he began to get a lump in his throat. It was a remarkable comeback that hardly seemed possible just days earlier. It not only gave the city prolonged hope for itself, but it also meant at least one more week of baseball, which meant one more week of distraction.

That one more week would not be an easy task. In the American League Championship Series, the Yankees were facing the Seattle Mariners, a team that had won a record-tying 116 games during the regular season. But despite starting the series in Seattle, the Yankees won the first two games. After dropping Game 3 back in New York, Game 4 saw more heroics from Soriano. Tied at one in the bottom of the ninth and with a runner on first, he came up against Mariners shutdown reliever Kazuhiro Sasaki and drilled a pitch over the right-center field wall for a two-run, game-winning home run. As an ecstatic crowd cheered, Soriano pumped his fist in the air. It would not be the last time he would come through that fall.

Up 3–1 in the series, the Yankees made Game 5 anti-climactic. The old guard led the way. Andy Pettitte pitched into the seventh inning and took home ALCS MVP honors. Tino Martinez; Williams, and O'Neill all homered—O'Neill's was the last of his career—and the Yankees won 12–3. "The one thought that did come to my mind strangely enough is, 'Boy, this city suffered a lot, and tonight they let out a lot of emotions,'" said Mariners manager Lou Piniella. "And I felt good for them in that way."

The 2001 World Series was one of the best Fall Classics in baseball history. It was a gut-wrenching, agonizing struggle that ended in heartbreak for New York. But although the end result was neither what the Yankees nor the city hoped for, the seven-game ride brought moments of sheer joy that had never been seen or experienced in the Bronx—not even in years where the team captured the title. While smoke was still billowing from southern Manhattan and a new threat put the country on alert, for eight days in late October and early November, the city and the United States were captivated by what was happening in Phoenix and New York City.

It certainly didn't look like it would be a captivating World Series after Game 1. Arizona led 9–1 before the fifth inning, putting the game out of reach early as the Yankees couldn't touch pitcher Curt Schilling. Game 2 remained a close contest between Pettitte and Randy Johnson until the bottom of the seventh. Clinging to a 1–0 lead, Matt Williams crushed a three-run home run, putting the matchup out of reach. Johnson finished off the game for a 4–0 shutout. The Yankees returned home down 2–0. In the first two games of the series, they had managed only six hits. It was the lowest total by any team after the first two games of the World Series since 1906. There didn't seem to be much magic in the desert air. But back in New York, the series took on its legendary status. And it all began with a moment that happened before Game 3 even started.

George W. Bush wasn't the most popular person in New York City pre-9/11. In the 2000 presidential election, he received less than 20 percent of the vote in New York. But in the immediate aftermath of the attacks, the entire country rallied around the president. Bush's speeches were broadcast during the middle of sporting events, and the action stopped so everyone could watch. Three days after 9/11, he visited the World Trade Center site. At one point he stood on top of a pile of rubble and put his arm around firefighter Bob Beckwith. The president began speaking through a bullhorn, thanking those who were part of the recovery effort. Someone in the crowd said they could not hear him. "I can hear you!" Bush said. "The rest of the world hears you! And the people— and the people who knocked these buildings down will hear all of us soon."

In later years these kinds of bombastic statements from Bush would draw sharp criticism from those who saw them as unbecoming of a president. But in that moment, in that place, it was exactly what the crowd and the country wanted and needed to hear. Those around him went crazy and began chanting "USA, USA." The image was broadcast across the country that weekend. For the American people, it was more than just a call to avenge those who'd been lost or to attack those who'd attacked us. It showed that we wouldn't be pushed around. We wouldn't be forced into seclusion or made to fear our surroundings. In short we weren't going to take any shit.

By the time Game 3 rolled around, the country was already taking military action in Afghanistan in response to the attacks. The actions were largely supported by the public and boosted Bush's popularity in the aftermath of the attacks. And the president was about to provide the public one more iconic moment by throwing out the first pitch before the first World Series game played in a now drastically different New York. Bush hung out in the Yankees clubhouse beforehand and then began warming up in the tunnel underneath the stadium. Beneath his FDNY fleece windbreaker, the president was wearing a bulletproof vest. Even though security was everywhere and snipers were present on the rooftops of the building, the Secret Service was taking no chances. In addition to Bush's vest, one more security measure was taken. Another umpire was added to the crew for the pregame ceremonies, and that umpire was an undercover Secret Service agent.

As Bush was warming up, Jeter strolled by. They made quick small talk, and then Jeter asked the president if he planned to throw from the mound or from just in front of the mound. Earlier in the year, Bush had thrown out the first pitch at Milwaukee's new Miller Park. Tossing from the mound, he had bounced his throw (though that didn't stop Brewers coach Davey Lopes from saying "perfect strike, Mr. President"). The incident had embarrassed Bush, a good athlete and huge baseball fan who had once owned the Texas Rangers. Not wanting to repeat the Milwaukee performance, he told Jeter he would throw from in front of the mound. Jeter told him if he did that, the crowd would boo him. Like any good politician, the president feared getting booed more than bouncing his throw, so Bush agreed to toss from the mound—not an easy thing to do considering the vest. Then as Bush was standing in the dugout just before he was about to head onto the field, Jeter walked by him again. "Don't bounce it," Jeter said, "or they will boo you." Jeter may have just been talking shit, but surely it was enough to make even the president a little edgy.

Bush headed out onto the field, and as his name was announced, a loud thunderous cheer went up from the stadium. The president took the mound and gave a thumbs-up to the crowd. Then he delivered a perfect strike down the middle of the plate to Yankees catcher Todd Greene. The catcher had no idea he was going to be on the receiving end of the throw until just before it occurred. Clemens had taken too long with his warm-up tosses, preventing Posada from leaving the bullpen and catching the first pitch. It was one of the serendipitous moments that forever linked Greene with history. "I didn't understand the implications or how cool or how big it was at the time," Greene said. "Then an hour later, I was like, *shit, that was pretty cool.* That was the coolest thing I probably did in my career."

Bush's toss only incited an already charged-up crowd even more. It was a picture-perfect throw in a situation that needed just that. "Our country has been struck, and it was wounded. Our people were hurt. And what that strike allowed us to do was what we do naturally as Americans: cheer for this country. It was such

Standing in between Yankees manager Joe Torre and Diamondbacks manager Bob Brenly, President Bush waves to the crowd before throwing out the first pitch of Game 3 of the poignant 2001 World Series.

a moment," said then-White House press secretary Ari Fleischer. "I remember the next morning I was at the White House, and Bush was talking about that game and the crowd. He said, 'No matter what happens to me in the course of the presidency, I will remember this all of my life.'"

After the president's surreal moment, the two teams got down to business. The Yankees, sporting American flag decals on the upper back of their jerseys, desperately needed a win, or the series was all but over. Clemens turned in a strong pitching performance, but the offense was flat again. The score was tied at one until the bottom of the sixth when Brosius knocked in a two-out hit to score the go-ahead run. Rivera came in for a two-inning save, held the lead, and the Yankees were now down two games to one in the series.

The next night was Halloween. Combine that with a full moon hanging above Yankee Stadium, and you knew some strange things were going to happen. It began in the top of the first inning when Orlando Hernandez got himself into a bases-loaded, one-out jam only to escape with the help of a strikeout and a pop-up. Schilling, who'd been nearly untouchable in Game 1, was about the same in Game 4. He made one mistake, an outside fastball to Spencer, which landed in the right-field seats. Other than that the Yankees simply couldn't hit him. With the game tied at one in the top of the fifth and Tony Womack on third, Luis Gonzalez lifted a fly ball to shallow left field. Spencer caught it and fired the ball to home plate. It short-hopped Posada, who was able to smother it in his chest, then grab it with his bare hand, and apply the tag to Womack just before he reached home plate, preserving the tie. Hernandez was so pumped up over the double play that he nearly punched Womack in the face while pumping his fist in excitement.

The game remained tied until the top of the eighth when Arizona scored two runs to take a 3–1 lead. Then in a move that some would question, Diamondbacks manager Bob Brenly took Schilling out of the game after just 88 pitches. In his place he brought in right-handed closer Byung-Hyun Kim, a 22-year-old submarine thrower. No one could complain, though, when Kim struck out the side in the eighth and retired Jeter to start the ninth. O'Neill singled into left, but after Williams struck out on a ball in the dirt, it got very quiet in Yankee Stadium. The crowd still held out hope, but Kim had now struck out four of the six hitters he'd faced, and coming to the plate was Martinez, who had yet to get a hit in the World Series. To that point the Yankees were hitting just .143 over the first four games. Many were hoping for something special, but it seemed like their team was about to fall into a three-games-to-one hole. The cameras quickly panned to Cashman, who looked forlorn over what appeared to be his team's fate. Just behind home plate, a fan in the front row began pointing repeatedly at right-center field as if he were trying to will Martinez to hit the ball there.

Martinez drilled the first-pitch fastball to deep center field. Immediately the crowd went from quiet to over-the-top screaming as they traced the flight of the ball, which landed in the first row of bleachers. O'Neill began screaming and pumping his fist as he crossed second base. Players jumped out of the dugout. The PA system began blasting Tag Team's "Whoomp There It Is." Yankee Stadium began shaking—literally—as more than 55,000 people stomped up and down. The Yankees had needed a special moment, and now they had it: a two-out, two-run, game-tying home run in the bottom of the ninth, only the third time in major league history that had happened during the World Series. Martinez crossed home plate and allowed himself some fist pumps to acknowledge the ecstatic crowd.

The camera panned twice to Schilling in the Arizona dugout. Before the start of the World Series, Schilling had famously dismissed the idea that there was some sort of supernatural presence around the Yankees. "When you use the words 'mystique' and 'aura,'" Schilling said, "those are dancers in a nightclub. Those are not things we concern ourselves with on the ballfield." Now Schilling stood expressionless, perhaps wondering if maybe there was something to all of that. "What a night," remarked Fox's Joe Buck. "Mercy," said his announcing partner, Tim McCarver.

Arizona was held scoreless in the top of the 10th, and with two outs in the bottom of the inning, Jeter stepped in against Kim. As Jeter was hitting, the center-field clock struck midnight. For the first time in history, Major League Baseball was playing a game in November. It didn't last long, though. On a 3–2 pitch, Jeter poked one down the right-field line. It wasn't a majestic shot, but at Yankee Stadium, it didn't need to be. The ball had just enough to clear the 314 mark, touching down on the walkway before the first row of seats. As Jeter circled the bases with his right fist in the air, radio announcer Michael Kay screamed, "See ya! See ya! See ya!" Seated down the first-base line and sitting with former Yankee Dave Winfield, Jeter's parents screamed, jumped up and down, and began hugging anybody in site. Though the month was only minutes old, a fan had already prepared and unfurled a sign: "Mr. November." It was Jeter's first career walk-off home run, the first home run ever hit in November, and the first time in World Series history that a team hit a ninth-inning home run to tie a game and then homered in extra innings to win it. It was yet another exhilarating moment for a city still reeling from the attack.

The Yankees were back. The city was abuzz with what happened the night before. Millions of groggy fans stumbled into work that morning in the tri-state area exhausted both mentally and physically from Game 4. It was immediately hailed as one of the greatest World Series games ever played, and anticipation was high for Game 5. But no one could realistically expect Game 5 to live up to what had just happened, could they? "I know everybody is waiting for that sort of ending again, but I think it's unfair to expect that because those happen once every 50 years," Kay said before the game.

For eight innings it did not live up to Game 4. Mussina was sharp for New York, but he gave up two fifth-inning home runs that put the team in a 2–0 hole. And the Yankees offense continued to struggle even against spot starter Miguel Bautista, who held them scoreless. The team entered the ninth inning down two runs just as the night before. And just as the night before, Brenly called on Kim to get the final outs and send his team back to Arizona. The announcement of Kim in the game brought immediate excitement to a crowd that hadn't had much to cheer about all game. With the exception of the seventh-inning stretch and chants of "USA, USA," the fans hadn't been able to get much going. Kim's entrance changed that as everyone began having visions of a ninth-inning repeat of Game 4. When Posada led off with a double, the crowd became even more boisterous. *This is going to happen again*, they thought. But then Spencer grounded out, and Chuck Knoblauch struck out and the crowd went eerily silent.

Up to the plate came Brosius. He'd had two at-bats against Kim the night before, nearly homering in the second one. That thought gave Torre some comfort as Brosius took ball one. Then Kim hung a slider, and Brosius clobbered it. As the ball sailed to left field, Brosius immediately thrust both arms into the air in celebration. Once the ball landed, though, almost 10 rows deep in the left-field stands, chaos ensued. "Holy shit! Holy shit! Holy shit!" Olney said.

"I don't believe it," said Yankees radio announcer John Sterling, "probably the most unbelievable feat in World Series history." "Do you believe it?" screamed announcer Gary Thorne. Echoed ESPN radio's Jon Miller: "They have done it again!"

The wings of the upper deck at Yankee Stadium actually shook. It was so loud that fans sitting in the bleachers could not hear Chumbawamba's "Tubthumping" and its "I get knocked down, but I get up again" lyrics, which provided an appropriated narrative for what just happened, over the loudspeakers. The Yankees poured out of the dugout, jumping like little leaguers. "Unbelievable," said Jeter in *The Yankee Years*. "You'll never see anything like that again. Never. We did it two days in a row. That was as exciting as anything that has happened here." On the mound Kim looked ashen. He was so shell-shocked that catcher Rod Barajas actually went to the mound and cradled his head. Media reports would later say (falsely) that Kim was in tears. In the Yankees dugout, Brosius could hardly contain his smile as many of the players looked around, still in disbelief. As the Vengaboys "We Like To Party" blasted over the PA system, Brosius allowed himself a few head bobs to the music. "Mike, I don't believe it and I'm here," Sterling said to Kay as Brenly removed Kim from the game. "Now let me ask you. How many games have we done together, one million? Do you believe it—that this could happen two nights in a row with two outs in the ninth inning?"

Sterling had not been far off. Before Game 4 only once in World Series history had a team trailed by two runs in the ninth inning, tied the game on a home run, and then won the game. Now it had happened two nights in a row. Never before in World Series history had a team won two games in which it trailed going into the ninth inning until the 2001 World Series.

The crowd was still buzzing as the game stretched into extra innings. Rivera worked out of a bases-loaded, one-out jam in the 11th. In the bottom of the 12th, Knoblauch led off with a single. Brosius played hero again by sacrificing Knoblauch to second. Up came Soriano. He'd already provided two big moments in the playoffs against the A's and Mariners. Now on a 2–1 pitch, he punched the ball out into right field. Reggie Sanders fielded the ball on a hop and fired to home, but the ball bounced off Barajas' glove. Knoblauch slid in safe and, like that, the Yankees led the series 3–2. The last time a team had hit a game-tying home run in the ninth inning of a World Series game and eventually won that game was in 1929. The Yankees had now done it two nights in a row.

The crowd of 56,018 stood and sang along to Sinatra's "New York, New York." This would be the last time they would see their beloved team on the field for the year. Most expected them to eventually win the championship, but even if they didn't, the last three nights had been an extraordinary experience that lifted the city's spirits. "The games fed off the emotion of a scarred and resilient city for which the Yankees had assumed a symbolic presence," Olney wrote. The Yankees had become America's team— if only for a week. "Coming back and winning those games in the fashion we did, it was unbelievable," O'Neill said. "And I really saw a change in the way New Yorkers treated each other. People in New York get such a bad rap of not being nice and this and that. But you really saw the city kind of change then. That was an unbelievable thing to see and be a part of."

To say that what had happened to the Diamondbacks was shocking would be an understatement. The expression on Brenly's face during the press conferences after Game 5 said it all. Arizona had been nearly perfect in New York. Their starters were flawless, they'd gotten clutch hits, and—with the exception of two bad pitches—their bullpen was nearly impeccable. And they had nothing to show for it but three losses.

Pettitte took the mound in Game 6 in the desert. The Yankees had to be hopeful. Pettitte had been the starting pitcher in five postseason series-clinching games for them. But Game 6 was a disaster in every sense of the word. The Yankees were down 12–0 by the end of the third, and Pettitte lasted only two innings. Reliever Jay Witasick gave up 10 hits and nine runs in just an inning and a third. Even the Arizona pitcher, Johnson, who'd come into the game with 38 hits in 315 career regular season at-bats, knocked in a run with a single. The Yankees scored two meaningless runs in a 15–2 drubbing, and their inability to generate much offense meant Brenly did not have to stress Johnson, meaning he could be available for Game 7.

The clubbing the Yankees took in Game 6, however, became almost irrelevant the next morning. Anthrax had been discovered in New York's City Hall. It was a sobering reminder of the dangers that still lurked. The first anthrax attacks had been launched just a week after the 9/11 attacks with several laced letters being mailed from a New Jersey post office to various media outlets in New York City as well as to two United States senators. Several people were infected, and at least two died as a result. Mayor Giuliani, who'd been in Arizona for Game 6, flew back to New York that night. After receiving an update on the anthrax situation and attending the kickoff of the New York City Marathon, he hopped on a plane and flew back to Phoenix.

Game 7 played out in a manner fitting of the drama of the series. Schilling and Clemens matched zeroes for five innings. Then in the bottom of the sixth, Arizona took a 1–0 lead on a double by Danny Bautista. Only a terrific play by Jeter prevented Bautista from reaching third with no outs. In the seventh the

Yankees fought back. Singles by Jeter, O'Neill, and Martinez tied the game. Rain began to fall in the desert as Soriano golfed an 0–2 splitter from Schilling deep into the left-field stands in the eighth inning, putting the Yankees ahead 2–1. The small groups of New Yorkers there, including several families of 9/11 victims that had been brought to the game by Mayor Giuliani, jumped in excitement. Torre had been talking to bench coach Don Zimmer as Soriano's at-bat progressed about who to bring in for the bottom of the eighth. Torre wanted to use Ramiro Mendoza; Zimmer was adamant about bringing in Rivera. With a tie game on the road, Torre did not want to use his closer. They went back and forth. Finally, Torre said if only Soriano would just hit a home run, it would solve the whole problem. As Torre expressed that thought to Zimmer, Soriano's shot left the playing field. Torre, who rarely displayed emotion in the dugout, enthusiastically pumped his fist in the air. The Yankees were six outs away from bringing another title to New York, and they had the best closer in the history of the game to finish off the Diamondbacks.

But the Yankees never got the six outs. In the bottom of the ninth, a single, an error, and a double off Rivera, who'd converted 23 straight postseason save opportunities, tied the game. After loading the bases with one out, Gonzalez popped a shot over the drawn-in infield for a single, giving Arizona the title. It was a crushing loss for both the players and the city. "I just remember feeling, *Gosh, we let down everyone in New York.* I just couldn't believe it. I was in a state of shock for a good week," Justice told Fox's Ken Rosenthal.

But in the end, the loss seemed small compared to what had happened and what was continuing to happen in southern Manhattan. And besides for nearly a month, the Yankees had given New York one of the greatest, gutsiest postseason performances in history. "Everybody doubted if we were going to get through this," said actor Steve Schirripa, who lost three close friends in the attacks. "People lost their fathers, their mothers, their kids. I know you say, 'Well baseball, big deal.' But I think it showed that, hey, maybe we will get through this. Maybe we will get back to some kind of normal life. It was the first positive thing that we had a chance to cling on to and get some people's minds off it—even if it was for an hour. And as trivial as baseball may sound to some people, I think it gave the city and New Jersey and the country a little ray of hope in them."

The memories would last a lifetime and helped bring some relief to a devastated city. "We did everything and beyond to bring some hope…[to] at least take their minds away from reality. We did. Even though we lost the series, we did," Rivera said.

Of course, the idea of the Yankees being America's team lasted about 24 hours after Gonzalez's hit dropped into left field. During the offseason they tossed out big money, landing free-agent first baseman Giambi, reinforcing their image as the team that spends whatever it takes to win. That, plus the natural passage of time, put the Yankees back where they were on September 10, 2011: America's most hated team. Even President Bush, who'd thrilled the country with his first pitch strike before Game 3, soured on the Yankees. Fleischer recalls being on a trip to China sometime after the 2001 season. Early in the morning, the president hopped on a treadmill, and the Yankees game happened to be on TV. In full view of a reporter running on the treadmill next to him, Bush actively rooted against the Yankees.

But for a small period of time in the fall of 2001, the Yankees were magically able to rally the country around them. They did it through one of the most extraordinary playoff runs that has ever occurred in baseball history. Their ability to constantly come back, to never give in no matter what the obstacles, helped inspire millions of people in New York City and the surrounding area. Baseball is just a game, yes. But for so many people during that time period, baseball was an escape.

12

Mayors and Managers

It is the world's most known position in local government. Those who attain it are almost instantly mentioned as candidates for higher office. They become national figures by virtue of their office. Mayor of New York City is not an easy job. You are the leader of 8.3 million people, a responsibility greater than the governors of 39 states. While many states don't even have their own media market, thus eliminating some of the media pressure, New York has CBS, ABC, NBC, Fox, and WPIX providing exclusive coverage of the Big Apple. The mayor must be media savvy, appreciate a good publicity stunt, and know how to relate to its constituents. Those who fail to do so will sink.

Being manager of the Yankees is no different. Dozens of reporters follow and question your every move. You are held responsible by millions of people and must deal with situations, which you did not create but for which you are accountable. If you fail to communicate well with your staff and your employers, you will sink. The men (yes, they've all been men) who have held the reins of power in city hall and Yankee Stadium have had similar experiences. Using the same attributes, they have either succeeded immensely or been tossed aside. And even those who have been popular and achieved much fall under the "what have you done for me lately?" culture of the city.

Fiorello LaGuardia and Casey Stengel are often mentioned as the greatest mayor of New York City and manager of the Yankees, respectively. That's not a coincidence. Each had similar qualities that made them successful. They were good with a quote, knew the value of positive publicity, and were harsh with subordinates who failed to live up to their expectations. Both were small in stature, which caused people to underestimate their tenacity and grit.

Known as the "Little Flower," LaGuardia was just 5'2" in height, and his look and persona brought comparisons with Napoleon. He became mayor at a critical time for the city. The Depression had caused massive unemployment. City Hall had become rife with corruption. The previous elected mayor, Jimmy Walker, was known for his extravagant nightlife, mistress, and association with known gambler Arnold Rothstein. Walker was forced to resign in disgrace in 1932. Though LaGuardia was a Republican, he embraced the New Deal principles put forth by Franklin Roosevelt, a Democratic president. It made him unpopular within his own party but popular with the people of New York. LaGuardia also dove headfirst into tackling corruption and incompetence within city government. His appointment of Robert Moses to head the parks department is one of the most well-regarded appointments in the history of the city as Moses shaped and molded New York into what we know it as today.

The Little Flower was tough on his staff, never failing to insult or slap down any subordinate who failed to perform to his expectations. According to biographer Lowell Limpus, LaGuardia "proceeded to browbeat his subordinates in the same fashion in which he had always bulldozed his little office force. That meant shrieking, screaming, and cursing at them—frequently when others were present. It was no rarity for the chief executive to hurl his pen on the floor and launch into a bitter tirade against the head of some great city department."

LaGuardia was also quick to exploit a good public relations gimmick. He was the first mayor to truly understand and adequately use the power of the media, something he'd begun doing

The diminutive but powerful mayor known as "Little Flower," Fiorello LaGuardia speaks to his constituents in 1941. (AP Images)

as a congressman. Vehemently opposed to prohibition, LaGuardia, while serving in congress, once mixed two legal cocktails into one illegal cocktail at a New York City drugstore, daring the police to arrest him. He did this in full view of the media and made certain they got pictures. He was not arrested for the incident. As mayor he would be seen at almost every major fire in the city, making sure his picture was taken as he played the role of decisive leader. LaGuardia hated slot machines, so when the city passed an ordinance outlawing them, he gleefully posed for the press—sledgehammer in tow—smashing the machines. When returning from a trip during his term, LaGuardia's flight landed at Newark Airport in New Jersey, even though his ticket said New York. Outraged that the city had no major airport, he demanded that night to be flown to a field in Brooklyn, where he held an impromptu press conference demanding a new airport be built in the city. The demand eventually yielded LaGuardia Airport.

The media and public also loved LaGuardia because he was quick with a good quote. According to H. Paul Jeffers' biography, *Napoleon of New York*, when discussing the proceedings of the board of alderman of which LaGuardia was president, he said, "Every member present must behave as a gentleman, and those who are not must try to." He referred to people who played slot machines as "boobs." When a National Education Association committee attacked him for interfering with the city's board of education, LaGuardia shot back that the committee simply wasn't smart enough to understand the complexity of New York's school system. He also detested the term "politician" and never referred to himself as one. Although he had campaigned against his late-night frolicking predecessors, he was often seen out and about—not necessarily partying but just being out and being seen. While he was proud of his Italian heritage, he was also a proud American who loudly supported the war effort during World War II. New Yorkers ate it all up, and LaGuardia easily won reelection in 1937 and 1941, becoming the first mayor of the city elected to three terms. Up for a possible fourth term in 1945, he declined to run, though he most likely would have won. He opted instead to retire. Just two years later, he died from cancer at the age of 64. "Dynamite and aggressive, he appeared to be everywhere at once, rushing to fires at times and at other times flying all over the country by airplane," wrote *The New York Times* after his death. "A fighter by nature he was always ready to take on all comers big or little, from Hitler to the man in the street." For his 1999 book, *The American Mayor*, Melvin G. Holli polled 160 historians, social scientists, and journalists and found that LaGuardia was regarded as both the greatest mayor in the history of New York and in the history of the United States.

Two years after the death of the Little Flower, another short, blunt, and soon-to-be-widely heralded man emerged in New York. Only this time he was manager of the Yankees. But at the peak of his popularity, Stengel could well have been elected mayor of New York.

Born Charles Dillon Stengel, Casey decided to drop out of dental school at age 20 to play baseball instead. He was a marginal player, perhaps best known for hitting an inside-the-park home run against the Yankees in the 1923 World Series. After retirement he began what started out as a rather lackluster career as a manager. He managed the Brooklyn Dodgers and then Boston Braves for nine seasons, only once finishing with a better than .500 record. He eventually went out to the West Coast to manage in Oakland. During these futile years of managing, Stengel became familiar with Yankees general manager George Weiss. The GM took a liking to Stengel as did others in the Yankee hierarchy. They appreciated Stengel's devotion to the game as well as the fact that he would not kowtow to veteran players. He would manage how he wanted to manage. When the Yankees dropped their manager after the 1948 season, Stengel was brought over from California to take charge.

Stengel's hiring didn't bring much enthusiasm. He certainly did not have the managerial stature of his predecessor, Bucky Harris. But Stengel had a few things going for him. First, the Yankees were in the midst of promoting their minor league talent, led by Whitey Ford and Mickey Mantle, to go along with an already star-studded lineup. These men were to Stengel what Robert Moses was to LaGuardia. Second, Stengel was a master tactician who understood the changing dynamics of the game and responded accordingly. He was the first manager to make effective use of the platoon system, playing right-handed batters against lefty pitchers and left-handed batters against righties.

Stengel's success on the field was matched by his amusing personality. He easily came up with zingers, puns, and quips that made covering him a pleasure for beat writers. Among some of the classics are:

"Good pitching will always stop good hitting and vice versa."

"There comes a time in every man's life, and I've had plenty of them."

"You have to have a catcher or you'll have all passed balls."

In *Damn Yankees* writer Roy Blount Jr. recounts a story Yankee outfielder Irv Noren told him about Stengel. Noren was sent up to pinch hit in a key situation. The count went full, at which point Stengel called time and came out of the dugout to talk to Noren. "If it's a ball, take it," Stengel told him. "If it's a strike, hit it." As a player Stengel once doffed his cap to a booing crowd at Ebbets Field, only to reveal a sparrow, which immediately flew away. Stengel's act would only intensify once he became manager of the hapless New York Mets, and part of his job became distracting fans from how bad the team was.

In some ways the jester image did Stengel no favors as fans came to see him as some sort of lovable clown in a baseball uniform. Many did not realize his sharp baseball acumen nor did they know how brutal he could be on some of his players. In *Dynasty* Peter Golenbock recalls how Stengel lost patience with rookies as he got older, chastising them for making errors, which only resulted in players becoming more tense and making more errors. "Stengel kept the young pitchers edgy by constantly second-guessing them every time they gave up a base hit," Golenbock wrote. "A batter would hit a curve, and Stengel would yell, 'How the hell can you throw that guy a curve?' If a batter hit a fastball, it was, 'How the hell can you throw that guy a fastball?'" Stengel was cold and merciless on the players he did not like and could be heard using the most derogatory of terms to describe people's race or ethnicity.

The Yankees lost the World Series in 1960 on a Game 7 home run by Bill Mazeroski in the bottom of the ninth inning. Shortly thereafter, the Yankees let Stengel go as manager, announcing the decision in a poorly crafted press conference, implying the reason for the firing was that he was simply getting too old for the game. Always ready with a line even in the midst of bad news, Stengel told the press, "I'll never make the mistake of being 70 again."

At the time of his firing, Stengel was second in team history in managerial wins. (He has since been passed by Joe Torre.) In 12 seasons as manager, he tied for the most in the history of the game with seven titles. Only twice did the Yankees fail to make the World Series under Stengel: in 1954 (when the team still won

Though he had a reputation as a jester, Casey Stengel won seven World Series with the Yankees while managing the team from 1949 to 1960. (AP Images)

103 games) and in 1959. Stengel remains a key part of Yankees history—perhaps the most famous and successful manager they have ever had. And much like LaGuardia, his memory lives on not only because of his success, but also because of the grandness of his character.

Although LaGuardia and Stengel enjoyed some of the most successful terms of any mayor or manager, others were not so lucky. New York City and the Yankees have endured their share of bad eras. Those in charge have often taken the blame—fairly or unfairly—for the turbulence. Confronted by a plethora of forces beyond their control, the mayors faced an angry constituency, and the manager faced an angry owner. The result was the same: a firing. For Abe Beame and David Dinkins, their lifelong goals of running New York were marred by a series of incidents that drew the ire of voters. For Dallas Green, Bucky Dent, and Stump Merrill, their dream of managing the most storied team in all of sports was marred by a meddlesome owner who created situations under which no one could have possibly become successful.

Beame grew up on the Lower East Side and spent decades working for the city. He served as city budget director during the 1950s. He ran for mayor in 1965 but lost to John Lindsay. During the 1960s he served as comptroller for the city. By all accounts Beame was a good man. But when he finally attained the role of mayor in 1973, the first Jewish mayor in New York's history was overwhelmed by the problems confronting the city. New York's fiscal house was in shambles. Beame had been elected in part because people felt the former comptroller had the expertise to solve the budgetary problems, but Beame discovered the issues were much worse than he'd realized. As detailed by *The New York Times* in their obituary of him, when Beame got into office, he discovered that his predecessor "had resorted to a stupefying array of gimmicks: juggling books to shift state aid from one year to another, using fictitious surpluses, deferring required payments, arbitrarily raising revenue estimates, borrowing against questionable receipts."

The law firm White and Case did an independent review of New York City's books in 1975 and discovered the city did not have the resources to borrow another dime from anyone for anything. Shortly thereafter, the teacher's union said it would not commit to its pension funds because of the city's finances. Investors refused to buy bonds from the city, realizing it was a far too risky venture.

Decades later national recessions meant more willingness to help big cities in fiscal crisis. That was not the case with New York in the 1970s. For the city back in 1975, "there wasn't a lot of sympathy from the federal government," CUNY Queens College labor historian Joshua Freeman told the *New York Daily News*. When New York went to President Ford to request the federal government help the city through a loan, Ford declined assistance. The *Daily News* responded with one of the most famous headlines in American history: "Ford To City: Drop Dead."

In order to resolve the crisis, Beame had to lay off thousands of city employees, a workforce that had ballooned by approximately 30 percent under Lindsay. Included in the layoffs were hundreds of police officers. The laid-off cops responded by holding various demonstrations and hounding Beame constantly. Crime was already a problem in the city and now it would only grow worse with a reduced police force. But Beame had little choice. If the city did not find ways to come up with revenue, it was going to be unable to pay its bills, and bankruptcy, which would have been catastrophic for the country's largest city, was an absolute possibility.

Eventually, city officials worked out a variety of plans to help New York avoid a near catastrophe. Although Beame would try to take credit, the people of New York simply weren't buying it. Beame was not an inspirational speaker. He delivered many speeches while standing on top of a brief case due to his small stature and he failed to connect with audiences or even individuals in one-on-one conversation. His speeches were often littered with policy details that could put even the most wonkish of people to sleep.

The arrest of the Son of Sam killer provided Beame a small boost, but he almost managed to screw that up. As the suspect, David Berkowitz, was being led through the police station, Beame, not recognizing who was the cop and who was the killer, almost shook the Son of Sam's hand to congratulate him. And not too long before the primary election, in which Beame was up against three other formidable Democratic candidates, New York experienced a blackout of epic proportions. It happened during a stiflingly hot summer evening, and the ensuing darkness brought on mass looting. Times of crises are usually great poll boosters for any politician, but Beame came off as unable to do anything about getting the power back on or stopping the crime. Shortly thereafter, a Securities and Exchange Commission report on the history of the city's fiscal crisis painted Beame in a harsh light. The mayor came off as aloof at times, ignoring the warnings of bankers about the extent of the problems, not knowing all the details, and embellishing his problem-solving actions. In the end, New York's financial problems, crime, and the overall discontent of life in the city sank Beame. He failed to garner enough votes to even make the run-off election in the primary, which became a contest between Ed Koch and Mario Cuomo. Beame, who rarely showed emotion in public, broke down and cried during his concession speech, saying he'd done the best he could. He faded from public view after leaving office, becoming an investment banker. Beame died in 2001 at the age of 94.

Dinkins had fought for a lifetime to climb through New York city politics and make his way to the top. He'd served as president of the board of elections, city clerk, and Manhattan borough president. In 1989 he won the mayor's office by first knocking off a three-term incumbent, Koch, in the Democratic primary. He then won a grueling campaign against former U.S. Attorney Rudy Giuliani. Dinkins became the first black mayor of the city, a historic accomplishment that many hoped would help heal the racial discontent that had permeated New York during the 1980s.

Race relations, however, only seemed to worsen as did a host of other issues that had been left for Dinkins to resolve from the Koch administration. Koch had made several important strides during his term, fixing up much of the budgetary mess he'd inherited and sparking economic development in the city. But as issues of crime and race were still overwhelming the city, New York's image was taking a serious hit around the world.

Dinkins did his best to handle these problems, but at times his administration appeared overwhelmed by the size and scope of it all. During the Crown Heights riots, Dinkins was slammed by the Jewish community for his seeming indifference to their plight. It was a charge that especially hurt the mayor, considering he'd gone to great lengths to court the Jewish vote in 1989. As tensions built over the course of several days of the riots, the mayor and his team seemed indecisive. Dinkins had been elected partially because he was the anti-Koch. His remarks were carefully thought out, and his decisions not impulsive. Koch's glib remarks and ability to speak on just about anything without knowing all the facts had grown tiresome to New Yorkers. But now they wanted some of Koch's chutzpah back. Dinkins' appearance of failing to lead, coupled with an inability to do anything about escalating crime rates, turned off many voters in the city, especially white, working-class voters in areas like Staten Island and Brooklyn. They were looking for someone to restore law-and-order in their city and they didn't think Dinkins was doing it.

In reality Dinkins began the process of hiring thousands of cops to watch over New York. It was the beginning of an initiative the next administration would reap the benefits of. In a similar vein, it was the Dinkins administration that started many of the conversations that resulted in much of the new development in and around the Times Square area. But Dinkins failed to receive credit for two reasons. First, much of the building and the ribbon cuttings and all the other pomp and circumstance that comes with new development did not happen until after he'd been voted out of office. Second, a little more than halfway through his term, the country was gripped by a national recession that caused large-scale unemployment. The recession was largely responsible for voters tossing President Bush out of office in 1992 and also played a role in other politicians losing their jobs.

Dinkins was no different. He faced a 1993 rematch against Giuliani that became extremely nasty with both sides playing the race card against the other. Giuliani also made quality of life an issue, stressing that he would go after the panhandlers and squeegee men who tormented New Yorkers and tourists. It was enough in the end, though barely, to oust Dinkins from office. Like Beame, Dinkins faced a torrent of issues that he did not create and in some ways were beyond his control. The image of him that voters had in 1993 should not be his lasting one. "Dinkins faced a very sharp economic downturn and he was in the very difficult position of coming in with high expectations from many constituencies," City University Graduate Center professor John H. Mollenkopf told *The New York Times*. "Yet he expanded the police force and rebuilt neighborhoods; he deserves more credit than he gets for managing that time." Dinkins remained marginally active in politics after leaving office, endorsing various candidates for mayor. He became a professor at Columbia University, a position he retains to this day.

Dinkins wasn't the only person in New York in 1989 on the hot seat. Green walked into a mess every bit as perplexing as the city's when he signed on to become manager of the Yankees for the '89 season. Green's selection was somewhat stunning as he was the first person outside the Yankees organization to take the reins in over a decade. George Steinbrenner was looking to go in a different direction. Who could blame him? Clearly the one he was going with wasn't working. Since losing the World Series in 1981, The Boss had chewed on and spit out six different managers over seven seasons. During that time he used Billy Martin thrice and Lou Piniella twice as well as bringing back Bob Lemon and Gene Michael for second servings. Amazingly, there were four separate times during that period in which a manger was fired and replaced with the exact same person they had originally replaced.

Then along came Green, known as "Discipline Dallas" for his unwillingness to take people's crap. Steinbrenner thought this would be just the thing his clubhouse needed. Instead it was the exact attribute that made Green unwilling to deal with the kind of Steinbrenner bullshit with which previous managers had put up. It didn't take long for Green to realize he was in trouble. "I remember during the offseason leading up to the '89 season I used to talk to Dallas a lot on the phone, just trying to get to know him leading into spring training," said Moss Klein, who covered the Yankees for *The* (Newark) *Star-Ledger*. "Dallas kept saying to me, 'Just wait and see. Things are going to be different. George told me he has learned from history. He knows what he is doing. He is going to be different.' I kept saying to him, 'Dallas, I am going to be shocked if he is any different.' It got to be the third week of spring training, and I was standing on the field in Fort Lauderdale one day, and Dallas came walking and motioned over to me. He said, 'You know what you kept telling me during the offseason about things aren't going to be different, that he isn't going to change?' I said, 'Yeah.' He said, 'You were right.'"

Steinbrenner insisted on retaining pitchers Ron Guidry and Tommy John, sentimental favorites to whom The Boss was attached. Guidry, however, was 39 years old and plagued by injuries. John would turn 46 in May and simply not a reliable pitcher anymore. Without seeking Green's input, Steinbrenner also traded away Rick Rhoden, one of the few durable pitchers the Yankees had during the last two seasons. Claudell Washington, a durable and productive outfielder in 1988, was allowed to sign elsewhere. Dave Winfield was out for the year with a back problem as was starting shortstop Rafael Santana. Rickey Henderson was unhappy and, some said, dogging it out on the field. His statements about the Yankees missing the playoffs the previous season because of too much drinking created resentment in the clubhouse. A few days later, Henderson told the *Daily News'* Michael Kay that the Yankees were a racist organization, remarks which Henderson later denied ever making. Jack Clark's 27 home runs and 93 RBIs were traded to the San Diego Padres, and no one was brought in to replace that production. Years of shoddy deals had left the farm system almost empty.

The team was a mess, and there was little Green could do about it. All the discipline in the world wasn't going to change the fact that Andy Hawkins would end up as the only pitcher on the team with double-digit wins (he also had double-digit losses) or that, outside of Don Mattingly, the entire infield would hit just 16 home runs and drive in less than 150 runs (and that includes backup players).

The Yankees won on Opening Day, then lost their next seven games by a combined score of 57–15. Then the phone calls started coming in and the complaints. But Green was having none of it. He neither needed this job nor was beholden to Steinbrenner. "He got a few months into the season and he didn't want any part of the job anymore and he did something that none of the other Yankee managers had done: he started going on the attack," Klein said. Green began referring to Steinbrenner as "Manager George" openly to the press, an act of defiance he knew would get The Boss' attention.

The Yankees beat the Kansas City Royals 10–1 to go a game over .500 on July 16 and were just six out of first. But over their next 29 games, they went 9–20, falling out of contention. Steinbrenner fired Green on August 18, a day after the Yankees beat the Tigers 2–1 in Detroit. Green didn't leave without a memorable parting shot at The Boss. "George doesn't know a fucking thing about the game of baseball," Dallas told the media. "That's the bottom line."

Steinbrenner called on Dent to replace Green. Dent had no managerial experience in the big leagues, having been at the helm of the Yankees' Triple A affiliate when he got promoted. He was still a hero for his home run against the Boston Red Sox in 1978, but that would earn him no collateral as manager. Dent was inheriting the same team that Green had managed and quickly found out it wasn't a matter of style; it was a matter of talent. In his first game in the dugout, the Yankees were losing 6–0 by the bottom of the fourth inning. The Yankees started out 2–11 with Dent, making people wonder if another firing was on the way. They rebounded to win nine in a row, then lost seven of their next eight, essentially canceling out any gains. They finished the year 74–87, fifth in the American League East.

Somehow, someway, the Yankees ended up being even worse in 1990. Mattingly's back finally gave out, resulting in the worst season of his career. The rest of the offense was anemic, with only one hitter, Roberto Kelly, batting better than .260. Mel Hall finished third on the team in RBIs *with 46.* Only four players had more than 100 hits, and outside of Jesse Barfield, no one on the team walked more than 50 times. The bad offense was matched by the pitching. No starter won more than nine games, and 13 different people started at least one game that year. Among them was Steve Adkins, who walked 29 hitters in just 24 innings, and Pascual Perez, who managed to lose two of his three starts for the season despite giving up a total of three runs in those three games.

The Yankees lost 9–4 in Kansas City on May 26. Hawkins gave up five runs in less than two innings that night, pushing his ERA to 7.52. The team was down 9–0 after four innings. The loss dropped the team into dead last in the AL East, a position they would not relinquish for the rest of the year. Somehow, all of this was Dent's fault. On June 5 the Yankees overcame a four-run deficit in the eighth inning at Fenway Park, tying the game at eight. But the bullpen lost it in the bottom of the inning, and the Yankees fell 9–8. Dent was let go after the game along with most of the coaching staff. It was the 10th time in his 18 years of owning the club that Steinbrenner had changed managers during the season. It remains the last time the Yankees have done so.

In Dent's place came Merrill, a man right out of central casting for a baseball coach. He had a belly that stuck out over his belt and once used a dirty sock to clean his teeth. Merrill had been in the organization for years and had dreamed of managing the Yankees. But the dream was tempered because of the club he inherited. The Yankees lost the first four games under Merrill and finished the year 67–95, their worst record in decades. On the final day of the season, they were on the wrong end of history when Detroit's Cecil Fielder clubbed two home runs against them, becoming the first player in 13 years to hit more than 50 homers in a season.

The next year, 1991, didn't prove much better for Merrill and the Yankees, though Merrill became the first manager in four years to last an entire season with the Yankees. But that had more to do with The Boss' banishment from the game. In reality the team was no better, and player discontent was off the charts. The team was riddled with players who'd had enough of New York and enough of Merrill. When Mattingly, who'd been named captain of the team before the season started, was benched on August 15th for refusing to cut his hair, many lost any lingering shred of respect for their manager. During the course of the year, players were actually telling members of the media that it was their job to try to get Merrill fired.

The season wasn't all terrible. In his first start with the club, pitcher Scott Sanderson took a no-hitter into the ninth inning in Detroit. He lost it when Tony Phillips doubled on the first pitch of the inning, but Sanderson was a pleasant surprise for the year, winning 16 games. The year also saw the debut of Bernie Williams, who singled and knocked in two runs in his first major league game on July 7. Two and a half weeks later, the Yankees stood at 45–45, not too bad for a team that had finished last the year before. But it all went downhill from there. Much of the young talent the team tested during the rest of the year didn't pan out. The Yankees went 26–46 the rest of the way, avoiding last place only because the Baltimore Orioles and Cleveland Indians were that much worse.

Not long after the season ended, Merrill got the boot along with the rest of his coaching staff. Third-base coach Buck Showalter was included in the firings. A short time later, though, Michael, now the GM, called and offered Showalter the managerial position. In the two decades before Michael made that call, the Yankees had 12 different managers. In the two decades since Michael made that call, they have had three.

13

Yankees Fans

I say the following, which I should mention includes me, with all the love, tenderness, and warmth possible: Yankees fans are assholes. Many people from other fan bases will tell you that. But there is something about this particular breed of asshole that is charming, and in this respect, Yankees fans mirror New Yorkers as a whole. Few would accuse New York as being the home of good manners. Yet there is something endearing about the taxi driver who flips you off for blocking traffic or the subway rider who drops F-bombs in front of your children like it's his official function. You come to New York expecting such things and leave disappointed if you don't hear them.

New Yorkers, for all their attitude, also don't accept bullshit easily. They know when they are being scammed and have no problem calling out the scammer. It's a unique talent that comes with living in one of the most crowded areas in the world and dealing with millions of tourists each year who clog the subways, ask stupid questions, and block the way to work. For all their swagger, though, New Yorkers are also amazingly compassionate and forgiving people. Forgiveness is a New York specialty. New Yorkers love a good comeback story, so they are always willing to embrace those who have been cast aside by others. And if the contrition is real, they'll have no problem building you back up.

Richard Nixon learned about that. The former president, who resigned in 1974 over the various Watergate scandals, moved out of California in 1980 to New York City. Nixon had spent nearly his entire life in California, but this was not the first time he moved to New York. After losing the presidential election in 1960 and the California gubernatorial race in 1962, his career was deemed dead. He set up shop in New York, reviving himself and beginning the process that eventually led to his being elected president in 1968. It was the culmination of perhaps the greatest comeback in American political history. A short while after moving to New York a second time, Nixon moved to New Jersey, but he maintained an office in Foley Square. It was there that Nixon worked—rather successfully—to rebuild his image. "Richard Nixon is back," wrote Julie Baumgold in a piece for *New York Magazine*. "He's out walking the early morning streets. Signing autographs at Yankee Stadium. On television. At 21. At Luchow's. At David K's. At Windows on the World. In Central Park. On 57th street." Nixon roamed the streets each morning on a two-mile walk through the city. He was seen attending Yankees games, including being present when Dave Righetti tossed his no-hitter on July 4, 1983. He was seen at Shea Stadium, congratulating David Cone as he came off the mound after having achieved his 20th win of the 1988 season. Nixon made good money, becoming a best-selling author many times over and was regarded as an elder statesman particularly in matters of foreign policy. By the time of his death, which occurred in New York City in 1994, he'd managed to rebrand himself in light of Watergate—thanks in part to his acceptance by the people of New York City.

Bill Clinton endured the Monica Lewinsky scandal during his second term in office. After leaving the presidency, though, he was welcomed with open arms when he established his new office in Harlem (despite the fact that he'd never lived anywhere near New York). Martha Stewart, born across the Hudson River in Jersey City, spent five months in prison for charges related to insider trading. Just a year after being sent to prison, she had a book on *The New York Times'* best-seller list, more ad space in her magazine, and shows on both television and radio, netting her millions of dollars. New Yorkers were clearly ready to forgive and forget a little petty crime.

But New Yorkers are only willing to forgive if the contrition is real. In 2011 then-congressman Anthony Weiner, who represented the Flatbush district, was embroiled in scandal when it was revealed that he tweeted sexually explicit pictures of himself to a woman who wasn't his wife. After initially saying his account had been hacked and the pictures were not of him, he later announced that they were of him and he had been sending them to several women. He resigned shortly thereafter. Two years later Weiner announced himself as a candidate for mayor in the city's Democratic primary. Initially, New Yorkers seemed to have no problem looking past his previous scandal, and Weiner was actually leading in the polls. But then word broke that Weiner had still been sending pictures to women even after he had resigned from Congress. New Yorkers immediately smelled bullshit. Weiner's poll numbers plunged, and he ended up with just 5 percent of the vote.

But back to my original point: Yankees fans are assholes. A simple Google search can tell you that. Start typing "Yankee fans" and "are annoying" will pop up. And dislike for Yankees fans isn't just relegated to New York Mets fans or New England. It goes nationwide. The reasons why are no mystery. Yankees fans are pompous, arrogant, and kind of douchey. Go to urbandictionary.com and look under the definition of "new york yankees." Here are just a couple of the descriptions you will find:

"They have the absolute shittiest fanbase EVER! They have like 70 million "fans" that probably can't name 5 players on the yankees roster and probably think a-rod was drafted by the team."
or
"A baseball team with fans (99% of them bandwagon) that doesn't shut up about their 26 world titles, and uses their

incredibly high paycheck to hire new players who either used to be good in the past."

For the record it's actually 27 world titles, but the point is accurate. Make any sort of knock on the Yankees to a fan, and their response invariably will be to ask you how many championships your team has won. They can't wait to tell you how Mariano Rivera is the greatest relief pitcher that ever lived or how legendary Derek Jeter is and will forever be. Right after the 2013 All-Star Game, in which Rivera pitched one inning and was named MVP, a couple of Yankees fans and I got the following email from my brother Mike, a Mets fan: "Can one of you guys just shoot me a text or email and let me know when the universe has crawled out of Mariano Rivera's anus?"

Yankees fans talk about Yankees mystique and aura, about the sacred history of sports' most storied franchise. They reference the true Yankees—Jeter, Rivera, Don Mattingly, etc.—and those who will never be true Yankees—A-Rod, Roger Clemens, etc.—a concept that is nauseating to most other fans. And the bandwagon fan reference comes up nearly all the time when people are asked why they hate Yankees fans. Again from Mets fan Mike Donnelly: "It's the Yankee fan that's always annoyed me more than the Yankee player. The Yankee fan, mostly fair weather who just like to be able to say they're a Yankee fan, will clap longest and loudest just so they can say how great of fans they are because they clap longest and loudest."

What bothers most people about Yankees fans, though, is that for all the team's success and history, they still find a way to complain. Most fans would be ecstatic sitting in first place. But for Yankees fans, that's not good enough. Even in first place, even in the World Series, something is always wrong: the bullpen sucks; Girardi is overmanaging; they can't hit with runners in scoring position. On and on it goes. For years Rodriguez has had to contend with fans citing his inability to hit in crucial situations, a notion that seems ludicrous to most fans given his career statistics.

While Boston Red Sox fans used to simply await the inevitable collapse, and Mets fans seem to take a perverse joy in lamenting the inferior product at Citibank Field, Yankees fans look for the imperfections in their team and use it as a crutch to bitch about during the season. It's never enough for them. It's what comes from a combination of being spoiled over numerous world championships and people's natural instinct to complain. "With such lofty expectations, the highs can never be high," wrote novelist Nathaniel Rich about the Yankees and their fans in the book, *Damn Yankees*. "A championship restores the team to its rightful place in the universe; never will it be, as it was in 2004 for the Red Sox, a euphoric, mind-exploding, once-in-a-lifetime glory. Will a Yankees fan ever tell his grandchildren about the World Championship of, say, 1999? Excessive winning…makes committed Yankee fans crabby, impossible to impress, bored."

The behavior of Yankees fans isn't something to hang your hat on sometimes either. When Chris Chambliss hit a home run to win the 1976 American League pennant against the Kansas City Royals at Yankee Stadium, fans immediately flooded the field. It was enough to actually prevent Chambliss from being able to reach home plate. Instead after passing second, he darted straight back to the Yankees dugout, knocking a few fans over in the process. Once order was restored, Chambliss went back to touch home and ensure the home run counted. On July 4, 1985, a woman sitting in the upper deck at the stadium was actually hit in the hand with a bullet by what police thought was a random shot. The bullet passed through her hand and ended up in her purse. She survived with no serious injury. *The New York Times* reported that the shooting was believed to have been the first inside a New York ballpark in 35 years.

During the 1995 playoffs, the fans, particularly those in the bleachers, tormented the Seattle Mariners. Seattle's Game 1 starting pitcher, Chris Bosio, recalled several objects being thrown at him as he warmed up in the bullpen—not to mention all sorts of taunts that were tossed his way. During the course of play, objects were repeatedly thrown on the field, including a walkman and a golf ball that nearly hit Mariners second baseman Joey Cora in the head. At one point a Mariners executive's son was hit with a shot glass. When

Mattingly homered in Game 2, the fans littered the field with debris in a misguided yet somewhat touching display of affection. Mariners manager Lou Piniella actually pulled his team off the field, fearing for his players' safety. As he motioned his players off, Piniella was hit in the stomach with a program. When the series moved to Seattle, fans in the Kingdome held up signs that read, "Welcome Back to Civilization" and another meant for George Steinbrenner that read, "Hey George, We Have Fans, Not Animals in the Stands." In 2010 a Yankees fan stabbed a Red Sox fan in the neck at a Connecticut restaurant, seriously wounding him. The Sox fan, based on his Boston accent, had been told he wasn't welcome in the place because it was "Yankee territory." The Yankees fan kept harassing him until he finally—and totally unprovoked—stabbed the man.

The greatest statistic, however, that proves how awful Yankees fans can be is this. According to a 2010 report by *The New York Times*, a person is more likely to commit a crime, particularly a violent crime, when wearing a Yankees hat or shirt then any other team. As *Damn Yankees* points out, "when Muammar Gaddafi was finally killed, one of the insurgents who claimed credit for shooting the Libyan dictator in the head appeared in a widely circulated photograph brandishing Gaddafi's pistol and styling a flat-brimmed, slightly tilted Yankee cap."

But for all that bad and irksome behavior, there is no denying the passion, fanaticism, and—yes—intelligence of Yankees fans. Every team with a modicum of success will have its share of bandwagon fans. And while the 2013 injury-plagued Yankees saw a decline in both attendance and television viewership, the fact remains that the team has consistently led the league in attendance or been at least in the top three. They drew four million a season from 2005–2008, amazing considering only nine times in baseball history has a team drawn over four million in attendance. "We won a World Series in Cincinnati and we had a wonderful parade," Paul O'Neill said. "Then when we won a World Series in '96. In that parade you see the amount of people. It blew me away to see how many people were involved because it was the first time that my eyes were open to the masses of people that are Yankees fans in New York."

The fans that come through the gates are part of what gives Yankee Stadium, both old and new, its character. Section 39 at the old Yankee Stadium and Section 203 at the new one is where the Bleacher Creatures, a staple for decades, call home. Although their antics may not thrill those who bring their families to the game, families should know better than to sit out there. The Creatures have provided loads of free entertainment while making life hellish for opposing outfielders. When Ichiro Suzuki (now on the Yankees) first joined the Mariners, the Creatures learned Japanese obscenities to taunt him. But even that relationship had a love-hate aspect to it. Opposing players who acknowledged the taunts and showed they respected the Creatures' sense of humor endeared themselves to the crowd. Fans of other teams who dared sit in that section wearing a visiting team's cap were almost always guaranteed to be serenaded with a chant of "Ass-hole! Ass-hole!"

A die-hard Yankees fan, former White House press secretary Ari Fleischer used to attend games in Yankee Stadium in the 1970s with his father. "Police would sweep the stadium," Fleischer said. "They would have cops in aisle after aisle walk up as a show of force. These were in the good seats. The bleachers were no man's land. You didn't go there unless you were prepared for what the Bleacher Creatures were going to give out." The Creatures even taunted other Yankees fans. It wasn't uncommon to hear them chant "Box seats suck" or ridicule the fans sitting just across the way from them in right field. The right-field fans would retort by chanting that at least they had beer, a reference to the fact that for the last decade of the original Yankee Stadium, alcohol was not sold in the bleacher section. But as *New York Daily News* writer Filip Bondy pointed out, "The Creatures will get drunk somehow despite the alcohol ban. Beer, rum, and vodka will appear from nowhere." When they are done with fans in other sections, they turn on each other. You might hear a "You are ugly, you are ugly," taunt or "You sell drugs, you sell drugs."

Tina Lewis is the queen of the Bleacher Creatures. Bondy wrote about annoying Jonathan, who "is so annoying that Tina doesn't mind when he sells his seats to interlopers on StubHub." You have got "Bald Vinny" Milano, the leader of the roll call chant, and Sheff-fan, and countless others. They have been leery of newcomers and outsiders. They would refer to new fans as "98ers" (i.e. people who didn't start attending games until after the Yankees won 125 games in 1998.) Even Supreme Court Justice Sonia Sotomayor, who grew up in the Bronx, joined the Creatures when she attended a game in 2012. "I pay homage to the Bleacher Creatures," she told the *Daily News*. "They are the greatest fans…they show it every game, every time they come out. And I felt very proud to be with them."

The Bleacher Creatures, though, aren't the only ones who get in on the fun. The whole crowd at Yankee Stadium loves a good taunt, and they never miss a chance to get on an opposing player for any shortcoming. Kansas City Royals third baseman George Brett, who battled the Yankees during several key playoff clashes, constantly had to deal with comments about his hemorrhoids for years. (Perhaps he thought Yankees fans were a pain in the ass, pardon the pun.) In 2001 after the Yankees won the first two games of the AL Championship Series in Seattle, Mariners manager Piniella guaranteed his team would play another game in Seattle that year. As the Yankees were clobbering the Mariners in Game 5 and about to win the Series, the hometown crowd broke out into chants of "No Game 6! No Game 6!" Then they turned to Ichiro and began shouting "Say-o-nara!"

Three years later Red Sox pitcher Pedro Martinez acknowledged he had trouble beating the Yankees by saying, "What can I say? I tip my hat and call the Yankees, 'My daddy,'" Yankees fans immediately pounced on it. During the ALCS that year, chants of "Who's Your Daddy?" sprung up across the stadium. Though Martinez's Sox would exact revenge on the team by overcoming a 3–0 deficit in that series, Martinez would continue to hear the chants whenever he appeared at the stadium in ensuing years.

Of course, there is also the Bronx Cheer, the term given to when fans sarcastically applaud the accomplishment of a mundane task. A pitcher who walks a few batters in a row will get a Bronx

Cheer for simply throwing a strike. A fielder who drops a fly ball might get one if, on the next ball his way, he makes a routine catch. And the cheers are more often than not actually directed at the hometown team, though the occasional opposing player and umpire might get one too.

But not all the fans' energy is focused on taunting opposing players. After the Yankees made little effort to re-sign him, Reggie Jackson signed with the California Angels, following the 1981 season. When the Angels visited Yankee Stadium, Jackson homered into the upper deck off of Ron Guidry. The home crowd gave him an ovation and then began chanting "Steinbrenner Sucks" in a sign of disapproval over the owner's failure to bring the star back to New York.

Catcher Mike Stanley was a popular member of the '90s teams that began the Yankees resurgence. When the team traded for Joe Girardi and didn't move to sign Stanley, Yankees fans were outraged. When Stanley returned the following season, even as a member of the hated Red Sox, he got a resounding ovation in his first at-bat back at Yankee Stadium. "There is literally no better place to play because, as a player, the fans just love their players," Stanley said. "That is all you could ask for. They are fair. They are not going to get on you to get on you. They are going to get on you because you did something because they demand winning, and there is just no substitute. They are not going to be satisfied with a halfway decent year. It's crushing to the fans in New York when they don't win. And I don't see that in other cities."

When Tino Martinez returned to Yankee Stadium in 2003, it was as a member of the St. Louis Cardinals during interleague play. His homecoming was overshadowed by Clemens seeking to win his 300th game. Just before Martinez was to come to the plate, Clemens also recorded his 4,000th career strikeout, becoming only the second pitcher ever to reach that number. The applause that followed was a mix of respect for Clemens and admiration for Martinez. Never getting the applause all to himself he surely would have received without Clemens' accomplishment, Martinez hit two home runs in a Cardinals loss the next day and received a warm ovation from the crowd. And no matter how bad the team might be, no matter what issue they are complaining about on any given day, Yankees fans will defend their team to the death. You might overhear two Yankees fans ripping A-Rod, but should you enter the discussion and not be a Yankees fan, prepare for a hostile reaction. Only we have the right to knock our team. "I would submit that New Yorkers love their hometown more complicatedly than a hometowner loves Kansas City or Detroit," wrote sports columnist Sally Jenkins. "For many of us, this love is complicatedly expressed in a grudging and complaining loyalty to the New York Yankees."

Courteous (at times) and cleverly funny, Yankees fans are also all about the game. While most newer stadiums have focused on frills that provide a diversion from the action on the field, the old Yankee Stadium and the new one are largely devoid of such things. At a Yankees game, it is the action on the field that matters. Fans are attentive and in tune with what is going on. Even a no-hitter broken up as early as the fourth inning will result in polite applause from the hometown crowd, commending the effort. And the littlest of milestones achieved—whether it's a 1,000[th] career hit or 50th career win—is met with vigorous appreciation.

And there is appreciation for the little things that help win games. In the third inning of Game 6 of the 1996 World Series, O'Neill led off with a double against Greg Maddux. The Yankees hadn't scored a run off Maddux in Game 2, so the crowd knew how important it was for O'Neill to score. That's why when Mariano Duncan hit an inside 0–2 pitch the other way, moving O'Neill to third base with one out, he got a standing ovation. Perhaps one of the most touching moments created by Yankees fans occurred during Game 5 of the 2001 World Series and also involved O'Neill. The Yankees were trailing in the game 2–0, heading into the top of the ninth inning. Regardless of the outcome, this was going to be the last home game of the season. O'Neill had already announced that this was going to be his final year. For nine seasons O'Neill had given New York his all, and the fans loved him for it. It was a far cry from the man who, when traded to the team in November of 1992, nearly broke down into tears. O'Neill was not excited about going to the big city. But he was going to a team that wasn't expecting much out of him. He'd hit for some power with the Cincinnati Reds and played good defense in the outfield, but O'Neill wasn't much above an average player at the time. In New York, however, he flourished. He hit .311 his first year there. Then in 1994 O'Neill hit over .400 for the first two and a half months of the season, eventually winning the batting title. He was usually good for 20-plus home runs, 100 RBIs, and a .300 average. Fans loved his intensity, the way he refused to merely give up an at-bat or how he bashed a water cooler when he failed to get a hit. Opposing fans hated him for the way he constantly complained about strike calls. Many thought he was a crybaby. But to New Yorkers that was all part of his unwillingness to ever give an inch on the field.

The result was that, as O'Neill jogged out to right field one last time at Yankee Stadium in the top of the ninth, the fans gave him a standing ovation. Then the chant started. First it was a smattering of fans. Then it was the entire stadium. Even though the Yankees were fighting for the championship, the fans remained focused solely on their beloved right fielder, chanting "PAUL-O-NEILL" throughout the entire inning. After a double play ended the top of the frame, O'Neill walked in from right and doffed his cap to the fans in appreciation. "I have had more people say, 'I was at Game 5 in 2001 when they chanted your name.' I have had so many people say that," O'Neill said. "Sports are kind of like songs. You have memories of certain times in your life by certain teams that won this year or that, and that's what people talk about—and what they were going through in their life during that period or that year. They always seem to get to Game 5 in 2001. That was a special moment obviously." (Little did the fans know, of course, that the Yankees would tie the game in the ninth, and O'Neill would end up playing three more innings in right field that night.)

The fans are also all about innovation. On June 17, 1978, as Ron Guidry began piling up strikeout after strikeout against the Angels, the crowd began chanting with every two-strike count in the hopes of putting another K into the books. Guidry ended up with 18, a single-game record for the Yankees and the most ever by a left-handed pitcher in an American League game. (Randy Johnson eventually broke that mark.) The two-strike clap was invented that night and became a tradition that has remained until this day.

The Bleacher Creatures, when not creating interesting new phrases with the English language or innovative ways to describe a Red Sox fan, have also developed their own traditions. Perhaps the most well known is the roll call. It began simply enough when the Creatures would call out to a Yankees outfielder. Then in 1998 they decided to chant first baseman Martinez's name. He responded with a wave of his right hand. Somewhat surprised that Martinez acknowledged them, the Creatures decided to expand it to everyone on the field—minus the pitcher and catcher, who are too into the game to respond. With that a tradition was born. Roll call now happens before every Yankees home game. A player's name or some variation is chanted until that player acknowledges the Creatures, who then move on to the next player. It carried on from the old ballpark to the new and still occurs today.

And what Yankees fan could forget Freddy Schuman, better known as Freddy "Sez." Schuman was a fixture at Yankee Stadium for decades. He would walk around carrying a shamrock-painted metal frying pan with a sign adorned to the top of it, usually with a message of encouragement for the team or fans. As he walked about the stadium, he would hand fans a metal spoon with which to bang the pan in hopes of starting a rally. One of his pans actually ended up on display in the Baseball Hall of Fame, and Schuman himself ended up appearing in a MasterCard commercial and a House of Pain video.

The new stadium has brought in more of a corporate crowd, and the design itself has pushed fans farther from the field, so the noise coming out of the ballpark does not compare to the old place. Some of the character of the old ballpark is sorely lacking, and certain traditions, especially the Cotton-Eyed Joe routine during the seventh-inning stretch, are just downright embarrassing. But the fans are just as passionate, clever, funny—and definitely as assholish—as ever.

14

A New Year
and a New Season

No matter how dreary one's life might be or what problems lie ahead, there are always two days in the year for residents of the tri-state area that fill you with hope: New Year's Day and Opening Day. Both represent new beginnings, a unique opportunity to start over and dream anew for the coming year or season. In theory the two are actually very different. Baseball's Opening Day is the definitive start to the season. From that point on, all games count in the standings. New acquisitions and returning stars bring about the possibility of a championship. Everyone starts with the same record. Everyone starts with the same chance (in theory at least) of winning it all.

New Year's is a little more arbitrary in terms of new beginnings. It is, of course, the start of the calendar year, but there is no concrete reason why you have to start over on that day. You could make a resolution any date: April 30, June 27, November 12—what's the difference? But New Year's has taken on a larger symbolic meaning that has become about more than just a day of the year. It has become a worldwide celebration of life, happiness, and tranquility.

Nowhere is this celebration more evident or grander than on the night of December 31st in New York City. Every major city in the world has its own New Year's Eve celebration. But what happens in Times Square always stands out from the rest. An endless sea of humanity spends hours crammed into a tiny space to watch a giant ball slowly descend before setting off a huge neon sign indicating the New Year has arrived. It's the same scene every year. The only thing that changes is the number. Every year people are stuck in place without much of a chance for a bathroom break and not even allowed to have a drink, though some most certainly find a way around that. Year after year, however, hundreds of thousands of people show up, and millions more watch on television to take part and see this event.

New Yorkers used to ring in the New Year in front of Trinity Church in lower Manhattan with bells and chimes. That changed when the first Times Square ball drop as we know it occurred on New Year's Eve in 1907. Adolph Ochs, the publisher of *The New York Times*, hired the sign maker Artkraft Strauss to build—then lower—a 700-pound wood and iron ball, five feet in diameter and illuminated by 100 25-watt bulbs, to mark the passage from 1907 to 1908. The ritual itself was copied from a ceremony that had started in Greenwich, England, in 1833 to help people synchronize time. As the years have gone by, the size and scope of the event has become much grander. The ball itself now weighs almost 12,000 pounds and is made up of Waterford crystals. Instead of being dropped by hand, it is now done by controls i.e. "one guy and a button for the winch," said Jeff Straus, president of Countdown Entertainment, which runs the event.

The event is always the same, and yet the allure of it never fails to bring in people from all walks of life and all parts of the country. As 2012 moved into 2013, hundreds of thousands of people crammed into midtown Manhattan. "I couldn't begin the new year in a more beautiful way," said Yvonne Gomez of South Dakota as she stood with her husband. "I married him two weeks ago, and here we are in the middle of Times Square celebrating the new year—two widowers who found each other." Taylor Nanz, a

Hundreds of thousands flock to New York's Times Square in 2013 to take part in the city's famous New Year's Eve celebration.

student at Syracuse University, arrived in Times Square at 1:20 PM and stood in the same spot until after midnight. "People want to be together. That's what the magic is. People want to be part of that official countdown," Straus said. Ryan Seacrest hosts ABC's New Year's Eve show. "I remember being in awe of the big event in Times Square and dreaming big and thinking someday I want to go to New York and see the ball drop," Seacrest said.

Opening Day at Yankee Stadium mirrors the excitement and energy of New Year's in Times Square. Every year 50,000 people cram into the stadium on what is usually a cold early spring afternoon. And it doesn't matter if it is the official Opening Day or just the home opener; the feeling is always the same. The conclusion of last season—whether it ended in a championship, a disappointing playoff loss, or no postseason at all—is washed away.

And no matter how cold the temperature, the sight of fresh green grass on the field, vendors walking through the stands, and players on the field is more than enough to remind people that the long, dreary days of winter are behind us.

Expectations run high. These are the Yankees after all. And few teams can trot out the kind of legends of the game that the Yankees can. On any given Opening Day, you could have seen a Joe DiMaggio, Mickey Mantle, Yogi Berra, Whitey Ford, or Reggie Jackson in the stadium. "It just meant something," catcher Mike Stanley said. "A lot of times, it meant Joe DiMaggio throwing out the first pitch. You don't get that greatness of what they can pull off in Opening Day. Other places just can't match that." The occasional celebrity could be spotted, usually in the better seats, taking in the game. In 2002 recently retired pitcher David Cone decided to watch the home opener from the right-field bleachers. Often the mayor, whoever it might be, can be spotted in seats right next to the Yankees dugout.

The Yankees have usually not disappointed on Opening Day, going 64–48 overall and 75–37 in home openers. Even the 1990 Yankees, regarded as one of the worst pinstripe teams ever put together, won their opener. From 1982 until 2013, the Yankees didn't lose a single Opening Day at the stadium. And it's not just the success on Opening Day that keeps bringing fans back. Some of the teams' most memorable moments have occurred on that first day.

At the first Opening Day at the original Yankee Stadium, Babe Ruth hit the very first home run at the new ballpark. At the home opener in 1978, the team handed out Reggie-brand bars, a candy named after right fielder Reggie Jackson. When Jackson homered during the game, the fans littered the field with the candy. On Opening Day of 1981, longtime Yankees player and fan favorite Bobby Murcer hit a pinch-hit, grand slam against the Texas Rangers. Four years later Don Baylor came to bat in the bottom of the ninth with the score tied at four. Against Chicago White Sox pitcher Dan Spillner, he drove one into the left-field seats for a walk-off home run.

The 1990s and 2000s brought a slew of memorable Opening Day moments. At the home opener in 1993, the Yankees showcased two new additions to the club against the Kansas City Royals. Outfielder Paul O'Neill went 4-of-4 with two RBIs. Jim Abbott, a pitcher born without a right hand, shut the Royals down in a complete game 4–1 victory. Against the Royals again in 1996, the home opener was played during a snowstorm. "I remember standing on third base about the eighth inning, and Mariano Duncan was hitting," Jim Leyritz said. "I actually could not see him at the plate because it was snowing so hard."

Two years later the oddest home opener in Yankees history took place. The atmosphere was more festive than usual as the club was celebrating the 75th anniversary of Yankee Stadium. After a long ceremony, the team proceeded to get bashed by the Oakland A's, falling behind 5–0 by the bottom of the second inning. The Yankees then scored 16 runs over the next four innings (and they did it hitting only one home run). Not to be outdone, the A's scored eight runs in the top of the fifth to make it 16–13 game. The Yankees eventually tacked on one more run and ended up with a 17–13 win, the largest amount of combined runs scored in the history of Yankee Stadium openers. The teams combined for 32 hits, four errors, and 10 pitchers.

The team brought over Japanese superstar outfielder Hideki Matsui in 2003 to play left field. After starting the season on the road, Matsui was introduced to the hometown fans on a dreary April afternoon home opener against the Minnesota Twins. Matsui did not disappoint. In his third plate appearance of the game, he came to the plate with the bases loaded and one out. Against Joe Mays, Matsui drilled a 3–2 pitch over the right-field wall for a grand slam. The fans went crazy, sparking a love affair with Matsui that would last all of his seven seasons in New York. In 2005 the Yankees hosted the hated Boston Red Sox for a Sunday night season opener. Randy Johnson made his much anticipated Yankees debut, pitching six innings and striking out six. Matsui hit a home run and took one away from Kevin Millar.

The festive atmosphere, winning, and history were all critical aspects of what made New Year's and Opening Day in New York special, but there was also something else to it. There were two men who made each of these events unique and specific to New York. Both were instantly recognizable by their voices. One helped introduce an entire generation to rock and roll. The other introduced generations to hundreds of ballplayers. Without Dick Clark and Bob Sheppard, New Year's in Times Square and Opening Day at Yankee Stadium just aren't the same.

There was a 40-year period during the 20th century when one man was synonymous with New Year's. His actions tied in the nightly and early morning festivities with music, celebration, and renewal. That man, at first, was not Dick Clark. It was actually Guy Lombardo. Born in Ontario in 1902, Lombardo formed Guy Lombardo and his Royal Canadians, and his big band-style group gained fame after appearing on the radio in 1929. His band played at Manhattan's Roosevelt Hotel on New Year's Eve that same year, and their performance was broadcast on radio across the country. It was the beginning of two traditions. The first was Lombardo's band officially becoming the sound of every New Year's Eve. The second was "Auld Lang Syne" becoming the official anthem of the night. The song had Scottish roots, and his band would strike up the ditty as midnight passed, embedding it forever into the traditions of that night.

By the 1970s Lombardo's style had become passé. Rock and roll had swept across the country in the 1950s and '60s, leaving the big band era far behind not just musically but also in appealing to a television audience. Someone needed to cater to a new generation of New Year's participants. In stepped Clark who was born in Mount Vernon, New York, and had made a name for himself in the 1950s as the host of *American Bandstand*, a television show that introduced millions of people to rock and roll acts. Those who made their television debuts on the show include Chuck Berry, Bill Haley and the Comets, James Brown, Buddy Holly, and the Everly Brothers. These were some of the biggest names and the founders of modern rock. As their music became the theme to a new generation, Clark's popularity skyrocketed. Well-dressed, well-spoken, and well-mannered, "he came across more like an articulate graduate student," wrote the *Los Angeles Times*' Geoff Boucher. Clark became so associated with the rock genre and credited with helping it spread that he was inducted into the Rock and Roll Hall of Fame in 1993, an impressive accomplishment for someone who never played music himself.

As the country headed into the 1970s, Lombardo's act had grown stale with a lot of viewers. "It was terribly boring to me," said Clark in 2003. "I wanted to make New Year's Eve a little more contemporary and exciting." And so on New Year's Eve in 1972, ABC launched a new program, *New Year's Rockin' Eve*. "Guy was the only choice for the older generation. That's why we put 'Rockin'' in the title to let everybody know this was going to be a different approach," Clark said. Three Dog Night helped host the show and Helen Reddy, Al Green, and Blood, Sweat and Tears all performed. The new show was an immense hit both because of the musical acts it showcased and the appeal Clark had to millions of fans. Clark soon became a familiar, comforting source as the clock wound down the old year and rang in the new. Eventually, Clark's name would be added to the title of the show, displaying both the appeal of his name and his longevity in hosting the event.

As the years went on, the musical acts grew bigger and bigger. In almost 30 years, Three Dog Night and Al Green turned into Lady Gaga, Pitbull, and Justin Bieber (for better or for worse, depending on who you ask). But Clark was the one constant. He dominated the night throughout the '80s and '90s and even into the 21st century as other networks launched their own versions of *Rockin'*. And he was so much a part of those 10 seconds of the year that even when Seacrest joined him as a co-host, it was written in his contract that Clark had to be the one to count down those last seconds. When asked in 2011, Clark reflected back on many memorable moments. "The year of the Iran Hostage Crisis, the ball almost didn't drop," Clark said. That was because the owner of the One Times Square building wanted to cancel the event in protest of Iran holding the hostages. On the musical front, Clark said, "One of the most memorable has been Barry Manilow, who has performed his song, 'It's Just Another New Year's Eve' several times."

Shortly before the end of 2004, Clark suffered a stroke. For the first time since 1972, he was unable to host *Rockin' New Year's Eve*. He returned in 2005, but the stroke had impacted his speech, limiting his role in the program. The man who had been dubbed "America's Oldest Teenager" suddenly appeared much older on the screen. For some his presence became a little unsettling, though for others he was an inspiration to those attempting to recover from similar health issues. When Clark died in April of 2012, there was no denying that his presence on the TV screen would be missed on December 31ˢᵗ. Over a period of nearly 40 years, Clark had become like an additional member of the family every New Year's Eve. You knew he would always be there, and somehow that made everything seem all right. Millions of those who watched him never actually met him, and yet he became an invaluable part of their lives for one night every year. He made the Times Square celebration—already an intricate part of everything that is New York City—that much more special.

———

"Good afternoon, ladies and gentlemen. Welcome to Yankee Stadium." These simple words took on a larger than life feel thanks to the man who said them. When you heard those words come out of Sheppard's mouth, you felt good. You knew it was a new day with new possibilities at the ballpark. Sheppard didn't do anything especially unique. He wasn't over the top or bombastic. He didn't stretch out certain players' names or try to milk the crowd. He simply read what was in front of him in crisp, clean English with perfect diction. "Mr. Sheppard could read Eminem lyrics and make them sound like the Magna Carta," wrote Clyde Haberman of *The New York Times*. Simple, elegant, and graceful. It was enough to place the microphone he used for 50 years into the Hall of Fame.

Sheppard was born in 1910, though he tried very hard throughout his long life to keep his age a secret. Raised in Queens, he was athletic as a youth, playing baseball and football. He earned a bachelor's degree in English and speech from St. John's University and a master's degree in speech from Columbia University. He served in the Navy during World War II and after returning from service became a speech teacher.

On April 17, 1951, Sheppard debuted as the Yankees public address announcer during Opening Day against the Red Sox. Sheppard called every Opening Day at the stadium from then until 2006 and—in total—announced the lineups for more than 4,400 games during his life. It is hard to pinpoint when exactly Sheppard gained his fame. Until 1967 he only announced the starting lineup and substitutions—not every single at-bat. But his fame was certainly helped by the fact that the Yankees were so successful during the 1950s and early '60s. His voice was heard more often, and he got to announce the game's best players whether they were the Yankees or whoever their opponent was in the World Series. Hearing Sheppard announce your name was almost as exciting as making it to the big leagues. "There was an elegance to the diction, a precision to the pronunciation, that was unique," said MLB.com's Mike Bauman. "It was not showbiz, it was not glitz, it was not over the top. But it was extraordinarily good and always pleasing to the ear—not to mention the hearts and souls on hand at Yankee Stadium."

Soon enough, Sheppard's clear and precise manner became a mainstay. He would announce the player's position first, then their uniform number, then their name, followed again by the uniform number: "Now batting for the Yankees, the first baseman, No. 23, Don Mattingly, No. 23." Even after Sheppard's death, Derek Jeter actually requested that Sheppard's voice continue to introduce him at Yankee Stadium when he stepped to the plate. "When you think of Yankee Stadium, he's the first thing that comes to mind," Jeter said in 2006. "It's not right playing here unless he's the one that's announcing." Ken Phelps said, "It kind of sends a chill down your spine because…there was no pomp and circumstance or any kind of fluff—just class."

Almost every person I asked about Sheppard couldn't help but do their own imitation of him. Often it left something to be desired, but no matter how good or bad, the imitation was always a sincere compliment to the man. Buck Showalter recalled how before his first Opening Day as manager in 1992, Sheppard came down to the field to learn the pronunciation of one of the Yankees' infielders. "To have him come down, it was like the Pope coming out of the Vatican or something," Showalter said. "He comes down and he says [in Buck's best Sheppard imitation] 'it is Stankiewicz or Stankevitch?'"

"I remember Steve Sax telling me, 'Wait till you hear your name announced at Yankee Stadium. That is going to be something special,'" Leyritz said. "I was standing on-deck and then starting to walk to the plate, and hearing his voice and hearing how he did it, I was just like, *wow, okay, now I know what these guys were talking about.*"

Sheppard branched out to other sports, announcing football games for the Giants for decades. Of course, he wasn't without an occasional error or two. During the first game he ever announced for the Giants at the Meadowlands, he opened by welcoming fans to Yankee Stadium. Still the mistakes were few and far between, and that wasn't a coincidence. Sheppard worked hard at his craft, ensuring in whatever way he could to make sure he got a player's name right. He also loved a good challenge. Some of his favorite names to pronounce included Shigetoshi Hasegawa and Jose Valdivielso. And, of course, there were some old favorites like Mickey Mantle. He also had his least favorites. "What can I do with Steve Sax? What can I do with Mickey Klutts?" He asked.

Sheppard even took to notable cameo appearances. He did voice work for *Seinfeld* on multiple occasions, including an episode where he calls Elaine's boyfriend (whose name is the same as a serial killer) over the PA system. He appeared as himself in the 2003 comedy *Anger Management.* And to this day it is his voice that still informs people that they are watching the YES network. He was also one of the few employees who was immune to George Steinbrenner's venom. According to Bill Madden's *Steinbrenner,* when singer Mary O'Dowd forgot the words to the Canadian national anthem before a series against the Toronto Blue Jays in 1985, The Boss was irate.

The next day he decided he wanted an apology read over the PA system. He had his secretary call Sheppard to his office. When The Boss called you to his office, that meant be there yesterday. Instead, Sheppard, who was eating, said he would be up after he was done with dinner. Steinbrenner was irate and had to wait 15 minutes for Sheppard to appear. When Sheppard finally did, Steinbrenner began instructing him on what he wanted him to say. Sheppard said he'd already written something. He then went on to ignore Steinbrenner's suggested additions. Perhaps he was the only man on the planet who could get away with such insubordination.

Sheppard died in July of 2010, just two days before Steinbrenner and just a few months short of his 100th birthday. The Yankees wore commemorative patches on their jerseys the rest of the season in his honor. Sheppard and Clark spent decades making significant moments all the more special. And while their legacies continue on after their deaths, New Year's and Opening Day just won't be the same without them.

Acknowledgments

First and foremost I must thank my mother Sandy, who charges uber-supportive, headfirst into any endeavor I undertake, and my father, Tim, whose hours of hitting fly balls to me and my brother didn't result in any big league contracts but helped solidify a love for the game. As always, nothing I take on is possible without the support of a great and ever-loving family. My thanks to my brothers, Tim and Mike; brothers-in-law, Glenn and Derek; and sisters-in-law, Julie, Jen, and Taylor. Much appreciation also to the Kassabs, DeMarcos, Donnellys, O'Connors, Salaznos, Dudas, Leahys, Dykers, Praschils, and Singers.

The friends who have been there for me throughout the years are too numerous to name, and I am destined to forget some. So to those who shared kickball games at Lincoln School, Puttin' on the Hits at Lakeside School, and sweltering hot assemblies at Pompton Lakes High School, you have my everlasting appreciation. The same goes for the friends and Sigma Tau Gamma fraternity brothers I made at The College of New Jersey. I never tire of sharing the same stories, told a thousand times, with all of you. The individuals I have come to work with over the past decade or so also hold a special place for me and have been as supportive in my writing efforts as anyone. Thanks for putting up with constant emails,

Facebook messages, texts, etc., all dealing with me shamelessly promoting myself.

The following people put up with numerous phone calls, emails, and questions in order to help me set up interviews or obtain information. I appreciate their professionalism and the amazingly timely manner in which they were able to help: Casey Wilcox, Steve Alexander, Joe Bick, Marc Goldman, Vickie McQuade, Michael Margolis, and Robbie Kass.

My thanks to Tom Bast at Triumph who helped get this entire process started one late winter's day. The same for my editor, Jeff Fedotin, who could not have been more helpful during the entire process or provided better guidance. Really, my thanks to everyone at Triumph for this experience.

Sources

Interviews

In order to help tell this story, the following people were gracious enough to grant me interviews for this book. I appreciate the time and candor of: Paul Amoroso, Wade Boggs, Rick Cerrone, Al Downing, Brian Doyle, Ari Fleischer, Todd Greene, Jeff Idelson, David Kaplan, Moss Klein, Jim Leyritz, Kevin Maas, Mitchell Modell, Paul O'Neill, Joe Pepitone, Ken Phelps, Dennis Rasmussen, Billy Sample, Steve Schirripa, Buck Showalter, Mike Stanley, and John Sterling.

Books

Ackerman, Kenneth D. *Boss Tweed*. Virginia, Viral History Press, 2011.

Ambrose, Stephen E. *Nixon: Ruin and Recovery, 1973–1990*. New York, Simon & Schuster, 1991.

Appel, Marty. *Pinstripe Empire*. New York, Bloomsbury USA, 2012.

Bascomb, Neal. *Higher: A Historic Race To The Sky And The Making Of A City*. New York, Random House, 2003.

Bouton, Jim. *Ball Four*. New York, Wiley Publishing, 1990.

David, Greg. *Modern New York: The Life and Economics of a City*. New York, Palgrave MacMillan, 2012.

Fleder, Rob. *Damn Yankees*. New York, HarperCollins, 2012.

Golenbock, Peter. *Dynasty*. Mineola, Dover Publications, Inc., 1975.

Golenbock, Peter. *George: The Poor Little Rich Boy Who Built the Yankee Empire*. Hoboken, John Wiley & Sons, Inc., 2009.

Golenbock, Peter. *Wild, High and Tight: The Life and Death of Billy Martin*. New York, St. Martin's Press, 1994.

Giuliani, Rudolph W. *Leadership*. New York, Hyperion, 2002.

Jeffers, H. Paul. *The Napoleon of New York*. New York, John Wiley & Sons, Inc., 2002.

Leavy, Jane. *The Last Boy*. New York, HarperCollins, 2010.

Lowry, Philip J. *Green Cathedrals*. New York, Walker & Company, 2006.

Madden, Bill and Moss Klein. *Damned Yankees*. New York, Warner Books, Inc., 1990.

Madden, Bill. *Steinbrenner: The Last Lion of Baseball*. New York, HarperCollins, 2010.

Mahler, Jonathan. *Ladies and Gentlemen, The Bronx Is Burning*. New York, Farrar, Straus and Giroux, 2005.

Olney, Buster. *The Last Night of the Yankee Dynasty*. New York, HarperCollins, 2004.

Pearlman, Jeff. *The Bad Guys Won!* New York, Harper Collins, 2004.

Shalin, Mike. *Donnie Baseball*. Illinois, Triumph Books, 2011.

Soffer, Jonathan. *Ed Koch and the Rebuilding of New York*. New York, Columbia University Press, 2010.

Spitz, Bob. *The Beatles*. New York, Little, Brown and Company, 2005.

Sullivan, Neil J. *The Diamond in the Bronx*. New York, Oxford University Press, 2001.

Torre, Joe and Tom Verducci. *The Yankee Years*. New York, Doubleday, 2009.

Vincent, Fay. *The Last Commissioner: A Baseball Valentine*. Simon & Schuster, 2002.

Wells, David with Chris Kreski. *Perfect I'm Not*. New York, HarperCollins, 2003.

Newspapers, Periodicals, and Websites

ABC News online
Associated Press
The Atlantic
Bloomberg
CBS MoneyWatch online
CNN.com
ESPN.com
The Examiner
FoxSports.com
The Gotham Gazette
Huffington Post
The Link
Los Angeles Times
MLB.com
National Register of Historic Places
NBCSports.com
New York Daily News
New York Post
The New York Times
Newsday
NPR.org
Nycrimecommission.org
The Observer
Obit Magazine
The Onion
The Palm Beach Post
PBS.org
People magazine
Reuters
Salon.com
Seattle Post-Intelligencer
Sports Illustrated
The (Newark) *Star-Ledger*
Time magazine
Urbandictionary.com

USA TODAY
The Vineyard Gazette
The Washington Monthly

Nature Guide
to Vermont's
Long Trail

Nature Guide to Vermont's Long Trail

Lexi Shear

Published by:
The Green Mountain Club, Inc.
4711 Waterbury-Stowe Road, Waterbury Center, Vermont 05677
(802) 244-7037
gmc@greenmountainclub.org
www.greenmountainclub.org

Ben Rose, *Executive Director*
Arthur Goldsweig, *Director of Finance*
Susan Shea, *Director of Conservation and Managing Editor*
Matt Larson, *Development Assistant*

GMC Publications Committee, 2008: Richard Andrews, Dave Blumenthal,
Ruth Hare, Lynda Hutchins, Steve Larose, Mary Lou Recor, Val Stori

The information in this guide is the result of the best effort of the
author and the publisher, using information available at the time
of printing. Changes resulting from maintenance and relocations
are constantly occurring, and therefore, no published route can be
regarded as precisely accurate at the time you read this notice.

Cover and book design by The Laughing Bear Associates, Montpelier, Vermont
Copyediting and indexing by Electric Dragon Productions, Montpelier, Vermont
Original Long Trail cartography by Map Adventures, Portland Maine,
revised by Dave Blumenthal

Photographs are by Dave Blumenthal, and Matt Larson unless otherwise
indicated, and are used with the permission of the photographers, and
remain the copyrighted work of each individual photographer.

Cover photo credits: Front cover: Steve Faccio; back cover: Clyde Smith

First Edition
ISBN978-188802121-9

Printed in U.S.A.

Acknowledgments

This book would not have happened without the
assistance of numerous people. Many people contributed
ecological and geological expertise on matters large and
small including, in no particular order, Liz Thompson,
Bryan Pfeiffer, Eric Sorenson, Dave Hardy, Rick Paradis,
Val Stori, Jim Andrews, and Peter Thompson. Thanks to
Matt Larson and Sue Shea of the Green Mountain Club
for their work taking and editing photographs. Special thanks
to Steve Larose of the Green Mountain Club's Publications
Committee for his patience and perseverance in guiding
this project. And finally, my heartfelt gratitude goes to my
husband Dave Blumenthal, without whom this book would
have never happened.

Lexi Shear

Contents

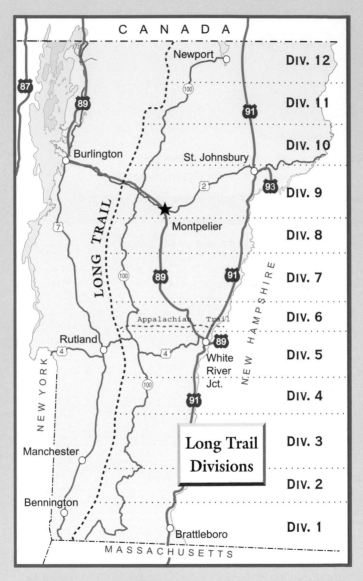

Vermont's Long Trail

Introduction

You've set aside a little time to get out in the woods. You've made your plans, driven to the trailhead, put on your hiking shoes, and up the path you go. Maybe you're out for a few hours, a few days, or even a few weeks. No matter your time frame, hiking gives you an opportunity to slow down and pay close attention to a birdsong, tree, or flower that you might overlook on a faster-paced day.

This guide will help you to identify the plants and animals that you'll encounter on a Long Trail journey. You will start to recognize interesting patterns and appreciate the natural history written in our forests, streams, and mountaintops.

The Long Trail

The Long Trail, Vermont's "footpath in the wilderness," winds through the woods, clambers over mountains, and skips across brooks and streams for 272 miles along the spine of the Green Mountains. Some hikers may choose to spend several weeks journeying the entire length of the trail from the Massachusetts border to Canada. Others may spend a relaxing autumn afternoon viewing the spectacular foliage.

The trail was conceived by James P. Taylor, then principal of Vermont Academy in Saxton's River, as he lingered on the summit of Stratton Mountain. In 1910, twenty-three people came together to form the Green Mountain Club and take the first step toward fulfilling Taylor's dream. By 1930, the trail was complete. Since then, the Green Mountain Club has

worked to maintain and manage the trail, build and rebuild
shelters and campsites, educate hikers, and permanently
protect the land surrounding the trail. The Long Trail is not
only the oldest long-distance hiking trail in the country,
but also the inspiration for the Appalachian Trail, with which
it coincides for its southern 105 miles.

Format of the Guide

Throughout the book, the
intention is not only to provide
information about the individual
species you might encounter,
but also to put those species in
context and reflect on how the
species interact.

Part I gives an overview of the
geology and climate of the Green
Mountains, which in turn determines the environment in which
the plant and animal communities
along the trail live. Part II describes the most common natural
communities found along the trail. This part will help you
identify similarities between different places along the trail
and anticipate which species you are most likely to see in a
particular location.

When you are actually hiking, you may want to read Part III,
which is a narrative of some of the notable natural features
found along the trail. It is not possible to describe everything
that might catch your eye as you hike. Some things, such as
beaver ponds, are described in only one of the many locations
where they occur along the trail. Once you learn to recognize
some of these features, keep your eyes open and you will see
them again and again!

If you want to identify a particular plant or animal that
you encounter, skip to Parts IV and V. These parts provide
a photographic identification guide to the most common
species found along the trail.

Learning about the flora and fauna and natural history
of the trail will increase your appreciation of the trail.
Keep your eyes open and happy hiking!

Part I:

The Geology, Climate, and Ecology of the Green Mountains

The Geology, Climate, and Ecology of the Green Mountains

Geology of the Green Mountains

The Green Mountains, whose spine the Long Trail traces, run from north to south and very nearly bisect the state of Vermont. Any description of their geology requires a basic understanding of rock types and geologic processes.

Rock Types and Geologic Processes

Rock Types

There are three basic types of rocks: igneous, sedimentary, and metamorphic. Igneous rocks are formed when molten rock cools. They are generally hard and crystalline. Sedimentary rocks are formed when sediments such as sand or mud are compacted over time. They are often relatively soft and contain visible remnants of the original sediments.

Camel's Hump

Metamorphic rocks are formed when there is enough heat and pressure to alter the minerals in the rocks but not enough to entirely melt them. This extremely variable type of rock is often visibly layered.

Geologic Processes

Scientists believe that the earth's crust, for all its solid appearance, is actually made up of about twelve individual large pieces, called plates. These plates float on top of a much denser, slightly plastic layer of material called the asthenosphere. Currents in the asthenosphere, caused by radioactive heating from the earth's core, cause the plates to move as though they were on a giant conveyer belt.

In regions where the plates have pulled apart from each other, forming gaps called rift zones, new material from the asthenosphere has bubbled up to fill the gaps, making a new crust. This process has caused the chain of midocean volcanoes, of which Iceland is a part, that runs the length of the Atlantic Ocean.

In some regions, denser oceanic plates and less dense continental plates converge. In this situation, the dense oceanic plate plunges under the continental plate in a process called subduction. At the point where the plates meet, there is a deep ocean trench. Water is pulled down into the subduction zone, which interacts with the surrounding crust. The high-pressure water lowers the melting point of the rock and causes portions of two plates to melt. The pockets of molten rock form volcanoes: Mount St. Helens and the other Cascade Range volcanoes of the Pacific Northwest are examples of this process.

In other parts of the world, for example, the Himalaya Mountains, continental plates collide into each other. In this case, neither plate goes under the other; instead, both plates are forced upward, forming huge mountains.

Geological History of the Green Mountains

Our story begins about 600 million years ago when a rift zone formed under present-day Vermont. Two halves of the ancient continent began to pull away from each other creating a basin, which filled with a shallow tropical sea, the Iapetus Ocean. The edge of the continental shelf lay along the western part of Vermont, with limestone reefs and sandy beaches bordering a deeper ocean basin toward the east, where silt and mud accumulated.

The ocean gradually widened as the plates pulled apart until about 500 million years ago, when the plates changed directions and began moving toward each other. At the point of convergence, the western plate began to subduct under the eastern one, forming a volcanic island chain similar to modern-day Japan just east of the present-day Green Mountains. Simultaneously, the easternmost plate acted like a bulldozer to scrape the sedimentary rocks on the ocean floor into a huge pile. This mass of rock was pushed up onto

GEOLOGY

the adjacent continental crust, forming the Green and Taconic Mountains of Vermont. This mountain-building event generated a tremendous amount of heat and pressure, causing the original sedimentary rocks between the continental crust and the island arc to become metamorphic schist. As subduction continued, the ocean crust was eventually completely consumed. Another island arc and small continent from the east collided with the young Green Mountains, deforming the rocks even further.

These mountains were more than twice as tall as our modern mountains. Over the millions of intervening years, erosion has slowly worn down their summits and sculpted their slopes into what we see today.

By around 200 million years ago, a new rift zone had formed to the east of Vermont and New Hampshire, whereupon the plates pulled apart, the Atlantic Ocean filled the basin, and the coastline began to take on its current shape.

Relatively recent phenomena have put the finishing touches on the current landscape of the Green Mountains: glaciers. The most recent glacial period reached its maximum 18,000 to 20,000 years ago when giant streams of ice more than a mile thick flowed roughly north to south over the Green Mountains. With tremendous power, the ice wore down mountains, sculpted valleys, moved huge boulders, and scraped off the soil.

Relatively recent phenomena have put the finishing touches on the current landscape of the Green Mountains: glaciers

As the glaciers retreated 13,000 years ago, boulders and debris were dropped in place, leaving behind the till that now covers the mountains. Large lakes filled the Champlain basin and the surrounding river valleys. The Long Trail briefly passes through lake deposits of sand, mud, and clay in the Winooski and Lamoille River valleys.

Evidence of this tumultuous geologic history is visible in numerous places along the trail and is described in more detail in Part III.

Lake of the Clouds

WEATHER

Weather and Climate of the Long Trail

Climate and weather have a great influence on the plant and animal communities of the Long Trail. Vermont has a temperate climate, with warm summers and very cold winters. In addition, as any seasoned Long Trail hiker will tell you, mountain weather can be extremely variable from one day to the next. This is largely because our weather comes from three distinctly different regions: the cold, dry Canadian subarctic; the warm, moist Gulf of Mexico; and the cool, damp North Atlantic.

The weather on the Long Trail, in particular, is greatly affected by the mountainous terrain. In general, the higher up you go, the cooler and wetter the weather becomes. In New England, the temperature decreases approximately 3 to 5 degrees Fahrenheit for every thousand feet of elevation gained.

The cool mountain temperatures can, in turn, cause increased rainfall. As the prevailing west wind blows into Vermont, air is forced up and over the spine of the Green Mountains, cooling as it rises. Often the air cools enough that the moisture in the air condenses to form clouds and rain. At times, especially in winter, the cold air in the mountains will cause persistent fog at higher elevations.

On hot, humid summer days, large columns of air rise and spark thunderstorms in the mountains. These storms are often accompanied by hail and wind and can be a major source of disturbance to the forest and a hazard to the hiker.

ECOLOGY

Mount Mansfield, looking south

Ecology of the Long Trail

Geology and climate combine to form the physical environment
in which plants and animals live. The geology of an area
determines the material (for example sand or clay) from which
soils form and the nutrient composition of the soils. Two such
nutrients are calcium and magnesium. Both are important for
plant growth and often in short supply. Limestone, and to
a lesser extent schist, are made of minerals high in calcium
and magnesium, and therefore often form nutrient-rich
soils, where plants grow extremely well. Other rocks, such as
quartzite, gneiss, and particularly granite, are harder and
produce soil that is poorer in nutrients and frequently acidic.

In addition, topography and soil type determine how much
water is available to plants. Sandy soil, for example, drains very
quickly and is therefore usually quite dry, while clay-rich soils
may prevent water from draining and is usually quite wet.
Basins and depressions in the bedrock can hold water,
creating wet areas.

Temperature, precipitation, geology, and topography
combine to create very different environments along the
trail. These differences are reflected in the varied natural

communities that you hike through. Certain plants and animals are best adapted for the cool, wet, acidic conditions found high up in the mountains. Others do better when they are warm and dry and so are only found on low-elevation south-facing slopes along the southern part of the trail. One of the most distinctive patterns, which you will see repeatedly as you traverse the Green Mountains, is the transition from the temperate-adapted northern hardwood forest (composed primarily of beech, birch, and maple) at lower elevations to a cold-adapted evergreen forest (dominated by spruce and fir) at higher elevations. This pattern is described in greater detail elsewhere in this book.

Physical differences are not the only factors that determine the composition of the forest. The forest's history makes a big difference as well. If all the trees in a particular area are downed by a disturbance, the woods will look different for a long time to come. The size of a disturbance can vary from one diseased tree succumbing to a windstorm to forest fire covering thousands of acres. In Vermont, natural disturbance is usually at the smaller end of the scale, affecting a few to several hundred acres. Wind, ice, snowstorms, and landslides are the most common natural disturbances along the trail. Very occasionally, thousands of acres are affected by large-scale disturbances such as hurricanes, forest fires, or ice storms. In 1998, an ice storm ravaged much of the Northeast and had a profound effect on much of Vermont's forest. Fire is uncommon in our humid forests; however, it is believed to play a substantial role on dry knolls and ridgetops. Flooding is quite common along Vermont's rivers, but has little effect on our mountain ecosystems.

Temperature, precipitation, geology, and topography combine to create very different environments along the trail.

No matter the type of disturbance, the plants that grow back immediately afterward will likely not be the same as those that were there before. When trees are removed, more sunlight reaches the ground. This allows fast-growing, light-loving plants to take hold. In a northern hardwood forest, these areas might be pioneered by grasses and raspberries. White pine, aspen, paper birch, and other light-requiring trees come in next. They eventually grow taller than the grasses and shrubs and

ECOLOGY

ECOLOGY

create too much shade for them to survive. The pine and
aspen may dominate the site for many years. Their seeds,
however, cannot grow on the now-shaded forest floor, so there
will be no pine or aspen seedlings growing beneath the mature
trees. Beech, spruce, and maple, however, are extremely
tolerant of shade, and their seeds will grow on the forest floor.
Eventually the birch and aspen, which are relatively short-lived
trees, die off, and beech and maple grow in to take their place.
Because young beeches and maples can grow in the shade
of their parents, the beech-maple forest type will predominate
until another disturbance starts the process over again.
A similar process, although with different species, occurs
in all our forests. In the mountains, spruce and fir trees are
the end result. This orderly progression of different plant
species is known as succession. Forests in a wide variety of
successional stages occur along the trail.

In Vermont, human activity, one of the biggest sources of
disturbances, has had a profound effect on our modern forests.
One hundred and fifty years ago, up to three-quarters of the
state was open land. The forests were cut to create fields and
pastures for farms and to provide wood. Farming the thin
rocky soils of Vermont is difficult at best, and as more fertile
land in the Midwest opened up, people left in droves. Most of
the forests that grew back were harvested again in the early
twentieth century. The majority of the forest you will pass
through is no more than one hundred years old, and some
of it is substantially younger, as evident by the species and sizes
of trees that grow there. Logging continues today, though,
with the protection of the Long Trail corridor, little is visible
from the trail.

Part II:

Natural Communities of the Long Trail

Natural Communities of the Long Trail

Natural Communities

A natural community is an "interacting assemblage of organisms, their physical environment, and the natural processes that affect them" (Thompson and Sorenson, 2000). Because physical characteristics (such as geology) and natural processes are hard to see, natural communities are most easily identified by the species, particularly the plants that inhabit them.

Natural communities occur at many scales. Some, such as the northern hardwood forest, extend for thousands of acres covering vast swathes of the landscape. Others are small, perhaps only an acre or two, and occur in response to localized changes in topography, climate, or soil. A forested swamp, for example, might occur in a small wet depression or an alpine meadow could be perched atop an exposed summit.

As you hike along the trail, patterns of natural communities become apparent. Every climb above 3,000 feet leads you into dark evergreen spruce-fir forest; every descent returns you to the northern hardwood forest. Rather than describing a community each time the trail passes through it, the book provides a detailed description of each natural community that the Long Trail passes through. Additional information about particular locations can be found in Part III.

The natural community descriptions here are a general guide. There can be considerable variation within one community type, and communities often shift gradually from one to another. Nonetheless, understanding natural communities will help you to understand the ecological patterns across the landscape. Identifying a natural community will also help you to know what sorts of plants and animals you might expect to see there. As in other parts of this book, the focus is on the naturally occurring communities visible from the trail. Farm pastures, ski slopes, roadsides, and other human-created openings are not included.

...understanding natural communities will help you to understand the ecological patterns across the landscape and what you might see there.

The natural community descriptions and classifications here are based primarily on the work of Elizabeth Thompson and Eric Sorenson in their book *Wetland, Woodland, Wildland: A Guide to the Natural Communities of Vermont.* A reader with a specific interest in natural communities should certainly consult their book for more information.

The communities are arranged in four broad categories: deciduous forest types (dominated by trees that lose their leaves); evergreen forest types (dominated by trees that do not lose their leaves); mixed deciduous and evergreen forest types (which have large numbers of both deciduous and evergreen trees); and nonforested communities.

Northern hardwood forest

Deciduous Forest Types

Northern Hardwood Forest

Most of the state of Vermont is blanketed by northern hard-wood forest. This is the classic New England forest whose vibrant fall foliage colors the region's identity. In general, beech, yellow birch, and sugar maple dominate the canopy, but the composition is quite variable and dependent on local conditions. On poorer soils, red maple may be more common. Red oak becomes common toward the south, especially on south-facing slopes; white pine occurs on drier sandy sites. Along the Long Trail, northern hardwood forest is found where the trail dips down below about 2,500 feet (2,900 feet in the south).

Often a tree's reproductive characteristics determine when and where it grows. Sugar maple can sprout and grow in the shade, and beech saplings sprout from the roots of mature trees and often dominate the understory. The ability to regenerate under the canopy of their parents makes these two types of trees a stable feature in the landscape. When the canopy opens up, however, due to logging or heavy wind, faster-growing, sun-loving species such as paper birch and aspen will take over temporarily.

The groundcover is as variable as the canopy in northern hardwood forests. A large variety of ferns, flowers, and shrubs make their home here. Many of the spring flowers, including trout lily and spring beauty, are only visible for a very short time. As soon as the ground is warm enough for them to grow, they send up leaves to take advantage of the light that floods the forest floor before the canopy trees put out their own leaves. In a few short weeks, these "spring ephemerals" sprout leaves, put out showy flowers, entice insect pollinators, make fruits and seeds, and store energy in their stout roots to get a head start on next year. By late June, the leaves have withered, and no sign of them appears until next spring. In the summer, few flowers are found in bloom, but the ground can be covered with lush patches of wood fern and Christmas fern or dotted with the heart-shaped leaves of Canada mayflower.

The majority of animals mentioned in this book can be found, at least occasionally, in this forest type. Hermit thrush, ovenbird, red-eyed vireo, black-throated blue warbler, chipmunk, porcupine, black bear, and white-tailed deer are all common. Many beech trees have sets of five parallel scars etched in their smooth bark: evidence of a black bear searching for a beechnut dinner.

Common trees: sugar maple, American beech, yellow birch, red maple, paper birch, bigtooth and quaking aspens, eastern hemlock, white ash, white pine, black cherry, red spruce

Common shrubs: hobblebush, striped maple, shadbush

Common herbs: intermediate wood fern, Christmas fern, shining clubmoss, sarsaparilla, whorled aster, painted trillium, red trillium, wild oats, Canada mayflower, spring beauty, trout lily, false Solomon's seal, starflower, common wood sorrel

Rich Northern Hardwood Forest

The rich northern hardwood forest looks, at first glance, similar to the northern hardwood forest that covers most of the lower slopes of the Green Mountains. However, one notable distinguishing characteristic is the abundance of spring wildflowers that covers the forest floor. The exact plant composition varies with the moisture content of the soil, but a broad diversity of species, up to twice as many as in common northern hardwood forest, is the rule. Maidenhair fern, sometimes in dense carpets, blue cohosh, wild leek, Dutchmen's breeches, hepatica, and wild ginger are all common. The trees here grow quickly and mature to be straight and tall. Sugar maple and white ash dominate the canopy and are frequently joined by hophornbeam, butternut, bitternut hickory, basswood, and yellow birch. Often there are few shrubs, and the forest has an open, parklike atmosphere. Where openings in the canopy (either from logging, blowdowns, or tree disease) allow light to reach the ground, there may be a significant shrub layer, including striped maple and alternate-leaved dogwood.

This forest type occurs on soils rich in mineral plant nutrients. Calcium, in particular, encourages tree growth and favors calcium-loving plants such as wild leeks and blue cohosh. Mineral enrichment occurs where nutrients are washed downhill and collect in coves at the bottoms of steep slopes. Occasional pockets of limestone bedrock, rich in calcium, can enrich the soil even more. Because the rich soil grows commercially valuable trees, there are very few places left in the state where rich northern hardwood forests remain unlogged.

As the trail heads north off Bamforth Ridge, just north of Camel's Hump, it winds through several steep outcrops before leveling out just before the Winooski River. This level area contains a typical example of rich northern hardwood forest.

Common trees: sugar maple, white ash

Common shrubs: striped maple, alternate-leaved dogwood

Common herbs: maidenhair fern, blue cohosh, wild leeks, Dutchmen's breeches, pale touch-me-not, hepatica, Christmas fern, wild ginger, white baneberry

DECIDUOUS FOREST TYPES

DECIDUOUS FOREST TYPES

Red Oak–Northern Hardwood Forest

In the southern part of the state, especially on warm, south-facing slopes below 2,500 feet, red oak finds a place in the canopy alongside sugar maple and beech. This forest type is very similar to the northern hardwood forest, but species such as witch hazel and low sweet blueberry may be found scattered through the understory in addition to oak. These species are indicative of warmer, drier, and poorer soils. These forests bear some similarity to forests further south, but true southern species such as white oak or hickory are not found on the Long Trail.

In this forest, an intriguing drama unfolds between red oak trees and squirrels. The acorns must be buried to sprout successfully. Conveniently (for the trees) red oak acorns are a favorite high fat food for many species including squirrels. Every fall, squirrels bury acorns over a wide area to store them for the winter. In a poor food year, almost all the acorns have been eaten by the end of the winter. Every two to five years, however, the oak trees outsmart the squirrels and produce a bumper crop of acorns—more than can possibly be eaten. In those years, the squirrels perform their gardening services but leave many of the acorns in the ground to sprout.

Common trees: red oak, sugar maple, beech

Common shrubs: witch hazel, shadbush, striped maple, beaked hazelnut, low sweet blueberry

Common herbs: intermediate wood fern, Indian cucumber, Christmas fern, white wood aster, starflower, wild oats, Canada mayflower, sarsaparilla

Dry Oak Forest

On scattered low hilltops along the southern part of the trail, the forest opens up to a parklike environment—a welcome change in a relatively homogeneous forest. The canopy is thinner, composed almost entirely of red oak. Low sweet blueberry and huckleberry, resilient members of the heath family, make up the sparse shrub layer. The limited ground cover is almost all grasses and sedges.

The soils here are thin, rocky, and acidic. The southern exposures and relatively low elevations create a warm micro-climate. These dry unfavorable conditions are tough for most trees, but oak does better than most. Lightning-caused fires may occasionally brush these hilltops and play a role in maintaining the oaks and heaths, which are adapted to survive, and even flourish, with fire.

This community is much better developed at lower elevations elsewhere in southern Vermont. Along the Long Trail, Bear Mountain in Wallingford has one of the few examples of this community.

As in the red oak-northern hardwood forest, acorns in a dry oak forest provide an important food source for many animals including squirrels and wild turkeys.

Common trees: red oak, white pine
Common shrubs: low sweet blueberry, huckleberry
Common herbs: grasses and sedges

Hemlock-northern hardwood forest

Mixed Deciduous
and Evergreen Forest Types

Hemlock–Northern Hardwood Forest

In lower elevation areas along the southern part of the trail,
concentrations of eastern hemlock, sometimes in almost pure
stands, occur in patches throughout the northern hardwood
forest. Hemlock is most prominent on steep-sided ravines
with thin, well-drained acidic soils. Pure hemlock forests are
very dark and have almost no understory vegetation since
shrubs and other low plants cannot survive with so little light.
When deciduous trees are mixed in with the hemlock,
more light reaches the forest floor, so understory plants are
more common.

Before European settlement, hemlock was present in
greater quantities across the landscape. In the eighteenth
and nineteenth centuries; however, it was widely harvested
to produce tannic acid for processing leather. Today, in many
places across the northern hardwood forest, it is present in
the understory. Eventually, these long-lived, shade-tolerant
trees will grow up into the canopy, restoring hemlock's original
place in our forests.

Hemlock forest occurs along the trail south of Vermont
Route 140 in Wallingford.

Common trees: eastern hemlock, American beech, yellow birch

Common shrubs: striped maple, hobblebush

Common herbs: painted trillium, partridgeberry, intermediate wood fern, Indian pipes, Canada mayflower, sarsaparilla

Montane Yellow Birch–Red Spruce Forest

As the trail makes its way up the mountainside, maple and beech dwindle and red spruce take their places. You have entered the montane yellow birch–red spruce forest. Generally this forest type is found between 2,000 and 2,500 feet in the north and up to 2,900 feet in the south. It is one of the most common forest types the trail passes through.

Yellow birch, with its peeling bronze bark, and red spruce, with bark that looks like burnt potato chips, dominate the canopy. Occasional maple, beech, or balsam fir are also present. Hobblebush, mountain maple, and striped maple are part of a thick shrubby understory: quite a deterrent to would-be bushwhackers. Hobblebush's long-arching stems sometimes root at both ends, forming a veritable trip wire, giving the plant its name.

These forests are often found on steep slopes where bedrock is close to the surface. The thin soils occasionally slide, leaving downed trees in their wake. Yellow birch has a particular ability to sprout in thin soils over rocks or on fallen logs. Occasionally, an old yellow birch can be found perched on the most unlikely rock with thick roots reaching down to the soil below.

Common trees: red spruce, yellow birch

Common shrubs: striped maple, mountain maple, hobblebush

Common herbs: mountain wood fern, bluebead lily, wood sorrel, Canada mayflower, sarsaparilla, whorled aster

Montane spruce-fir forest

Evergreen Forest Types

Montane Spruce-Fir Forest

Eventually, as the trail climbs toward the summits, the forest becomes almost entirely coniferous. From about 2,500 feet (2,900 feet in the south) to about 3,500 feet, red spruce and balsam fir dominate the forest canopy. Heart-leaved paper birch (a subspecies of the more common tree found at lower elevations) is the most common deciduous tree. Sometimes it can be found in nearly pure stands indicating relatively recent disturbance of the site, often due to shallow, wet soils.

Shrubs such as American mountain ash, striped maple, and hobblebush are scattered throughout the understory. The ground cover is often a thick carpet of mosses dotted with occasional herbs such as wood sorrel, bunchberry, or bluebead lily. In other places, where the thick evergreen canopy provides abundant shade, there is little or no groundcover.

Abundant wind and rain, prevalent fog, cold temperatures, thin, acidic soils, and landslides on steep slopes are the harsh forces that shape this forest type. Yet spruce and fir are well adapted to survive here. Their conical shape and flexible branches allow them to withstand the snow load that burdens them throughout the winter. In spring, their evergreen needles allow them to get energy from the sun without having to wait to make leaves. Mosses also flourish here. They easily absorb moisture from clouds and fog wrapping the mountaintops but can also withstand desiccation during extended dry periods.

Many birds nest in the spruce-fir forest, including blackpoll warbler, yellow-rumped warbler, red-breasted nuthatch, and Bicknell's thrush. Bicknell's thrush is a special bird of the New England mountains. It nests only in spruce-fir and krummholz forests above three thousand feet in New England, New York, and eastern Canada.

Common trees: red spruce, balsam fir, heart-leaved paper birch

Common shrubs: mountain maple, striped maple, hobblebush, American mountain ash

Common herbs: whorled aster, wood sorrel, bluebead lily, bunchberry, shining clubmoss, mountain wood fern

Subalpine Krummholz

Above 3,500 feet in Vermont's mountains, and higher in some places, the spruce-fir forest becomes shorter and the trees take on a gnarled appearance. This is krummholz, the land of "crooked wood" in German. Balsam fir dominates the trees here. Red spruce is replaced by its hardier cousin, black spruce. The trees have a distinctly untreelike shape. Some are bent over to the ground in low, dense mats through which trails must be aggressively chopped. Bushwhacking through this thicket is arduous, if not downright impossible!

Weather is extreme at this elevation. Wind, snow, and ice together shape this collection of oddly shaped trees. Wind seems to be the predominant shaping force physically limiting how tall a tree can grow. Wind and ice damage often kills the growing shoot at the top of the tree. If this happens repeatedly, the tree will no longer grow upward, but send out lateral shoots instead. Where the winter wind is from a consistent direction, particles of ice sandblast trees over time, killing all the branches on one side and creating a flagged appearance. In addition to stresses posed by the weather, the soils here are very thin, poor, and water-saturated for much of the year.

Balsam fir and black spruce are sometimes joined by mountain ash and heart-leaved paper birch. Common shrubs include velvetleaf blueberry and various other blueberries and cranberries. In the wettest hollows, mosses carpet the forest floor. In slightly drier places, you will see familiar inhabitants of the spruce-fir forest: Canada mayflower, bunchberry, wood sorrel, goldthread, and bluebead lily.

Krummholz is not common in Vermont. The best examples all occur along the Long Trail on the upper slopes of Jay Peak, Mt. Mansfield, Camel's Hump, and Killington.

Common trees: balsam fir, black spruce

Common shrubs: velvetleaf blueberry, Labrador tea, mountain maple

Common herbs: Canada mayflower, bunchberry, wood sorrel, goldthread, bluebead lily

Alpine meadow

Nonforested Communities

Alpine Meadow

On the highest summits of the Green Mountains, the trees
recede, the views open up, and you reach the alpine meadow.
This community exists only in three places along the trail:
Mt. Abraham, Camel's Hump, and Mt. Mansfield. Here, the
climatic forces that limit tree growth in the krummholz
are even greater, and trees cannot survive at all, except in
occasional sheltered pockets.

This community is a mosaic of several different plant
types. Dense shrub mats composed largely of alpine bilberry,
mountain blueberry, and black crowberry grow next to

sedge-dominated lawns and lichen-covered rock. The harsh environment shapes the plants here, forcing them to grow densely together and low to the ground. Some plants such as diapensia or mountain sandwort grow in hemispherical cushions. Other plants, such as mountain cranberry, have thick leathery leaves. These features offer some protection against the harsh wind and cold of the mountain summits.

Lichens, each of which is actually a close association between a fungus and an alga, are also extremely well adapted to the inhospitable mountain environment. They grow on bare rock where other plants are unable to get a foothold. Their splotches of yellow or grayish green brighten Vermont's highest summits.

The plants of the alpine zone may be well adapted to survive harsh weather, but many species are fragile and easily crushed. In addition, the soils they grow in are very thin and easily eroded. The alpine communities are, therefore, very easily damaged if stepped on. The large numbers of visitors to these scenic summits compound this problem. To help protect this unusual community, please be careful where you step and stay on the trail.

Common shrubs: alpine bilberry, black crowberry, mountain blueberry

Common herbs: mountain sandwort, three-toothed cinquefoil, Bigelow's sedge, hairgrass

Pond Shores

Along the trail there are few ponds of any size. Ponds that do exist fall into two general categories: beaver ponds and glacially scoured basins. Despite these two very different origins, the common shrubs around these ponds are the same: mountain holly, velvetleaf blueberry, meadowsweet, and leatherleaf. These shrubs form a narrow ring a few feet wide around the pond, separating the water from the surrounding forest. On some very steep-sided ponds, such as Sterling Pond, there is practically no shrub area at all.

Jenn Karson

Pond shore

It is interesting that many of the shrubs found on these pond shores, including Labrador tea and sheep laurel, are the same as those found high on the mountains in the krummholz and on open outcrops. Labrador tea, named for its popular use as a beverage by backwoodsmen, has leaves that are covered beneath with white or brown wooly fuzz. Sheep laurel has leathery oblong leaves. These traits are characteristic of dryland plants trying to inhibit water loss from their leaves, yet they are found along wet pond shores. These shrubs are also all evergreen, which is an advantage in these acidic, low-nutrient environments, as plants do not have to waste precious resources on leaves only to lose them. The hazard of evergreen leaves, however, is that on bright warm winter days, they will be active, but no water is available to the plant roots in the frozen ground. During these times, the plants are growing in a sort of a desert, and they are well prepared for it.

Beaver ponds, especially those that have been abandoned for some time, often have extensive grass and sedge meadows.

NONFORESTED COMMUNITIES

Generally the trail is routed quite far from these areas, and their plants are not covered in this book.

Many of these ponds, especially the higher elevation ones, are quite acidic due to the tannic acids produced by the slowly decaying needles and leaves in the surrounding forests. The acidity and small size of these ponds preclude the development of a large aquatic community. Some fish, however, are present, as well as an occasional snapping turtle. Frogs are common, especially around the beaver ponds.

Common shrubs: mountain holly, velvetleaf blueberry, wild raisin, meadowsweet, leatherleaf, sheep laurel, pink azalea

Part III:

The Length
of the Trail

Steven D. Faccio

The Length of the Trail

Hiking the Trail

The Long Trail begins at the Massachusetts–Vermont state line. Whether you're out for a day to hike a few miles or a month to hike to Canada, the trail will take you on a journey through a great variety of landscapes and natural communities. The following narrative is by no means intended to describe every feature along the trail. Rather, it will describe and explain some particularly interesting features you will see. Many phenomena are described at a particular location on the trail but are visible frequently. Keep your eyes open for these patterns.

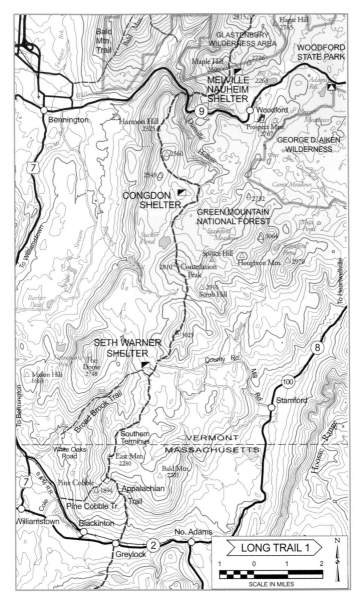

Division 1: Massachusetts Border to Vermont Route 9

Division 1:
Massachusetts Border to
Vermont Route 9

It's likely that, if you're standing on the southern terminus of the Long Trail, you've already encountered one of the most unusual spots on the southern portion of the trail. To get to where you are, you've probably walked from Williamstown, Massachusetts, passing over or near Pine Cobble. Even to the most inexperienced outdoorsperson, Pine Cobble looks very different from the surrounding forest. There is little soil. Large boulders of Cheshire quartzite are strewn across the ground. This hard, acidic rock does not easily weather into soil and does not provide minerals that plants need to survive. The low elevation and south-facing slope make for a hot, dry environment.

In this barren place, only the hardiest trees survive, and these are small and stunted. Pitch pine grows abundantly here. It is found nowhere else on the trail and so is not pictured in this book. It is easily recognized, however, by its bundles of needles packaged in threes. It is likely that occasional lightning-induced fires sweep across this hilltop and are instrumental in maintaining pitch pine here. Fire burns competing hardwood trees but leaves the pine unscathed thanks to its thick, fire-resistant bark. In addition, pitch pine cones require the heat of a fire to open and release their seeds. The seeds, once released, do relatively well in dry, inorganic soil. These attributes combine to make pitch pine the king of this hill.

By the time you reach the official beginning of the Long Trail, the rock type has changed to a slightly more forgiving gneiss. The elevation has increased, and the slope has flattened, so the climate is slightly cooler, and any soil that does form has a chance to accumulate. These conditions support the northern hardwood forest that now surrounds you. You will become very familiar with this forest type on your journey. Beech, yellow birch, sugar maple, and red maple are the most abundant trees. The shrub layer is thick with hobblebush and striped maple.

From here, the trail meanders along a broad ridge toward Seth Warner Shelter. Along the way, you pass numerous large boulders that appear to have been dropped here by some careless giant. In fact, we have to thank a force not so magical but no less awesome: glaciers. Ten to twenty thousand years ago, giant sheets of ice a mile thick flowed across New England. Like enormous bulldozers, the ice sheets scoured the surface of the earth. Often large boulders would become embedded in the ice, and as the ice slowly flowed south, the boulders were dragged along for the ride. When at last the climate warmed and the glaciers melted, these boulders, called glacial erratics, were left behind. Some remained balanced quite precariously on the outcrops beneath.

Another thing you may notice here are groups of red maple trees growing so closely together that their sizeable trunks are intertwined. If you look closely, you'll see that all the trunks are growing out of a rounded hummock. The forest you are walking through, like most of the forest you'll encounter in Vermont, has been logged. When red maple trees are cut, the stumps that remain send up several small sprouts. This allows the red maples to take advantage of the light made available by the removal of the canopy and get a jump on the competition. Often, numerous sprouts from a single stump survive, and sometimes, while they are still flexible, they weave around each other. As the trunks grow wider and more solid, what remains are several trees arrayed in a most unlikely position.

The trail sticks mostly to the crest of the ridge passing through hardwood forest of varying composition and age. Occasionally, the forest opens up to small wet areas and abandoned beaver ponds. In late summer, be on the lookout for jewelweed here, a common plant of wet areas all along the trail.

The last opening, before descending down to Vermont Route 9, is Harmon Hill. This area has been kept open by periodic fires set by the U.S. Forest Service to promote wildlife habitat. After a fire, numerous shrubs, including raspberry, pin cherry, and serviceberry, come back in the opening, providing important food for birds, bear, deer, and other animals. The opening itself, which is relatively unusual in the forest, provides habitat for rabbits and some ground-nesting birds.

Steven D. Faccio

Hermit Thrush

Vermont's state bird, the hermit thrush, is rarely seen but frequently heard. Its beautiful flutelike song begins with a long relatively low introductory note followed by several higher-trilled phrases. This medium-sized reddish brown bird can be distinguished by its distinctive white eye-ring and its habit of flicking up and then slowly lowering its tail after landing.

Hermit thrushes in the east nest on or near the ground in evergreen or mixed evergreen and deciduous forest along the length of the trail. Their nests are small cup-shaped structures on or near the ground. Like its larger cousin the robin, the hermit thrush forages on the ground for worms, insects, and other invertebrates.

Populations of the hermit thrush are increasing in many places. It is the only spotted thrush that winters in the southern United States. It has thus avoided the devastation wrought by destruction in the tropical forests of Central America and the Caribbean which has plagued the Bicknell's thrush and other species.

Jewelweed

In wet places along the trail toward the end of summer, you may find large masses of jewelweed. The plants have delicate, almost ranslucent stems three to four feet high. Bright orange or yellow (the color varies by species) cone-shaped flowers with conspicuous lips dangle down below the leaves and are frequently visited by hummingbirds and bees. In the fall, the flowers wither, and a dry seedpod takes their place. When ripe, the pods explode their seeds at the slightest pressure, giving the plant its other common name, touch-me-not. The stems, when crushed, exude a gooey sap, which is said to soothe the irritation caused by nettles and poison ivy — though I have had little luck with this remedy.

Division 2:
Vermont Route 9 to Kelley Stand Road

North of Vermont Route 9, the trail ascends for the first time into more mountainous terrain. Above Melville Nauheim Shelter, you cross Hell Hollow Brook and enter a small spruce-fir bog. Wet depressions like this are common as you traverse the high ridges of the Green Mountains. The ground is a lumpy array of hummocks and troughs. In the troughs, where there is often standing water, the only plants that flourish here are sphagnum mosses and certain grasses and sedges. The hummocks are slightly elevated and just dry enough for balsam fir and red spruce trees to survive.

Gradually, as you continue your climb, the number and variety of deciduous trees declines. Sugar maples are the first to disappear. Then, the beech trees become smaller and less numerous. Soon, the only big deciduous trees left are yellow birches with their deep bronze bark. Conifers, particularly red spruce, arrive to fill in the canopy. The understory is thick with hobblebush, wood fern, shining clubmoss, and wood sorrel. This new forest type, montane yellow birch–red spruce forest, is a prolonged transition zone between the deciduous forest below and the spruce-fir forest above.

At last, even the yellow birch leaves the forest, and balsam fir becomes abundant. You have entered the true montane spruce-fir forest. The dense evergreen canopy allows little light to filter through the needles, so the flowers and shrubs are often less numerous. Bluebead lily, shining clubmoss, wood fern, and mosses are most common. The summit of Glastenbury Mountain is dense with balsam fir and thick with their Christmasy fragrance. From the opening at Goddard Shelter, you can see the distinctive conical shape of the balsam fir trees, which makes them so easy to identify from afar. As you continue along the ridge north from Glastenbury, the trail pops in and out of spruce-fir islands, perched on the mountaintops above a sea of northern hardwood forest.

Between Kid Gore and Story Spring Shelters, you will pass several beaver ponds. Beavers were once hunted to the edge of extinction across much of eastern North America by Native Americans and early settlers, who received excellent prices for the thick waterproof pelts. In 1921, and again in 1932, beavers were released into Vermont's forests. Within only a few years, beaver populations were again well established across the state.

The beaver is second only to humans in its ability to alter the landscape to suit its own needs. When beavers move into a stream basin, they quickly begin building a dam to create a pond. The pond provides protection from predators. On land, these somewhat awkward animals are easy targets, but once in the water, they are agile and safe. Ponds also create marshy wetlands that fill with aquatic plants, a beaver's favorite summer food. In addition, a pond creates easy access to trees, which beavers use for dam building and store for winter food (they eat the inner bark).

DIVISION 2

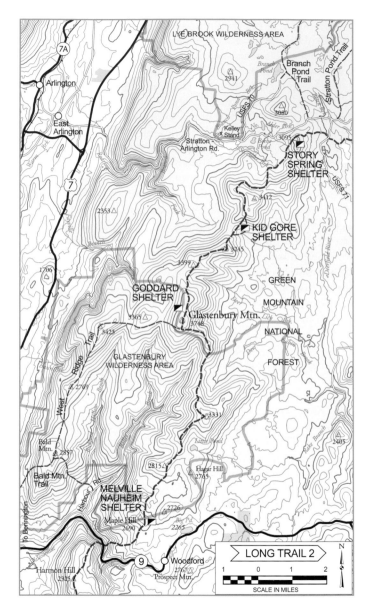

DIVISION 2

Division 2: Vermont Route 9 to Kelley Stand Road

Beaver dams are a feat of engineering. The biggest can be over one hundred feet long and ten feet high. The structural foundation of a dam is sticks and logs, placed to catch as much sediment as possible. The pond side of the dam is sealed with mud, which is inspected nightly and reinforced. Active beaver dams are remarkably watertight and hold water up to the very brim. If the water level falls below the top of the dam, then that is a sure sign that the area has been abandoned.

The pond closest to Story Spring Shelter is likely to be in active use. The water fills the dammed area to the brim, and the lodge has no vegetation on it, indicating recent reconstruction. A quiet evening stroll to this spot from the shelter may yield a view of its inhabitants.

DIVISION 2

Sphagnum Moss

Sphagnum moss, commonly known as peatmoss, is the quintessential moss of wet places in Vermont. Although there are few extensive sphagnum bogs along the trail, these mosses are commonly found in smaller wet pockets in the spruce-fir forest. There are many species of sphagnum, which will not be differentiated here. All of them have a distinctive star-shaped head (called a capitulum) with small branches drooping down the stem. The different species come in a rainbow of colors from bright red to pale green.

Sphagnum can absorb a tremendous amount of water in a network of large specialized cells in the leaves and stem. Some species can retain up to twenty-five times their own weight in water. This trait has been utilized by many different people, including Native Americans, who used sphagnum as diapering material; soldiers in World War I, who used the moss for field dressings; and modern horticulturalists, who use it to improve a soil's ability to retain moisture.

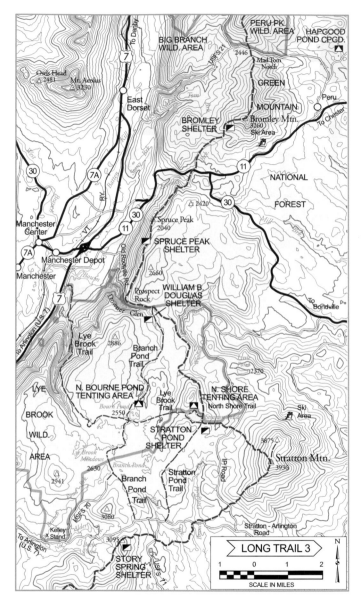

Division 3: Kelley Stand Road to Mad Tom Notch

Division 3:
Kelley Stand Road to
Mad Tom Notch

Past the Kelley Stand Road, the trail begins its ascent of
Stratton Mountain, the highest summit so far. Again you
are taken through the transition from deciduous northern
hardwood forest, up into the dark cool spruce-fir forest of
the mountain summit. What makes these evergreen trees so
well adapted to harsh mountain life?

The most obvious adaptation of these trees is their thick,
fleshy evergreen needles, which the trees keep for five to ten
years before shedding them. Because of their design, they
are tolerant of extreme cold and can remain on the tree
throughout the winter. It is believed that the needles do little
photosynthesis (capturing of sunlight to make food energy)
during the winter. Keeping its needles, however, allows the
tree to get an accelerated start in the spring. Long before their
deciduous neighbors have made leaves, spruce and fir are
actively converting light energy to sugar in their needles.
Saving needles from one season to the next also allows the
trees to conserve precious nutrients, which are in short supply
in the thin, acidic mountain soils.

Another adaptation of these trees is their distinctive
Christmas-tree shape, which allows them to resist the extreme
snow burdens of the mountains. As the snow loads each
branch, it droops down until it rests on the one below it,
gaining added strength. The conical shape also allows the
tree to shed snow more easily, much like a pitched roof.

From the summit of Stratton Mountain, you can climb the
fire tower and appreciate the view of the mountains running
northward that inspired James P. Taylor to create a "footpath
in the wilderness" the length of the state. (He was actually on
the north summit of Stratton, but the view is much the same.)

After descending the mountain, you reach Stratton Pond.
This spring-fed forty-six-acre pond, the largest pond on the
trail, is a popular site for weekend getaways. The basin was
likely hollowed out by glacial action. The pond is relatively
shallow and acidic. Acid in the pond is both naturally

Black Bear

Susan C. Morse

As you walk along, you may
see a large beech tree scarred
with regular sets of claw-marks.
Each mark is a set of five dots
arranged in an arc. Look up
and perhaps you'll see a
large cluster of broken limbs,
where a bear has snapped off
nut-laden branches for easier consumption.
This is a bear tree! Another bear sign to look for
is a large, chunky pile of scat. The contents of the
bear's most recent meals are often readily apparent.
I once found a bear scat reminiscent of a mound
of steaming applesauce! Occasionally, you may see
a bear track in a muddy trail. Their rear prints
resemble a human footprint with claws.

Bears survive the winter by hibernating in rock
crevices, caves, hollow logs, or any other protected
place. Females, who give birth during hibernation
every other year if food is abundant, are substantially
more particular about their dens than males.
Unlike smaller animals, chipmunks, for example,
a bear's body temperature lowers only slightly
during hibernation, so it is quite easily roused
should danger be imminent. A bear in Vermont
typically goes into its den in November or December
and does not eat, drink, urinate, or defecate until
it emerges in early spring at which time it may have
lost 15 to 30 percent of its body weight.

Long Trail hikers may wonder whether bears are
dangerous. According to state biologists, the risk of
attack is extremely slight. In the whole country there
is an average of only one black bear attack a year.
Unlike other places in the Northeast, Vermont bears
are very wary of humans and likely to run away from
you before you ever see them. In the unlikely event
of a bear encounter, speak to the animal to let it
know you are there and back off slowly.

occurring, from tannic acids produced by slowly decaying evergreen needles, and human caused, from acid rain. This acidity prevents the development of a large fish population, but keeps the water clear of algae. The steep sides of the pond harbor only a thin border of shrubby water-tolerant plants, including mountain holly, velvetleaf blueberry, and sheep laurel. If you are visiting at the end of June, you may see the bright pink fragrant blossoms of the mountain azalea.

The trail skirts the edge of the Lye Brook Wilderness Area, designated by Congress in 1975 to protect the forest and maintain it in a wild, unaltered state where "man . . . is a visitor who does not remain." This 15,680-acre wilderness is habitat for animals that do not like human disturbance: black bear and bobcat. Look at the trunk of a large beech tree, and you may find bear claw marks—groups of five holes arranged in an arc. These marks show where a bear climbed to reach a reward of nutritious beechnuts.

From Prospect Rock, the trail meanders gently along the sides of Spruce Peak. Occasionally, the trail dips into hollows with a greater diversity of plants. Look for the odd blue-green foliage of blue cohosh, the delicate branched stems of Canada violet, dark glossy green Christmas ferns, and lush, but stinging, patches of wood nettle. All these plants indicate the presence of more nutrient-rich soil. Through this area, the trail crisscrosses a thin band of rock known as Tyson formation quartz mica schist. This rock is softer and more mineral rich and so produces better soils. In addition, many of these plants are found in small hollows where soil nutrients collect. Small patches like this are particularly rewarding in the springtime when their flowers are most abundant.

One last climb in this section takes you over Bromley Mountain and back into the spruce-fir forest before you end at Mad Tom Notch.

Division 4:
Mad Tom Notch to Vermont Route 140

From Mad Tom Notch, the trail reenters federally designated wilderness. Peru Peak Wilderness together with the nearby Big Branch Wilderness, which you will cross shortly, cover 13,640 acres. The trail over Peru and Styles peaks takes you through the largest area of intact and undeveloped spruce-fir forest in southern Vermont. Along this high ridge, numerous small swamps form where depressions in the rock trap water. In these spots, lush green sphagnum moss carpets the ground.

After a long traverse, the trail descends from Peru Peak down to Griffith Lake. This pond has a narrow, shrubby wetland ringing it similar to the one at Stratton Pond. Mountain holly is most common, but wild raisin, meadowsweet, and a few other plants are also present.

A short section of trail and a brief, exposed scramble take you to the top of Baker Peak, an open rocky bald. Wavy layers of alternating light and dark rock are visible in places. This striped rock, called gneiss, is formed when the intense heat and pressure of mountain-building forces the minerals of the rock to deform into layers. On a clear day, from your perch on top of Mt. Baker, you can see west across the Valley of Vermont. This valley, the path of U.S. Route 7 from Rutland to Pownal, channeled huge streams of glacial ice, which sculpted and eroded it, leaving behind a typical glacial valley with a flat bottom and steep sides.

From the summit of Mt. Baker, the trail descends gradually to the road (USFS 10) and then climbs slightly to Little Rock Pond. Just past the pond lie the remains of the hamlet of Aldrichville. As you walk down the trail, you are following the route of what was once the main road to Wallingford. For nineteen years from 1879 to 1898, this was a thriving village of as many as sixty people who operated a lumber operation, sawmill, and blacksmith shop.

Once the best lumber was removed, the sawmill was deconstructed, and the settlement was abandoned. One hundred years later, all that remains of this once-bustling village are a few walls and cellar holes, which are hard to discern through

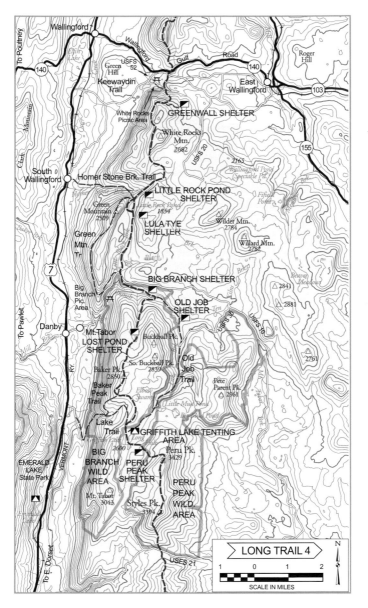

Division 4: Mad Tom Notch to Vermont Route 140

the trees and shrubs. The forest has returned to the denuded hillsides. The forest of deciduous trees that you see today, however, is very different from the virgin tracts of enormous red spruce, yellow birch, and hemlock that the Aldrich brothers found in 1879. Perhaps in several hundred years, the trees will return to their former grandeur. It is a good reminder that however wild the woods around the trail seem, they have all, with the exception of some of the spruce-fir forest, been altered by human activities.

After Aldrichville, the trail gradually ascends White Rocks Mountain. It is well worth the detour to the rocky lookout above the White Rocks Cliffs. Here, you are sitting on the same Cheshire quartzite that was at the start of the trail at Pine Cobble. The steep cliffs and hard unforgiving rock make this a tough place to grow. The knob itself has mostly birch and shrubs: mountain holly, velvetleaf blueberry, and sheep laurel. It is interesting that, although this area is stressful in a very different way from the wet edges of a pond, many of the plants that are found around Griffith Lake or Stratton Pond also grow here.

As you ascend from the White Rocks vista, the bedrock beneath your feet takes a huge leap back in time. The bulk of the southern Green Mountains is formed from ancient gneiss and quartzite that are close to a billion years old. Along the edges of the mountains are bands of younger rocks, schist, and quartzite from around 550 million years ago. How did this pattern occur? The ancient rocks, which were here before the Green Mountains, subsided into a basin that filled with ocean water. Sand beaches formed along the edges, and the bottom of the basin was covered with silt and mud. Eventually, these sediments became schist and quartzite. The clean white Cheshire quartzite, so distinctive of White Rocks, was once beach sand at the edge of the continental shelf. During the formation of the Green Mountains, these many layers of rock were pushed upward in a gigantic fold. Erosion took its toll on the mountains, wearing the younger rocks away in the highest places on the mountains' crests. Eventually, all that was left of the younger layers were the narrow strips of rock around the edge of the mountains that remain today.

The trail descends from White Rocks Mountain and, just before Route 140, passes between two sharply contrasting forest types. On the right-hand side of the trail is a dark forest of large hemlock trees. The ground is covered in a soft blanket of needles and dotted only sparsely with shrubs, herbs, and the occasional white finger of Indian pipe. Left and downhill of the trail is a multilayered northern hardwood forest with a thick shrubby understory and a full complement of now -familiar herbaceous plants. The proximate explanation of this striking difference is that the low light that filters through the thick evergreen canopy of the hemlocks, in combination with the acidifying effect of the hemlock needles, makes the ground beneath the hemlock forest a most inhospitable place to grow.

But what, ultimately, is responsible for these two such different populations of trees? It is likely that soil composition, moisture, and human history all are a piece of the answer to this puzzle. Hemlock is an extremely long-lived slow-growing tree that can reproduce in its own shade. On the uphill side of the trail, these traits allow the hemlocks to persist. The forest downhill of the trail was almost certainly harvested in recent history. The northern hardwoods grow back faster than the hemlocks and so currently dominate the site. It is possible, however, that eventually, if left alone, both sides of the trail will be inhabited by hemlocks.

Indian Pipe

Throughout the woods, particularly in moist shady spots, you will see the ghostly form of Indian pipes sticking their waxy white stalks above the soil. A nodding bell-shaped flower sits atop each stem. Without chlorophyll (the pigment that makes most plants green and allows them to photosynthesize), Indian pipes cannot use energy from the sun to make food. Instead, with the help of a fungus, they absorb nutrients from dead and decaying matter in the ground. There is some evidence that, through the fungus, Indian pipes suck nutrition parasitically from the roots of living trees.

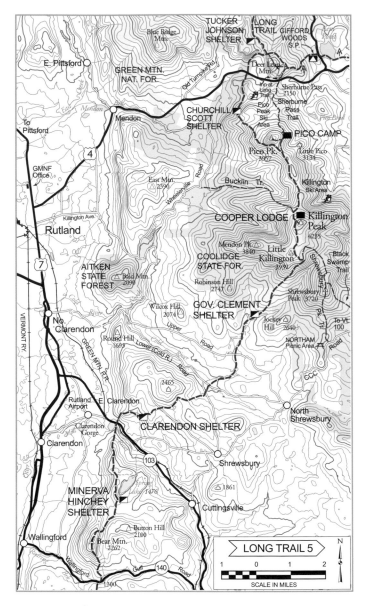

Division 5: Vermont Route 140 to U.S. Route 4

Division 5:
Vermont Route 140 to U.S. Route 4

From Route 140, the trail gradually ascends the southern slopes of Bear Mountain. Numerous rock walls through the woods attest to the human impact on this stretch of forest. These walls were built not to delineate property boundaries but to enclose livestock, most likely sheep. There are more clues to this history than just the walls. Scattered throughout the forest, often close to a wall, are occasional very large trees. Not only are these trees bigger than their neighbors, but they have a very different shape. Thick, spreading branches encircle the trunk almost all the way to the ground. Trees that grow in a forest put all their effort into growing upward toward the light as fast as possible. Any side branches that sprout are quickly self-pruned, as they are of little use in the dark forest. Trees that grow in the open (in a pasture, for example) take advantage of the light around them and grow thick branches in all directions. The unmistakable form of these "wolf trees" is a sure sign that the land was once open. Often these trees were left to provide shade for grazing animals when the land was cleared.

The numerous white pines in this forest also are a result of the land's history. White pine is so common now in Vermont that few people realize that its preferred habitat is restricted to relatively dry sandy soil. In an abandoned field, the soil condition is artificially dry, which gives white pine seedlings the advantage over some of the hardwoods, and the seedlings have the light they need to grow robustly. Most places where we see white pine today are abandoned fields like this one. Over time, if left undisturbed, the process of succession will take its course, and hardwoods will grow up under the pines and resume their dominance in the canopy.

As the trail proceeds up the hill, the forest becomes more and more mature. In one of the old upper pastures, you encounter a stand of pure spruce. Close inspection will reveal that this is a different species from the familiar red spruce. These trees have branches that droop characteristically toward the ends; their needles are longer (up to one inch long);

the cones are longer; and the bark is smoother. This is a stand of Norway spruce, a European tree that is frequently planted in pure plantations. No doubt these particular trees are the result of such an endeavor.

As you proceed up the hill, the patchwork of abandoned pastures, fields, and plantations becomes less distinct and the forest is more homogeneous. At the top of Bear Mountain, the forest opens up again into a rocky woodland dominated by oaks and lowbush blueberry. The summit of this mountain is made up of the now-familiar Cheshire quartzite. This poor rocky substrate and the warm southern exposure prevent most plants from growing here. Scattered oak trees, which are well adapted to warm, dry climates, and extremely tolerant blueberries are all that can make it.

The trail makes its way gradually down the ridge past Minerva Hinchey Shelter and Spring Lake. Oaks are still prevalent in the forest, though now they are joined by other deciduous trees. Acorns from the trees on the top of Bear Mountain made their way down hill with assistance from gravity and animals and sprouted to grow the oak trees here.

Continuing north, you dip down into the steep-sided Clarendon Gorge. The action of Mill River over millennia has cut this cleft through the rock. For the next five miles, the trail passes by networks of stone walls, over numerous woods roads, and through a mosaic of forests and pastures in every stage of use and abandonment. Signs of human habitation are everywhere. Eventually, past Governor Clement Shelter, the forest grows older and wilder looking, though this forest, too, has served human uses; the evidence is just harder to see.

The trail begins to climb in earnest to reach the top of Killington Peak. This 2,500-foot ascent is one of the longest sustained climbs on the trail. Soon you leave behind all signs of human history and again enter the spruce-fir zone. These mountains are primarily composed of the same ancient gneiss that you've been walking on. The peaks of Killington, Little Killington, Mendon, Pico, and Little Pico are all capped with just as ancient but slightly harder quartzite. This erosion-resistant rock contributes to the height of Killington Peak, which at 4,235 feet is the second tallest mountain in Vermont. From the summit of Pico,

DIVISION 5

the trail descends through a section of very rich hardwood forest. Delicate maidenhair fern and blue cohosh carpet the understory. Spring flowers, including Dutchmen's breeches, are abundant.

Dutchmen's Breeches

These enchanting little flowers can be found in the springtime in many places along the trail where the soil is high in mineral nutrients. The name comes from the shape of the flower, which, to some imaginative observers, resembles pairs of old-fashioned underwear hanging upside down to dry. Each delicate flower has two long spurs on top (the legs of the pantaloon), a balloon-shaped middle (the waist), and small yellow petal ends dangling below.

At first glance, it's hard to imagine how this strange shape benefits the flower. As with so many flowers, its pollination method holds the key to the mystery. The stamens, male parts of the flower, are pursed inside two yellow petals. Here they are protected from the wind and weather. Bumblebees, the flowers' main pollinators, are attracted by nectar, which is stored at the very top of each spur. The bee's tongue is just long enough to reach the sugary prize but only if its head nestles into the flower where it is covered in pollen.

By midsummer, no sign of these whimsical little flowers can be found. The flowers and foliage of these "spring ephemerals" have all died back waiting for another season.

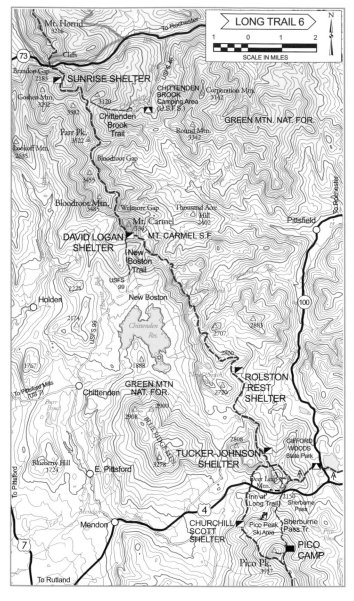

Division 6: U.S. Route 4 to Vermont Route 73

Division 6:
U.S. Route 4 to Vermont Route 73

The trail ascends gradually from Route 4 to Maine Junction where the Appalachian Trail heads east. It is only a short side trip from here to Deer Leap Cliff, which, on a clear day, offers spectacular views of the surrounding mountains all the way to the Adirondacks. The outcrop itself is composed largely of younger rock than what you have been recently traveling on. (It is a mere 530 million years old instead of close to 1 billion!)

From here, the trail takes you on a relatively level journey through a forest of beech, birch, and maple. This section is one of the longest stretches of purely deciduous forest along the trail.

Through this section, keep your eyes (and your ears!) alert for ruffed grouse. The males, in an effort to mark their territory and attract females, make a low droning drumming sound whose beats gradually accelerate. The bird performs by beating his wings against his body, preferably from the vantage of an easily visible old log.

The female grouse does not drum, but has her own display, occasionally witnessed by an observant hiker. Females nest and raise their young on the ground at the base of a tree or under low branches. (The males do not participate.) If you stumble upon a grouse family, the mother will do her utmost to lure you away from her brood by whining piteously and stumbling along the ground as though her wing were broken. Predators are attracted by the apparently easy prey of an injured bird and follow her through the forest. Once a safe distance from the chicks, the female quickly drops the charade and flies off.

The trail meanders along the ridge to the east of Chittenden Reservoir. Occasional breaks in the forest offer views of the water-filled basin below. Farther along the ridge, the trail crosses a deeryard. In the winter, deer, with their long skinny legs, have trouble maneuvering in deep snow, which leaves them exhausted and easy prey. To overcome this difficulty, deer group together in dense coniferous forest areas. Here, the snow depth is typically substantially lower as much of the snow remains supported by the evergreen branches above.

DIVISION 6

The thick snow-covered branches act like a blanket to provide protection from wind and cold. Deer prefer places with abundant deciduous shrubs whose tender bark and buds provide winter forage.

From here, the trail ascends the flanks of Mt. Carmel to the David Logan Shelter. Look for wood sorrel and mosses as you pause at the shelter. These plants of the spruce-fir forest will become ever more common as you walk northward. The trail skirts the edge of the spruce-fir zone around Bloodroot Mountain and other unnamed peaks and then descends into Brandon Gap.

Bryan Pfeiffer

Red Eft

Bright orange salamanders are visible along the trail on wet days in the spring and summer. These creatures, the most easily seen amphibians on the trail, are actually juvenile red-spotted newts called red efts. (Newts are a subset within the larger class of salamanders.) The newts start their existence as yellowish green aquatic larvae in ponds and pools. After several months, they develop lungs and change into the vivid terrestrial eft.

The efts travel through the forest to colonize new ponds and pools. They can travel safely during the daytime (and so are often encountered by hikers) as they are protected from predators by their extreme toxicity. Newts in the eft stage have skin secretions that are ten times more toxic than adult secretions. As with other poisonous creatures, their bright coloration is a warning.

After two to seven years on land, the efts transform again into yellowish green aquatic adults. These drab creatures retain the characteristic red spots of the eft, but blend in much better with a brown pond bottom. Their tails, now shorter and fin-shaped, are also more suitable for watery living.

Susan Shea

Wood Sorrel

One of the many pleasures of hiking into the spruce-fir zone in midsummer is finding wood sorrel in bloom. The single delicate white flowers dance above the leaves on slender stalks. The five petals have bright

pink veins radiating out from the center. These vivid lines, called bee guides, attract flies and bees to the center of the flower where pollen coats the insect, which it then transfers to other flowers.

The leaves, with three bright green heart-shaped leaflets, emerge from the base of the plant and give it another of its common names, mountain shamrock. When sun hits these normally shaded leaves, they fold down along the stem to protect themselves from undue water loss. The leaves themselves are edible and have a refreshing sour flavor for a thirsty hiker. They should be consumed sparingly, however, since their sourness derives from oxalic acid, which is toxic in large quantities.

DIVISION 7

Division 7:
Brandon Gap to Cooley Glen

The ascent out of Brandon Gap is one of the steepest climbs the trail makes in many miles. Through the trees to the east, the imposing face of the Great Cliff of Mt. Horrid is just visible. The rocky top of the cliff, accessible by a short side trail, is home to several uncommon plants, one of which is the three-toothed cinquefoil. Enjoy them, but watch your step and stay on the rocks.

These cliffs are often home to nesting peregrine falcons. If birds are nesting on The Great Cliff, the area will be posted

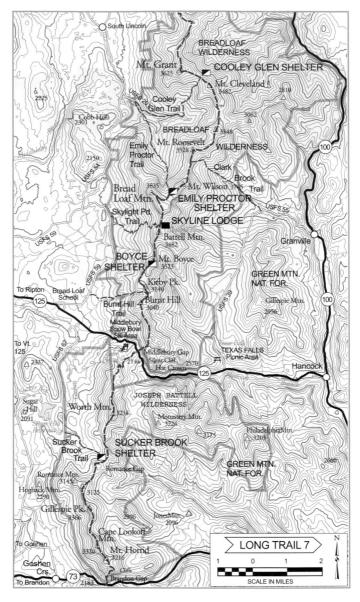

Division 7: Brandon Gap to Cooley Glen

as closed until the young birds fledge (usually August). Please respect all closure notices and, when necessary, appreciate the cliffs from afar.

From the cliff, the trail takes you over Mt. Horrid and then meanders up and down along the ridge. Throughout this area, lots of ice storm damage is visible. Many of the birches are broken and leaning; their branches snapped under the heavy load of ice deposited during the winter of 1998. Just north of Sucker Brook Shelter, the forest is open enough to support a large growth of blackberry bushes. Be on the lookout for signs of wildlife. Bear, deer, and moose all make use of this abundant food. Many times in this section, you pass from deciduous beech and maple forest into spruce-fir and then back again as your elevation changes. Soon you reach the summit of Worth Mountain and begin your descent through the Middlebury College Ski Bowl to Middlebury Gap.

Just before the gap, a short side trail leads to Lake Pleiad. This beautiful rock-rimmed lake is nestled between the steep slopes of the mountain on the southwest side and a bare rock ledge on the northeast. Thousands of years ago, the erosive force of glaciers carved this bowl out of the rock, leaving behind the bare schist streaked through with large sparkling white chunks of quartz.

Ascending north out of Middlebury Gap, you pass through a beech forest. The larger trees here have bark that is pock-marked, rough, and in places broken and cracked. This bark is so different from the familiar smooth gray beech bark that it is almost unrecognizable. The trees are suffering from the ravages of beech bark disease. The disease is caused by a scale insect (similar to the white scabby scales occasionally found on houseplants) and a fungus. The insect bores through the bark to get to the sap underneath. This opening into the tree allows the fungus to enter where it slowly destroys the integrity of the thin bark. Once the bark has been compromised, other fungi and wood-boring insects are able to do their damage. Often the trunk is so weakened that the tree simply snaps in a strong wind.

When the beech trees are under stress from disease, they frequently respond by reproducing. Beech trees have the ability to send up shoots from the roots of larger trees. This allows the saplings to grow quickly in the shade where

DIVISION 7

DIVISION 7

Peregrine Falcon

This powerful, elegant falcon is easily recognized by its distinctive dark gray hood and mustache. Peregrines are among the fastest animals in the world. They prey on medium-sized birds, which they catch midair, descending on them suddenly at speeds of up to two hundred miles per hour.

Peregrine populations were decimated, and in eastern North America completely eliminated, by the widespread use of the insecticide DDT. The birds consumed large amounts of the chemical, which was concentrated in the bodies of their prey. As a result their eggshells were weakened to the point where successful reproduction was impossible. A captive breeding program was begun in 1975, and in the 1980s, the birds were released into the wild at several sites in Vermont. A successful breeding population has been reestablished, and in 2005, a record sixty-one surviving peregrine chicks were recorded in Vermont. Because of this recovery, the peregrine falcon was removed from the Vermont endangered species list in 2005.

Peregrines typically nest on bare rock ledges high on cliff faces. In addition to Mt. Horrid, you may find peregrines at Smugglers' Notch and Hazen's Notch. Please observe signs asking hikers to stay away from peregrine nesting sites.

other seedlings could not get a foothold. Often, for the hiker, the first sign of a disease-infested forest is the dense growth of beech saplings sent up by the dying trees.

This disease is a relatively new occurrence in Vermont forests. The fungus has been around for a long time, but the insect, which begins the damage, was introduced from Europe around 1890. Since that time, it has spread throughout New England and into New York, New Jersey, Pennsylvania, and even parts of West Virginia. What the ultimate effect of the disease will be on the composition of our forests is still unknown.

Soon you pass into the Breadloaf Wilderness, which, at almost 21,500 acres, is the largest federally designated wilderness area in Vermont. The wilderness was designated in 1984, so signs of logging and other human disturbance are still evident; however, with time, this forest will return to something that may well be close to its original state. You remain in this large wilderness area for many miles and eventually reach Cooley Glen Shelter.

Division 8:
Cooley Glen to Birch Glen Camp

From Cooley Glen, still in the Breadloaf Wilderness, you descend to the road at Lincoln Gap. From there, you ascend quickly and steeply out of the yellow birch–beech forest into yellow birch–red spruce forest, and finally into the now-familiar montane spruce-fir forest. The trail crosses over many slabs of rock as it climbs. In these spots, you can look to the side of the trail and appreciate just how little soil covers the bedrock. It is not hard to imagine that a heavy rain on these steep slopes could cause the thin soil layer to slump down the mountain, pulling trees and shrubs down with it.

On some of the slabs and boulders that you pass, if the light is just right, you can see subtle parallel grooves in the rock, generally oriented in a north–south direction. (There is a particularly good example of this less than a mile from the Lincoln Gap road where the trail descends and quickly ascends two sets of rock staircases.) These grooves are called glacial

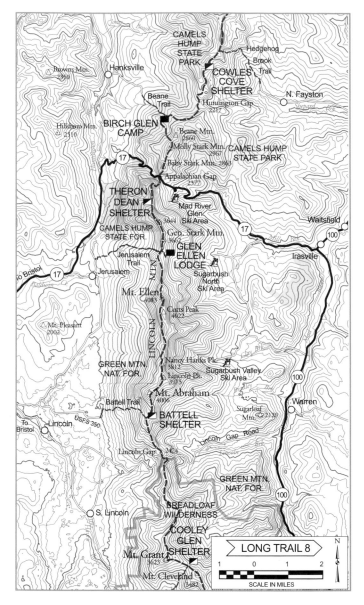

Division 8: Cooley Glen to Birch Glen Camp

striations. The massive ice sheets that flowed over these mountains during the last ice age dragged rocks and boulders along with them. The rocks scraped the bedrock surface below the ice and etched the grooves you see today. The rocks of the Green Mountains have so many layers in them that the subtle striations are often hard to see.

Eventually, the trail finishes its climb, and you are on the summit of Mt. Abraham, your first truly alpine summit if you have been hiking from the south. Here, the weather is harsh enough that even the hardy spruce and fir trees cannot survive. Occasional twisted trees can be found scattered in the more protected hollows, but the vast majority of the summit is bare rock or patches of alpine "lawn" composed of grasslike sedges. This fragile alpine plant community is found only at three locations in Vermont: Mt. Abraham (the smallest example), Camel's Hump, and Mt. Mansfield. Although the plants are amazingly tolerant of harsh weather, they are extremely vulnerable to damage from foot traffic, and care should be taken to hike only on the bare rocks.

Leaving Mt. Abraham, you travel along an extremely narrow ridge northward toward Mt. Ellen. Here, the Green Mountain ridge is at its narrowest. Downhill to the east through the trees you can catch glimpses of the steep slopes that result from the force of erosion on the narrow ridge.

The trail zigzags across the ridge through spruce-fir forest carpeted with mosses and bedecked with lichens. Occasional bunchberry and bluebead lily add spots of color to the forest floor. The wet spongy mosses are a testament to how much precipitation falls on these mountaintops. They are extremely effective at absorbing not only the water that falls as rain, but also droplets of water from the fog that so frequently obscures the summits.

Lichens in the forest are abundant. Old man's beard hangs down in scraggly greenish gray locks from the trees. Various species of pixie cups, one with bright red tops, sprout in miniature forests on decaying logs. Great starbursts of green and gray adorn the bark of the spruce and fir trees. All these seemingly dissimilar species are lichens. A lichen is actually not an individual organism. Instead, it is an intimate relationship between a fungus and an alga. The fungus provides physical structure and absorbs water and nutrients from the substrate (rock, wood, or soil). The alga photosynthesizes (using the same chemical reactions that plants accomplish) to turn energy from the sun into usable sugars to feed itself and its fungal host. This stunning example of biological cooperation creates a superbly resilient organism. Lichens can grow on bare rock or wood where nothing else has a chance. They can survive complete desiccation and extreme heat and cold. This stretch of trail is an excellent place to appreciate this fascinating life-form.

The trail descends abruptly from General Stark Mountain into Appalachian Gap. It quickly rises again along a steep boulder-lined route to the top of Baby Stark Mountain. From Molly Stark's Balcony, there is a sweeping view of the mountains northward, where the bare rock islands of Burnt Rock Mountain rise above the surrounding sea of green. The trail then dives back down underneath the canopy and descends to the shelter of Birch Glen Camp.

Bunchberry

This mountain forest flower, known also as dwarf cornel, is a diminutive version of the flowering dogwood. Its four conspicuous white "petals," which are actually modified leaves, surround a cluster of tiny greenish flowers. The flowers open extremely suddenly sometimes as the result of disturbance from a passing bumblebee. Inside the petals, the anthers, which contain the pollen, are set to spring. They explode outward catapulting the pollen into the air covering the unsuspecting bee. This movement, which was recently recorded using high-speed video observation, is the fastest known movement in the plant world.

Late in the summer, the flower cluster matures into a bunch of bright red edible berries. The berries, to most human palates, are sweet but not particularly flavorful; they are an important source of food, however, for deer, grouse, and other forest animals.

Division 9:
Birch Glen Camp to Bolton Mountain

From Birch Glen Camp, the trail ascends the ridge and then contours around to Cowles Cover Shelter. A lovely beech-birch-maple forest surrounds the shelter. Massive old yellow birches with their magnificent bronze bark are scattered about.

The trail gradually ascends from the shelter, passing lots of pink lady's slippers. Just before Burnt Rock Mountain, there is a short spur trail to one of the highest glacial potholes in New England. This small pond was formed by the high-pressure meltwater that swirled beneath the sheets of glacial ice. The water, laden with sand, scoured out this rounded basin. Past the pothole, the trail attains the open cobbles of Burnt Rock Mountain. This boreal outcrop is free of forest due to wind exposure and lack of soil. Velvetleaf blueberry, tucked into cracks between the rocks, mountain ash, and stunted spruces, sheltering tenuously behind boulders, offer a glimpse of the alpine vegetation soon to come. Although similar to the alpine meadows on Camel's Hump and Mt. Mansfield, the environment here is not so cold, wet, and harsh, and thus the rare alpine plants do not grow here.

From there, the trail ascends to the heavily wooded summits of Ira and Ethan Allen, and then descends to Montclair Glen. The forest here, composed almost exclusively of paper birch, is a testament to history, for those who know the story. In the late 1800s, much of what is now Camel's Hump State Forest was heavily logged for its valuable timber and later for pulpwood to make paper. What remained was a dry, scrubby, highly flammable thicket of shrubs and small trees. In 1903, a huge fire ravaged the forest, sparing only a few pockets on the western side of the mountain.

The scorched soil was an excellent breeding ground for the light-loving fast-growing paper birch. Their small seeds prefer the bare mineral soil, which provides more nutrients and moisture than layers of forest litter. The trees that sprouted over a hundred years ago remain to dominate the canopy. This incarnation of the forest will, however, soon be lost to the inevitable process of forest succession. Young birch trees cannot

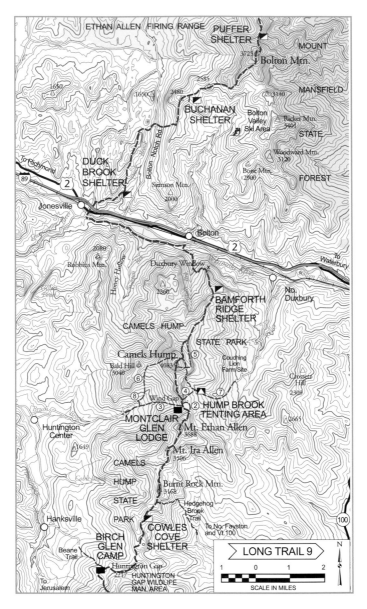

Division 9: Birch Glen Camp to Bolton Mountain

sprout in the shade of their parents. If you examine the under-story, you will see the saplings of those trees that can survive the shade: red spruce and balsam fir. As the relatively short-lived birch trees die off (few live longer than 150 to 200 years), the spruce and fir in the understory will grow to take their place.

The trail leads from the graceful birches at Montclair Glen up to Wind Gap and then starts a scrambling ascent of the steep south face of the mountain. Soon you break out onto an open knob—an inviting place to rest. From here you have a clear view down to a series of beaver ponds on the eastern slope of the mountain.

The forest below is largely paper birch, again the result of the 1903 fire, except for the conspicuously dark green spruce and fir ringing each pond. Beavers are responsible for this curious pattern. They eat the bark of deciduous trees and shrubs, in this case birch, which they harvest from around their ponds. Once they removed the birch, the spruce and fir left untouched in the understory grew to replace them. The beavers simply accelerated the process that will take place in the entire forest over the next hundred years. The beavers likely abandoned their handiwork long ago. They do not stray far from water, and as soon the only available trees were unpalatable conifers, they left in search of more abundant resources.

From the open ledges above Wind Gap, the trail continues to ascend the mountain, skirts the formidably steep south-facing cliffs, and eventually reaches the summit. The iconic silhouette of Camel's Hump—the steep cliffs on the south and the more gradual double hump descending to the Winooski River on the north—owes much of its shape to glacial erosion. The glaciers flowed over the mountain from the north, round-ing and smoothing the northern Bamforth Ridge. As the ice surged over the summit, it caught rocks on the lee side of the slope and plucked them away leaving the steep south cliff as evidence of its passing.

The summit of Camel's Hump is home to a ten-acre patch of alpine vegetation, the second largest such site in Vermont. (The largest, on Mt. Mansfield, is yet to come.) Small hardy shrubs such as mountain cranberry, alpine bilberry, and black crowberry crowd into cracks and behind boulders and put down roots where they can. Few plants can survive the harsh

DIVISION 9

Steven D. Faccio

Porcupine

Occasionally, as you wander through the woods, you might see trees (white pine, beech, and young hemlock are frequent targets) with large quantities of bark chewed off. These irregular patches of bare trunk have neatly gnawed edges. The tops of hemlocks are often also strangely shaped by the repeated clipping. This is porcupine damage.

These slow-moving forest waddlers are well protected by their quills, which are really modified hairs, and have little need for speed or agility. Armed with minute barbs at their tips, quills work their way deeper and deeper into the flesh of unlucky attackers and are extremely difficult to remove. If threatened, a porcupine may slap its spiny tail, but it cannot throw its quills as is commonly believed. Curious dogs are often the victims of a porcupine encounter. If you hike with your pet, it is recommended that you bring along pliers to remove the quills promptly.

Their only major predator is the fisher, who is adept enough to flip a porcupine over and attack its unprotected abdomen. In the 1940s fishers were nearly exterminated from Vermont. Old-time members of the Long Trail Patrol report killing ten porcupines a night at Montclair Glen. Fishers were reintroduced in the 1950s, and porcupine populations have subsequently diminished.

I was once sleeping out in the open to be awakened by the snorting and snuffing of a nocturnal porcupine. After my aggressive rock attack, it wandered off. In the morning, however, I found it curled up at my feet contentedly chewing through all the straps of my backpack. Porcupines love salt and will gnaw anything, including backpacks, plywood glue, and the edges of shelter bunks, to get it. This propensity causes occasional damage to shelters.

climate of this exposed alpine peak. Those that do have tough leathery or waxy leaves that help them to survive the extreme wind and cold so common on the summit. (For more on adaptation of alpine plants, see Section 10 Bolton Mountain to the Lamoille River.)

Because this is such an unusual environment for Vermont, some eighteen plant species here are extremely rare, including Boott's rattlesnake root, which grows nowhere else in the world outside the alpine summits of New England and New York. Please be sure to walk on the rocks and leash your dogs to protect this fragile place. The Green Mountain Club has taken a lead role in protecting the alpine vegetation by placing summit caretakers here to educate passing hikers.

Spruce-fir forest blankets the slopes of the mountain to the west. The trees of this forest, red spruce in particular, suffered from a dramatic decline in health in the 1960s and 1970s. Needles turned brown and dropped off; branches, and sometimes, whole trees died. It is believed that acid rain in the soil and acid cloud drops bathing the foliage significantly weakened the trees leaving them vulnerable to freezing and other cold damage on the bitterest winter nights. In addition, increased acidity leaches calcium and other plant nutrients out of the soil and releases the normally insoluble aluminum, which can be toxic. Currently the trees seem to be making a comeback, but whether this is temporary or permanent is not known, as the phenomenon is not well understood.

From the summit, look to the northwest, and you'll see bands of dead gray trees alternating with green live trees. This is a fir wave. Harsh conditions high on the mountains gradually take their toll on the balsam fir trees. When the trees finally succumb, they leave a more open forest, even though they often remain standing. The trees on the windward edge of the opening are more vulnerable, and soon they, too, die. The leeward edge is protected, allowing fir seedlings to flourish there. Eventually, the seedlings mature and replace the original trees. These openings migrate progressively up the mountainside in the direction of the prevailing wind.

From the summit of Camel's Hump, the trail begins its 3,500-foot descent to the Winooski River, the largest elevation change on the length of the trail. The trail descends, sometimes steeply, over the open knobs of Bamforth Ridge and then enters the woods. A view opens across the Winooski River at the Duxbury Window.

Soon after, the trail enters one of the best examples of rich northern hardwood forest along its length. This forest type, although not uncommon in the state as a whole, is rare along the high mountain ridges of the Long Trail. Soil nutrients wash down from the steep slopes above and collect in the flat valley bottom, allowing a host of plants not seen elsewhere to grow. In the spring, the forest floor is alive with wildflowers: delicate Dutchmen's breeches, primeval-looking blue cohosh, and dainty hepatica are interspersed with the more common spring beauties, trout lilies and trilliums. In the summer, the finely wrought leaves of maidenhair fern flow across the forest floor. Trees, too, benefit from the abundance of nutrients. Sugar maple and white ash grow unusually straight and tall. There are fewer shrubs here, giving the forest an open, parklike feel. Take a few minutes to enjoy this spot, one of my favorite places along the trail, before descending to the road.

Val Stori

Boott's Rattlesnake Root

In midsummer, look for the nodding white flowers of this diminutive alpine plant. It can be identified by the ragged edges of its petals, long curly stamens, and heart-shaped leaves surrounding the base of the flower stalk. It is believed that the plant grows only leaves for several years and then flowers once and dies. The only place in the world where it can be found is on the highest mountaintops of northern New England and the Adirondacks. In Vermont, it grows only on Camel's Hump and Mt. Mansfield. This limited range makes it very rare, so it is legally protected in all four states that it inhabits. The greatest threat to these plants is trampling by unwary hikers, so watch your step!

The trail follows the road toward Jonesville along the Winooski River. The general path of this river is older even than the mountains that surround it. As the mountains rose up by the force of two pieces of earth's crust colliding, the river cut its path downward through the mountain like a saw blade. The headwaters of the river are well east of the Green Mountain chain in the hills of Cabot.

At last, after several miles of road walking, and another road crossing soon after, the trail begins its ascent of Bolton Mountain. Climbing steeply at first, and then more gradually, the deciduous trees are left behind. Eventually, you reach the thick spruce-fir forest on the summit of Bolton Mountain.

Division 10:
Bolton Mountain to the Lamoille River

The summit of Bolton Mountain is one of the best spots along the Long Trail to see and hear the rare Bicknell's thrush. This bird lives exclusively in the high-elevation spruce-fir forests of New England and adjacent New York and Quebec.

From the summit of Bolton Mountain, the trail descends to Puffer Shelter and a great view of the rugged mountains to come. Past the shelter, you wind up and down the ridge formed by Mt. Mayo and Mt. Clark before dropping into Nebraska Notch. Just past the Clara Bow trail, you encounter a small long-abandoned beaver pond. Much of the basin has been filled in by wet meadow. In the late summer fluffy pink joe-pye weed and flashy jewelweed blanket the meadow. The old dam has several lines of shrubs along it, each marking the location of a different water line. Though the beaver may be gone, other animals are still here. Look closely, and you will see saplings with long fresh scrapes in their tender bark, and buds chewed off, sure signs of browsing moose.

The trail contours around Dewey Mountain, through a forest of beech, birch, maple, and scattered spruce. The forest floor is dotted with the now-familiar shining clubmoss, blue-bead lily, mountain wood sorrel, goldthread, and bunchberry.

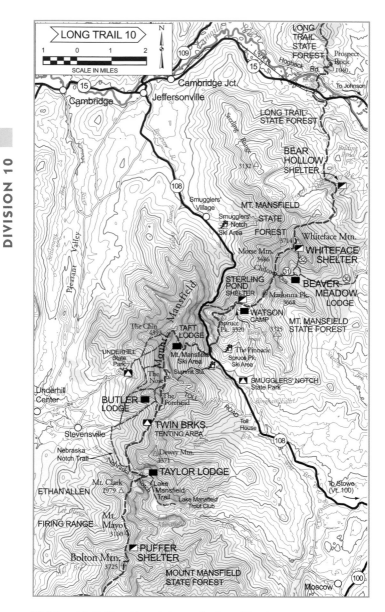

Division 10: Bolton Mountain to the Lamoille River

As you ascend from the tenting area toward the forehead of Mt. Mansfield, the spruce and fir again replace the deciduous trees. The trail winds whimsically between two large boulders that have fallen from the cliffs above.

At last, after some effort, you reach the Forehead, the first of Mt. Mansfield's open summits. Here, trees are sparse. Those that exist, balsam fir and heart-leafed paper birch, are shrubby, gnarled versions of their lower elevation selves. The trail enters the forest again, and then comes out into the open near the summit station, entering the largest area of alpine vegetation in Vermont.

The trail ascends from the summit station to Frenchman's Pile. Here mats of alpine bilberry, with their round, toothless, blue-green leaves, are the most abundant vegetation. In the fall, the bilberry leaves turn deep purple making them readily identifiable at some distance. A careful look under the bilberry mats reveals the waxy small dark green leaves of mountain cranberry, which, later in the summer produces edible bright red berries. Labrador tea, black crowberry, and three-toothed cinquefoil can be found in and under some of the shrub mats.

Occasional gnarled trees grow wherever boulders and bedrock hollows offer slight protection against the wind. Just past Frenchman's Pile, matted black spruce trees can be found along the trail. The shorter blue-green waxy needles distin-guish this spruce from its more familiar cousin, red spruce.

Farther on, you pass through several patches of alpine bog. Mt. Mansfield's alpine ridge is the only place in Vermont where you can find this unusual community. These diminutive wetlands form where water from rain, snow, and fog accumu-lates in small bedrock depressions. Because the water comes entirely from precipitation, it has no opportunity to percolate through rock or soil and pick up minerals. The water also cannot drain out of these depressions, so the largely acidic waste products of the organisms living there accumulate. Therefore, the environment here is mineral poor and extremely acidic. The wet, acidic conditions prevent decompo-sition, so layers of dead vegetation, known as peat, accumulate. The peat layer in these alpine bogs is generally one-half to two feet thick, much less than what is found in lowland bogs.

The plants in the alpine bog must not only tolerate the wet acidic conditions typical of all bogs but are also confronted

with the extreme cold and wind of the alpine environment.
Few plants are up to this challenge. The most distinctive and
abundant vegetation here is the bright red sphagnum moss,
which forms, in some places, a nearly continuous carpet.
The distinctive fluff-capped stalks of cotton grass are scattered
throughout. The shrubs here are all members of the heath
family. Small cranberry, with long narrow rolled-in leaves, and
black crowberry, with tiny needlelike evergreen leaves and black
berries, creep over the sphagnum. Taller shrubs are bog laurel,
with shiny green elliptical leaves and pink starlike flowers, and
Labrador tea, with thick, leathery evergreen leaves that are
coated underneath with conspicuous rust-colored wool.

In several places, particularly toward the summit of the
Chin, the trail passes by grassy lawns composed primarily
of Bigelow's sedge. In the saddle just below the Chin, keep
your eyes out for dense green cushions of diapensia. Another
cushion plant, mountain sandwort, is scattered throughout.

The plants of the alpine zone are similar and in some cases
identical to plants of the arctic tundra thousands of miles to
the north. This similarity is not coincidence. When the glaciers
retreated 10,000 years ago, all of New England and eastern
Canada was blanketed with one relatively homogenous tundra
ecosystem. Gradually, the climate warmed, soil developed, and
trees filled in the valleys and lowlands. All that remains now
of that continuous prehistoric vegetation are the islands of
tundra now on our mountaintops.

Because the alpine environment is so unique, many of these
plants are extremely rare. Diapensia, with its striking white waxy
flowers, and bearberry willow find their sole perch in Vermont
near the summit of Mt. Mansfield. Boott's rattlesnake root,
which grows nowhere else in the world except the alpine
summits of New England and New York, also grows here.

Many of these plants have thick leathery or waxy leaves
and grow densely, low to the ground. Other plants, such as
Labrador tea, have leaves coated in wooly hairs. These features
help protect the plants from the worst of the winter wind and
may also help to form a layer of slightly warmer air around
them. In addition, these adaptations help the plants survive a
less obvious stressor: drought. Though rainfall at certain times
of the year is abundant, water runs quickly off the rocks and
thin soils leaving a relatively parched environment for the

plants to cope with. The dense mats of plants absorb water and thick small leathery leaves help to minimize evaporation.

Another commonality among these alpine plants is that they are all perennials, lasting year after year. Annuals—which must sprout from seed, grow, flower, and fruit all in one year—simply don't have enough time to complete their life cycle in the short alpine growing season.

Though these plants are well adapted to the brutal weather, they, and the thin soil upon which they depend, are extremely vulnerable to foot traffic. The summit of Mt. Mansfield is the most accessible alpine area in Vermont, thanks to road and ski resort development. It was once the site of a hotel! Over the years, large areas of the summit have been denuded by visitors. In the late 1960s, the Vermont Department of Forest, Parks and Recreation and the Green Mountain Club started a ranger naturalist program (now the summit caretaker program). Volunteers and staff educate hikers about the fragile mountain environment and have erected physical barriers, such as string and low walls, to keep people on the trails. This substantial effort has lead to a remarkable recovery of the alpine ecosystem. Please do your part to protect this fragile ecosystem: watch where you step and stay on the trails.

Few animals can survive in the harsh alpine environment. Birds are the most easily visible wildlife. Ravens sometimes nest on cliffs northeast of the Chin and can frequently be seen wheeling and playing above the summit. White-throated sparrows are more easily seen than heard, and may greet you with their "Oh sweet Canada Canada Cadada." Yellow-rumped and blackpoll warblers also nest at or near tree line and can be seen near the summit.

No mammals breed on the alpine summit, though snowshoe hares will venture into the open from their homes farther down. These nocturnal creatures, about the size of cottontail rabbits, are rarely seen but commonly leave their distinctive large bounding tracks in the snow.

The trail descends from Mt. Mansfield to Smugglers' Notch, a narrow, precipitous mountain pass. This route acquired its name in the early 1800s when President Thomas Jefferson declared a trade embargo on Great Britain and Canada. The hardship imposed by closing legal trade with Montreal drove northern Vermonters to break the embargo.

Steven D. Faccio

Bicknell's Thrush

This reclusive little bird has only recently been identified as a separate species and has been the focus of much attention in the conservation world. It breeds exclusively in montane spruce-fir forests (generally above 3,000 feet) of New England, New York, and adjacent Canada. It winters primarily in high-elevation forests in the Dominican Republic and, to a lesser extent, on Haiti, Puerto Rico, and Cuba. According to extensive research by scientists from the Vermont Institute of Natural Science, the birds from the Mt. Mansfield area winter exclusively in the Dominican Republic and return to their Vermont breeding sites year after year.

These limited habitats, both summer and winter, mean that there are few places where it can live; hence, its population is relatively small and vulnerable. Habitat degradation from ski area and other ridgeline development in New England and forest harvesting in the Caribbean further imperils the survival of the species. This bird has been listed as a species of special concern in Vermont and has been given the highest priority by conservation organizations.

Bicknell's thrush prefers the dense, almost impenetrable thickets of spruce and fir so common on our mountains, so spotting it can be quite a feat. Its inconspicuous brown plumage and heavily spotted breast make it even more difficult to find. You're much more likely to hear its nasal trill than see it.

They passed through the notch on an arduous and illicit route north to market their goods. In 1922, an improved road was built here, and the route was again used for smuggling; this time liquor traveled southbound into the land of prohibition.

The notch is believed to have been primarily created by the action of streams coming off the surrounding mountains. In this case, one ancient stream flowed eastward and one west-ward. Over time, those streams wore their way deeper and farther up into the mountains. Eventually, the streams etched valleys all the way up to the ridge, forming a V-shaped notch. In more recent geologic history, glaciers continued the work of the water, eroding the notch to make it deeper and steeper.

The Long Trail begins a steady climb out of the notch and finally reaches a short spur trail, which leads to an excellent view from the outcrop at Elephant's Head. The cliffs below the outcrop are sometimes home to nesting peregrine falcons. The spur trail may be closed during the breeding season. If this is the case, please respect the closure and give the birds the space they need to thrive (for more on peregrine falcons, see section 7). From here, it continues to Sterling Pond, which sits in a steep-sided rocky alpine basin created by glacial scouring. The pond begins abruptly, with no wetland vegetation along the shore. This alpine bowl collects lots of snow and keeps it late into the spring. The balsam fir and heart-leafed paper birch are slightly small and twisted, reflecting this stressful environment.

The trail follows the rim of the pond over thin alpine soil. Slight depressions in the bedrock hold water and support miniature, moss-carpeted wetlands filled with false hellebore. The trail continues, traversing across a steep west-facing slope on the ascent to Madonna Peak. Here, the fir forest gives way to a patch of young paper birch. It's likely that fir trees extended across this area but were swept away by a landslide some years ago. The birch grew up quickly in the bare rocky spot. In a few decades, however, the birch will begin to decline, and young fir trees, now in the understory, will grow tall. Eventually unbroken fir forest will again cover the slope, until the next disturbance.

You finish your climb of Madonna Peak on the ski slope. Right next to the stairs to the summit house, there is an excel-lent example of clearly folded rock (schist). Hot semiliquid rock flowed and buckled as the mountains pushed upward 350 million years ago, creating this solid wave.

The trail descends to Chilcoot Pass and then climbs again up Whiteface Mountain. Near the top, a brief pause at the shelter affords an excellent view of Madonna Peak. The clearing in front of the shelter is thick with chokecherries, a favorite food of many animals including bear.

From Whiteface Mountain, the trail again crosses through the gradual transition from spruce-fir forest back to northern hardwood. A slight hollow, just past Bear Hollow Shelter, is home to a woodland flower garden. Plant nutrients from the steep slopes above wash down into the cove and enrich the soil. Blue cohosh, Canada violet, Solomon's seal, and Dutchmen's breeches are among the many plants that bloom here. In early summer, just past mud season, the white and purple Canada violet is the most eye-catching. Enriched flower-filled areas like this are scattered throughout this section of the trail, rewarding the alert hiker.

Old logging roads follow the trail down to the Lamoille River. Here you'll notice familiar garden weeds like dandelions, which are not seen elsewhere on the trail and are not listed in this book. Even a very lightly used dirt road can act as a conduit for weeds into the forest. The road creates just enough of an opening that these species can get a foothold here, and their seeds may get here by hitching a ride on logging trucks and machinery.

Still on old roads, you pass through a recently harvested area that is dense with young saplings. This forest has a very different feel. The thick growth of trees prevents all light from reaching the forest floor. Consequently, there are almost no understory plants here. As these trees grow, they will take up more and more space. Some will grow just a little faster and shade out their neighbors, and some will die. Eventually, just a few much larger trees will remain.

The trail crosses Route 15 and descends on a new section of trail, toward the Lamoille River. Before reaching the main channel, you cross an overflow channel of the river. During the spring flood, the river escapes its banks and takes over this subsidiary channel. Each year, the water scours its path and sweeps many of the plants away. Watch out for a large patch of poison ivy in this stretch. This irritating plant thrives in warm moist disturbed settings such as this.

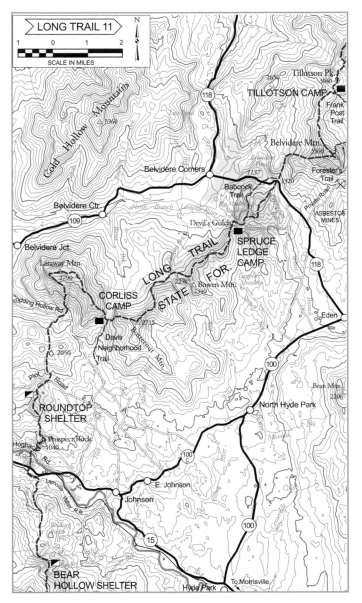

Division 11: Lamoille River to Tillotson Camp

Division 11:
Lamoille River to Tillotson Camp

Ascending out of the Lamoille River Valley, your first destination is Prospect Rock. Looking down on the flat river valley, it's possible to imagine it filled with water. At the end of the last ice age, meltwater blocked by ice remnants in the Champlain Valley formed the glacial Lake Winooski. The lake backed up into this valley and left behind fine sediments, which created the fertile agricultural soils below you.

Look around from this perch, and you'll notice that the vegetation is very different from anything you've seen in a while. Red pine and red oak are scattered around the summit and western slope of the rock. Relatively low elevation and great exposure to southern and western sunshine make this place just warm enough to support these species.

Next the trail meanders up Roundtop Mountain. In late spring and early summer, keep your eyes peeled for the exotic pink lady's slippers. Appreciate them, but don't pick them! Lady's slippers grow only in particular conditions. In order for a seed to sprout, a specific fungus must be present in the soil to help provide nutrition for the embryonic plant. Once the seed does sprout, it takes ten to seventeen years for it to grow into a flowering plant. After a single season of blooming, it can take up to four years for the plant to recover from its energy-intensive floral extravagance.

For the next several miles, you travel mostly through northern hardwood forest. Here, red trillium is noticeable in the springtime. Just before crossing Plot Road, you'll pass an active sugar bush, recognizable by the plastic tubing, visible year-round, attached to the trees for sap collection. In this rather sparse-looking forest, all the trees that are not maples have been removed, giving the maples more room to grow and yielding an increase in sap production.

During the steep climb up Laraway Mountain, you pass under several cliffs. Early in the summer, clumps of delicate wild red columbine cling to the rock face. Although it's often hard to get close to their cliff-side habitat, a good look at them will reveal their exquisite shape. Each of the five petals is formed into an elongated tube that stands up above the flower. At the very tip of each tube, the flower stores its sweet nectar, accessible only to hummingbirds, who eagerly drink the sugary offering and in the process pollinate the flower.

After Laraway Mountain, the trail traverses the ridge to Butternut Mountain and finally to Bowen Mountain. Along this stretch, the forest periodically opens up. Many of the large trees have branches broken at odd angles. Sometimes, whole treetops have partly snapped and are hanging on by only a few fibers. This is damage caused by an ice storm that devastated much of New England in January 1998. Prior to this event, ice

DIVISION 11

Red Squirrel

As you enter a spruce-fir forest, a noisy, high-pitched scolding chatter reaches your ears. There is no doubt that you have met a territorial red squirrel who is none too pleased to see you. These feisty little creatures eat mostly nuts and buds from evergreen trees. They clip twigs off these trees, eat the succulent bud on the end, and discard the remainder. Piles of four- to eight-inch-long twigs surrounding the base of a red spruce tree are sure signs of red squirrel activity. The squirrels will drop the cones out of the tree, as well, and take them to a favorite place to eat the nuts. Mounds of cone scales mark these favored snacking spots.

Red squirrel tracks leave distinctive marks in the snow as they bound from tree to tree. Like other bounders, the squirrel places its two small front feet down first. Then the larger rear feet swing forward and land in front of the front feet. If this distinctive set of four prints is about three and a half inches wide and five inches long, then chances are good that you're seeing a red squirrel track.

damage was not considered by ecologists to be a major source of disturbance in our forests. After walking through a few of these patches, it will not surprise you to hear that this attitude has changed. With the canopy largely gone, the understory plants grow rapidly in the light now reaching the forest floor. A thick shrub layer of raspberry, hobblebush, and birch saplings has developed, and ferns abound.

The next diversion is Devil's Gulch. This narrow cleft in the rock was once the outlet of a temporary glacial lake that formed when the northern Lamoille Valley was still choked with ice. The bottom is a jumbled mass of truck-sized boulders with steep cliffs rising on either side. Mosses, one with the descriptive name stair-step moss, and ferns carpet the boulders. As you enter the notch from the south on a hot summer day, you are greeted by a cold blast of air. The spaces between the boulders trap ice, snow, and cold water into the summer. This phenomenon acts as a natural ice box refrigerating the damp ravine. The plants that you see here, especially the mosses, reflect this cool, wet environment.

From the lookout at Spruce Ledge Camp, there is a great view of Belvidere Mountain, your next summit, and the white gash on its side that is an asbestos mine. The asbestos formation is the result of unusual geologic history. A large mass of the mountain, contains the mineral serpentine and amphibolite, a magnesium- and iron-rich rock that originated in ancient oceanic crust. This is very different from the less-dense, silica-rich continental crust you have been walking over. Four hundred and fifty to 350 million years ago, two ancient continents riding on tectonic plates collided to create the Green Mountains. Most of the existing oceanic crust between the two continents was consumed in this process. In localized regions, however, largely where the continents curved inward, slivers of oceanic crust together with the underlying mantle survived and were pushed up into the developing mountains. The oceanic crust became amphibolite, and the remnant of the mantle became serpentine.

The serpentine deposit is of interest both to ecologists and industrialists. Botanists are drawn to the spot because the unusual mineral composition creates difficult growing conditions for most plants. A few plants, however, have specifically evolved in this environment and are found nowhere else in the state. Industrialists have been interested in the spot because it is the source of a particularly fibrous form of serpentine: asbestos. In fact, in the 1940s the Belvidere mine produced 90 percent of all asbestos in the United States.

The trail largely circumvents the bulk of the serpentine deposit to avoid the mine. The occasional serpentine outcrop near the trail is recognized by its light greenish white color and silky, soft texture. The amphibolite is visible in the exposed rock under the fire tower.

In the saddle just north of Belvidere, you skirt around the diminutive Lockwood Pond, which is the headwaters of the Missisquoi River.

Red Trillium (Stinking Benjamin, Wake Robin)

The deep crimson of red trillium flowers is relatively common in northern hardwood forests in the late spring. All parts of this plant—from the leaves, to the petals, to the sections of the fruit—come in threes, giving it its name. Next time you see these flowers, get down on your hands and knees and take a good sniff. You'll find out why this plant has another common name, stinking Benjamin. The color and smell of these flowers, which are evocative of raw meat, attract carrion flies. The flies, who usually feed on garbage and rotting corpses, fly into the flower looking for dinner and come out covered in pollen, which fertilizes the next flower it visits.

Animals play a role in distributing the seeds of this plant as well. Each seed is attached to a fatty morsel— a treat to an ant. Ants collect the seeds, eat the fatty part, and leave the rest to sprout wherever they are dropped. Other trilliums also employ this tactic, but the fats in red trillium are particularly tasty to ants, so these plants tend to be spread faster than their relatives.

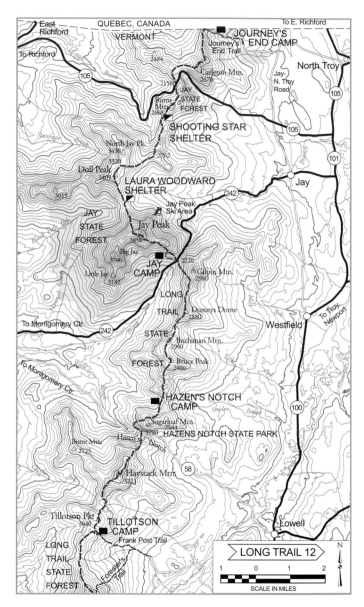

Division 12: Tillotson Camp to Journey's End

Division 12:
Tillotson Camp to Journey's End

As you wind your way down Tillotson Peak, you have several good views of a large pond, just to the north. The trail passes fifty yards or so to the east of the pond's edge, and a short bushwhack will have you standing on an enormous beaver dam that stretches across the valley. The pond must be abandoned as there are no signs of recent activity and the water is very low. Already, the far side of the pond has become a wet meadow. Gradually, the water will continue to drain, and the basin will fill in with sediment. Eventually one broad meadow will stretch where the pond once was. Following the path of forest succession, the meadow will give way to shrubs, which will be followed by birch. Eventually a mature forest of spruce and fir might stand here, as though the beavers had never built a dam.

Near the summit of Haystack Mountain is a small serpentine outcrop. This greenish fibrous mineral contains unusually large amounts of magnesium and iron as well as nickel and chromium, which can be toxic to plants. Few plants can survive here, so the outcrop is grassy and sparsely vegetated. Two extremely rare plants, Green Mountain maidenhair fern and serpentine sandwort, have adapted to the chemical challenges here and grow only on serpentine in northern New England and adjacent Quebec. (See Section 11 for more on the geology and ecology of serpentine.)

Descending north of Haystack toward Hazen's Notch, you pass through a classic stretch of mature spruce-fir forest. The ground is carpeted with mosses, bunchberry, and Canada mayflower. In the spring, white goldthread blossoms stick up on long stalks above the greenery. Little spruce and fir saplings are scattered throughout the understory, waiting for their chance to grow when a blowdown opens up the canopy.

The trail continues downhill into the last of the notches, Hazen's Notch. This spot, similar to Smugglers' Notch, was likely originally eroded by the action of running water. During the last ice age, the stream valleys were sculpted and enlarged to create the cliffs that are visible today. The trail passes west of the main cliff face, which has small deposits of serpentine.

Historically, it has been home to the rare peregrine falcon. Just after Highway 58, a steep ravine contains one of the most intact sections of northern hardwood forest. These trees have been sheltered by surrounding mountains and are, on account of the steep slopes, relatively inaccessible to logging.

Traversing the ridge along Bruce Peak, Buchanan Mountain, and Domey's Dome, you glimpse occasional views

Susan C. Morse

Moose

Hiking the Long Trail just south of Jay Peak, I once encountered a mother moose with two young. She stamped and snorted her disapproval at my presence, until I turned around. Moose are the largest mammals in Vermont, and though they are not predators, an angry moose can be very dangerous.

At the beginning of the last century, when the countryside was largely deforested, moose were rare. Over the last forty years, the moose population has increased dramatically as forests have regrown. The population in Vermont is now estimated to be about 5,000, a number large enough to be a hazard to unwary motorists.

Moose tracks are large, heart-shaped prints four to seven inches long. Their scat in the winter, when they eat mostly dry woody material, is composed of pellets. In the summer, succulent vegetation loosens the system to form something resembling a cow pie.

of Jay Peak. From here, you can see how much taller Jay is than anything in the vicinity. The peak is made of harder rock than the surrounding regions. Over millennia, erosion stripped the softer rock away and left Jay standing tall and alone. Also visible are several steep-sided bowls, the result of more recent erosion caused by glaciers.

After viewing Jay Peak, you descend into Jay Pass and begin climbing the mountain. The steep trail requires occasional scrambling and lands you, at last, on the summit. Here, for the last time, if you've been traveling northbound, you encounter the small twisted trees of the krummholz. If you're on the summit on a windy day (which is likely!) you'll have no trouble understanding the forces that deform these trees. Wind stress on these trees is compounded by deep snow. Jay's northern latitude and relative isolation from other tall mountains combine to make it one of the snowiest places in Vermont.

The summit of Jay Peak is believed to have supported an alpine plant community similar to the ones found on Camel's Hump and Mt. Mansfield. It was largely destroyed in the 1960s when the summit area was dynamited to facilitate the construction of the summit station and restaurant of the Jay Peak ski resort. If you look carefully in the rocks, you may discover an isolated plant still clinging to existence here.

On a clear day, the summit affords expansive views. To the southwest lies Big Jay, which is the second tallest trail-less peak in the state (Mendon, near Killington, is the tallest). A deep bowl-shaped valley lies between the two peaks. This glacial cirque is unusual in Vermont. The steep sides were carved by alpine glaciers eroding backward into the ridge during the last ice age. It is now a much-loved destination for intrepid backcountry skiers.

The trail descends the mountain and ascends Doll Peak for one last foray above 3,000 feet, and then meanders along the ridge and descends gradually to North Jay Pass and Route 105. On the ridge north and south of the pass, the numerous broken tree limbs are the result of severe ice storm damage from the 1998 storm.

The trail ascends slightly to Carleton Mountain. From the lookout, there is a great view of Jay and the surrounding mountains. Notice here, that the dark green spruce-fir forest through which you have traveled so far descends down the

mountains to an elevation of around 2,500 feet. This is 400 feet
lower than the first spruce-fir forest that you encountered on
the side of Glastenbury Mountain, over 250 trail miles south
of here. The harsher climate here gives the spruce and fir
the advantage over hardwoods at lower elevations.

Your last expansive view on the trail is from a rocky perch
just at the U.S.–Canadian border. Look north, and you'll
see that, although the trail ends here, the mountain range
(called the Sutton Mountains in Quebec) continues on.

Part IV:

The Plants and Fungi of the Long Trail

The Plants and Fungi of the Long Trail

Trees

Trees are arranged by leaf type. Needle-leaved trees, such as pine and spruce, are separated from broad-leaved trees, such as oak and maple. Needle-leaved trees, also called conifers, have seeds in cones and generally are evergreen (with the exception of larch). Broad-leaved trees produce flowers and have seeds that are enclosed in some kind of fruit. Fruits may be soft and fleshy, like an apple, or hard, like an acorn. In our region, the leaves of most broad-leaved trees change their color in the fall and eventually fall off (the word "turn" in the species descriptions indicates the colors that the leaves generally turn in the fall). Trees that lose their leaves are deciduous.

Key

L = leaf or needle length (for compound leaves, the length of the entire leaf, not the individual leaflet, is indicated)

T = height of mature tree

NEEDLE-LEAVED TREES

White Pine

White Pine

Red Pine

Red Pine

Balsam Fir

Balsam Fir

Needle-leaved Trees

White Pine

Pinus strobus / Pine Family

Long flexible needles, five in a bundle. Cones long and slender up to six inches. Bark thick and deeply furrowed. L 2–4 in. T 80–110 ft.

Habitat: Naturally, this tree is found on well-drained sandy soils and would be quite rare along the Long Trail. It grows extremely well in abandoned fields and can occur there in nearly pure stands until it is eventually replaced by hardwood forest. This is its most commonly occurring habitat along the trail.

Red Pine

Pinus resinosa / Pine Family

Stiff needles, two in a bundle. Short squat cones (1½–2½ in.). Bark reddish and broken up into big plates. L 4–6 in. T 50–80 ft.

Habitat: Dry woodlands; often grown in plantations; uncommon along the trail.

Balsam Fir

Abies balsamea / Pine Family

Short flat needles with two white stripes on the back and a circular base, which leaves a circular scar on the twig when the needle falls off. Needles often spread into two distinct rows, especially on lower branches. Bark light gray with resin-filled bumps. Cones upright and cylindrical. From a distance has a distinctly conical shape, except near tree line, where it can take a low matted form. L ½–1 in. T up to 75 ft.

Habitat: Ubiquitous at higher elevations along the trail, sometimes in pure stands.

NEEDLE-LEAVED TREES

Red Spruce

Red Spruce

Black Spruce

Norway Spruce

Eastern Hemlock

Eastern Hemlock

Red Spruce

Picea rubens   /   Pine Family

Short, stiff needles squarish in cross-section pointed at the tips.
Twigs rough where needles have fallen off. Bark of mature
trees breaks into large flakes resembling burnt potato chips.
Cylindrical reddish brown cones fall off when mature.
L ⅝–¾ in. T 60–70 ft.

Habitat: Extremely common in mid and high elevation forests
along the trail.

Black Spruce

Picea mariana   /   Pine Family

Needles very similar to red spruce but shorter, slightly bluer, and
somewhat waxy. Bark is dark and scaly. Cones short, egg-shaped,
and remaining on the tree for many years. L ¼–½ in.
T 25–30 ft. (but always shorter along the trail)

Habitat: Along the trail, only found at higher elevations just at
tree line in low twisted mats.

Norway Spruce

Picea abies   /   Pine Family

Needles similar to red spruce but generally longer. Bark rough
and scaly. Branches droop distinctively. Cone long (4–6 in.)
and slightly curved. L ½–1 in. T 80 ft.

Habitat: Not native to Vermont. Found in several plantations
along the southern part of the trail.

Eastern Hemlock

Tsuga canadensis   /   Pine Family

Needles short and flat with white stripes on the bottom. Short
stalks and a tendency to lie flat along the twig distinguish these
needles from balsam fir. Bark thick and grooved. Cones small
(<1 in.) and hanging down. Historically harvested because
it contains tannins used in leather production. L ⅜–⅝ in.
T 60–70 ft.

Habitat: Mixed in with northern hardwood forest, sometimes
in pure stands in cool acidic soils.

NEEDLE-LEAVED TREES

Northern Red Oak

American Beech

American Beech

Broad-leaved Trees

Broad-leaved trees are separated by leaf arrangement and shape.
Leaves can either be placed opposite each other along a twig or
alternating. Leaf shape is either simple or compound. In a simple
leaf, the blade is one connected piece. In a compound leaf, the
leaf is composed of distinctly separate leaflets. Leaflets can be
arranged radially around one point (palmately compound)
or in pairs along a stem (pinnately compound).

Alternate Simple Leaves

Northern Red Oak
Quercus rubra   /   Beech Family

Leaves shallow lobed and pointed at the tips, turning dark red
in the fall. Dry brown leaves often remain on the branches during
the first part of the winter. Bark with distinctive flat ridges. Fruit is
a one-inch-long acorn. L 4–10 in. T 70–80 ft.

Habitat: More common on the southern end of the trail on
warmer south-facing slopes.

American Beech
Fagus grandifolia   /   Beech Family

Leaves are toothed, turning yellow to brown and often remaining
on the tree during early winter. Distinctive long slender buds are
said to resemble cigars. Bark smooth and light gray. Fruit is a
prickly bur containing two to three nuts, a favorite food of many
animals, especially bears. L 3–6 in. T 60–80 ft.

Habitat: Ubiquitous in deciduous woods along the trail.

BROAD-LEAVED TREES

Paper Birch

Paper Birch

Yellow Birch

Yellow Birch

Hophornbeam

Basswood

Susan Shea

Paper Birch
Betula papyrifera   /   Birch Family

Leaves toothed, turning light yellow. Bark is white and peeling, sometimes showing light pink or orange where older bark has peeled away. Fruit is a slender drooping catkin. L 2–4 in. T 70–80 ft.

Habitat: Common in deciduous and coniferous forests throughout the trail; common in places that have been logged or burned.

Similar Species: Heart-leaved paper birch. Considered to be a subspecies of paper birch, this variant is found only at higher elevation in spruce-fir forest and krummholz. It is distinguished by its heart-shaped leaves and its dark pink inner bark.

Yellow Birch
Betula alleghaniensis   /   Birch Family

Leaves similar to but slightly wider than paper birch, turning yellow. Mature bark is bronze colored, peeling in thin strips. Fruit is an erect oval catkin. Young twigs have a distinct wintergreen aroma when the bark is scraped off. L 2–4 in. T 70–80 ft.

Habitat: Common in northern hardwood and montane yellow birch–red spruce forests.

Hophornbeam
Ostrya virginiana   /   Birch Family

Small tree. Leaves toothed, egg-shaped, and pointed at the tip, turning yellow. Bark is brown, flaking off in small vertical strips. Fruit is a hoplike cluster of many small nutlets enclosed in a flat papery shell. Buds are finely grooved under magnification. L 1–5 in. T 20–30 ft.

Habitat: Most common in warmer drier forests along the southern part of the trail; often with oak.

Basswood
Tilia americana   /   Linden Family

Leaves round, slightly heart-shaped, and toothed, turning yellow. Mature bark is distinctly ridged. Fruit is a cluster of small nutlike pods hanging below a leaflike structure. L 3–6 in. T 50–80 ft.

Habitat: Rich woods.

BROAD-LEAVED TREES

Quaking Aspen

Susan Shea

Quaking Aspen

Bigtooth Aspen

Bigtooth Aspen

Black Cherry

Pin Cherry

Quaking Aspen

Populus tremuloides   /   Willow Family

Leaves small, roundish, and finely toothed, turning yellow.
Leaf stems are flattened causing them to "quake" in the breeze.
Bark is chalky white, sometimes slightly greenish, maturing to
brown and furrowed in the oldest trees. Fruit is a small drooping
catkin that produces many cottony seeds. L 2–6 in. T 20–50 ft.

Habitat: Deciduous forest with a history of logging or fire.

Bigtooth Aspen

Populus grandidentata   /   Willow Family

Leaves larger and more coarsely toothed than quaking aspen,
turning orange. Bark and fruit similar to quaking aspen though
bark slightly darker when young. L 1–4 in. T 30–40 ft.

Habitat: Deciduous forest.

Black Cherry

Prunus serotina   /   Rose Family

Egg-shaped minutely toothed leaves, turning yellow or reddish.
Dark brown bark is smooth when young, resembles burnt potato
chips when mature. Beautiful white flowers, clustered in slender
cylindrical spikes, resemble those of chokecherry. Often the
flowers are only noticeable when the petals fall to the ground.
Fruit a small black edible cherry. Twigs have an acrid bitter cherry
aroma when the bark is scraped off. L 2½–5 in. T 60–80 ft.

Habitat: Deciduous forest.

Pin Cherry

Prunus pensylvanica   /   Rose Family

Small tree or shrub with leaves similar to black cherry but more
slender. Red-brown smooth bark. White flowers are loosely
clustered. Fruit is a red, very sour cherry. Twigs have a similar
aroma to black cherry when bark is scraped off. Seeds can
remain viable in the soil for fifteen to twenty years, allowing this
tree to sprout and grow quickly after a fire or clear-cut.
L 2½–5 in. T 10–30 ft.

Habitat: Deciduous forest after fire or clear-cut.

BROAD-LEAVED TREES

Chokecherry

Pringle Herbarium/UVM

Downy Serviceberry

American Mountain Ash

Chokecherry
Prunus virginiana

Small tree or shrub. Leaves serrated and rounder than the other cherries. Relatively smooth bark growing scaly in the biggest stems. Small white flowers in a cylindrical cluster similar to black cherry. Fruit small, very dark red, edible but sour. Twigs have a similar aroma to black cherry when bark is scraped. L 2–4 ½ in. T 2–20 ft.

Habitat: Forest edges and open places.

Downy Serviceberry
Amelanchier arborea   /   Rose Family

Small tree. Leaves toothed, rounded at the base, and hairy in early spring, turning orange. Bark light brown, striped or slightly flaky when mature. White flowers with slender petals are among the first blossoms of spring. Fruit is dry and dark purple ripening in June giving the tree the alternate common name Juneberry. L 1 ½–4 in. T 20–40 ft.

Habitat: Dry rocky woods.

Similar Species: There are several shrubby species of serviceberry along the trail. These look similar to downy serviceberry but never grow to be tree sized (not pictured).

Alternate Compound Leaves

American Mountain Ash
Sorbus americana   /   Rose Family

Small tree or shrub. Leaves pinnately compound with eleven to seventeen serrated leaflets, turning yellow. Bark is smooth and light colored with horizontal markings. Numerous tiny white flowers occur in a dense flat-topped cluster. In early summer, petals often carpet the trail. Fruits are small, red-orange, and clustered. Fruits often remain on the tree into the winter providing food for numerous birds and mammals. L 6–9 in. T up to 40 ft.

Habitat: Primarily found in montane spruce-fir forests.

White Ash

White Ash

Sugar Maple

Sugar Maple

Bitternut Hickory (not pictured)
Carya cordiformis   /   Walnut Family

Leaves pinnately compound with seven to nine very finely toothed leaflets, turning yellow. Lower leaflets much smaller than upper ones. Bark with many narrow ridges. Fruit is a round, four-parted, smooth, greenish nut. Buds are bright yellow and pungently aromatic. L 6–12 in. T 50–60 ft.

Habitat: Dry woods; more common along the southern part of the trail.

White Ash
Fraxinus americana   /   Olive Family

Leaves pinnately compound with five to nine very finely toothed leaflets, turning yellow or sometimes purplish. Bark with distinct, smooth, criss-crossing ridges. Fruits contain a small, plump, dry seed with a long, slender, dry wing hanging in clusters. L 8–12 in. T 70–80 ft.

Habitat: Rich moist woods.

Opposite Simple Leaves

Sugar Maple
Acer saccharum   /   Maple Family

Leaves familiar shaped lacking the many small teeth that characterize red maple leaves. (One way to remember this distinction is that if you eat lots of sugar, you lose your teeth!) Notches in the leaves U-shaped. Leaves turn yellow, orange, or red and are largely responsible for Vermont's famous fall foliage. Bark in indistinct ridges. Buds brown. Flowers small and greenish. Fruits a plump seed with a broad, brown, dry wing paired to form a V. L 3½–5½ in. T 70–100 ft.

Habitat: Very common in deciduous woods.

BROAD-LEAVED TREES

Red Maple

Red Maple

Red Maple

Striped Maple

Striped Maple

Mountain Maple

Red Maple

Acer rubrum   /   Maple Family

Leaves generally smaller than sugar maple, toothed, and with V-shaped notches, turning red. Bark flakier than sugar maple. Twigs and buds reddish. Flowers tiny and reddish in loose clusters, visible in the very early spring from a distance as a reddish haze around the tree. Fruits similar to sugar maple but red and in a tighter V. L 2½–4 in. T 60–90 ft.

Habitat: Deciduous woods; more tolerant of wet or poor soil than sugar maple.

Striped Maple

Acer pensylvanicum   /   Maple Family

Small tree or shrub. Leaves rounded at the base and toothed with very shallow notches, turning yellow. Bark of young trees green and white striped, becoming darker, but still distinctly striped with age. Fruits similar to sugar maple. Buds long and very red. Buds and bark of this tree are a favorite food of moose, giving it another common name, moosewood. L 5–7 in. T up to 30 ft.

Habitat: Very common in the understory along most of the trail.

Mountain Maple

Acer spicatum   /   Maple Family

Small tree or shrub. Leaves similar to striped maple but more coarsely toothed. Bark brown and not noticeably striped. Twigs and small branches show distinct mottling that goes from light brown near the trunk to reddish at the tips. Fruit similar to sugar maple. L 2½–41/2 in. T up to 20 ft.

Habitat: Common in the understory higher up in the mountains.

BROAD-LEAVED TREES

Common Lowbush Blueberry

Common Lowbush Blueberry   **Velvetleaf Blueberry**

Alpine Bilberry   **Alpine Bilberry**

Shrubs

Although there is no scientific difference between trees and shrubs, they have been divided into two sections to aid in identification.

Key
L = leaf length
H = bush height

Alternate Simple Leaves

Common Lowbush Blueberry
Vaccinium angustifolium / Heath Family

Small shrub. Leaves very finely toothed. Small, white (sometimes pinkish) bell-shaped flowers in a small cluster. Fruit a sweet, blue berry enjoyed by many animals (including humans!).
L ½–1 ¼ in. H 4–24 in.

Habitat: Dry rocky soil.

Similar Species: Mountain blueberry (Vaccinium boreale) (not pictured) is less than four inches tall and grows above tree line.

Velvetleaf Blueberry
Vaccinium myrtilloides / Heath Family

Similar to common lowbush blueberry. Leaves not serrated and hairy beneath. Young twigs also slightly hairy. Small bell-shaped greenish flowers. Fruit a blue berry, edible, but not as sweet as other blueberries. L ½–1 ¼ in. H 8–20 in.

Habitat: Moist or dry soil, bogs, and pond edges.

Similar Species: Common lowbush blueberry.

Alpine Bilberry
Vaccinium uliginosum / Heath Family

Low matted plant. Leaves almost round, bluish, turning purple in the fall. Small pink bell-shaped flowers. Fruit a sweet, dark blue or black berry. L ⅜–1 in. H 4–12 in.

Habitat: Open alpine areas.

SHRUBS

Mountain Cranberry

Mountain Cranberry

Labrador Tea

Leatherleaf

Crowberry

Crowberry

Mountain Cranberry
Vaccinium vitis-idaea / Heath Family

Creeping, mat-forming shrub. Leaves small leathery and evergreen. Tiny pink bell-shaped flowers. Edible fruit is bright red and quite sour. L ¼–⅜ in. H 4–8 in.

Habitat: Open alpine areas.

Labrador Tea
Ledum groenlandicum / Heath Family

Small erect shrub. Leathery evergreen leaves rolled under at the edges with dense orange hairs beneath. Twigs also hairy. Small white flowers in loose clusters at the top of the plant. The aromatic leaves can be used to make a tea, though large amounts of it may be toxic. (Make sure you positively identify it first!) L 1–2 in. H <3 ft.

Habitat: Acidic bogs and open alpine areas.

Leatherleaf
Chamaedaphne calyculata / Heath Family

Leathery evergreen leaves with small rusty scales beneath. Tiny, white bell-shaped flowers dangling along one side of stem. Fruit a dry capsule. L ½–2 in. H <4½ ft.

Habitat: Bogs, pond margins, and open alpine areas.

Crowberry
Empetrum nigrum / Crowberry Family

Matted alpine shrub with tiny needlelike evergreen leaves. Tiny, purple flowers. Fruit a black, sometimes waxy berry. L ¼ in. H <6 in.

Habitat: Open alpine areas.

SHRUBS

Meadowsweet

Mountain Holly

Beaked hazelnut

Speckled Alder

Speckled Alder

Meadowsweet

Spiraea alba / Rose Family

Egg-shaped, coarsely toothed leaves. Many white or occasionally pinkish flowers in a pyramid-shaped cluster. Twigs smooth and red brown. L 1–3 in. H 1–6 ft.

Habitat: Dry to wet meadows and fields.

Similar Species: Hardhack (Spirea tomentosa) has dark pink flowers and hairy leaves (not pictured).

Mountain Holly

Nemopanthus mucronata / Holly Family

Oval, smooth-edged leaves with distinctly purple stalks and a tiny needlelike tip. Inconspicuous greenish white flowers. Round, dark red fruit on long stalks. L 1–2 in. H 2–9 ft.

Habitat: Cool wet places.

Beaked Hazelnut

Corylus cornuta / Birch Family

Relatively broad, coarsely toothed leaves. Female flowers inconspicuous; male flowers in drooping catkins. Fruit an edible nut surrounded by a bristly husk that extends into a long beak. L 4–5 in. H 3–9 ft.

Habitat: Deciduous forests and forest edges.

Speckled Alder

Alnus incana / Birch Family

Tall shrub. Oval, toothed leaves with distinct, slightly sunken veins. Male flowers cylindrical and drooping; female flowers in small, erect cones that remain on the shrub throughout the winter. Bark dark with light, elongated speckles. Provide food for deer and moose. L 2–4 in. H 3–20 ft.

Habitat: Wet soils of stream and pond edges.

Alternate-leaved Dogwood

Red Raspberry   **Red Raspberry**

Alternate-leaved Dogwood

Cornus alternifolia / Dogwood Family

Tall shrub. Leaves glossy green with distinct, sunken veins that curve to meet the leaf edge on a tangent. Many small white flowers in a loose flat-topped cluster. Berrylike blue-black fruit on a reddish stem. Bark smooth becoming scaly with age. L 2–4 in. H 3–18 ft.

Habitat: Rich woods.

Prickly Gooseberry (not pictured)

Ribes cynosbati / Gooseberry Family

Small shrub. Leaves lobed somewhat like small maple leaves. Small, greenish yellow flowers in clusters of two or three. Flowering branches prickly. Fruit green or reddish and prickly. Stem with occasional spine at the joints. L 1–2 in. H 1–5 ft.

Habitat: Moist rocky woods.

Similar Species: Skunk currant (Ribes glandulosum) (not pictured) has stems without spines or prickles and bright red skunky-smelling fruit.

————————

Alternate Compound Leaves

Red Raspberry

Rubus idaeus / Rose Family

Familiar, thicket-forming shrub. Leaves with three or five leaflets pinnately compound. Flowers white. Stem whitened, prickly. Fruit a juicy, sweet, red berry that separates from the base leaving behind a hole in the fruit. L 4–6 in. H 3–6 ft.

Habitat: Open areas and forest clearings.

Similar Species: There are several species of raspberry and blackberry along the trail. The two listed here are the most common.

Common Blackberry

Common Blackberry

Pringle Herbarium/UVM

Poison Ivy

Sheep Laurel

Common Blackberry

Rubus alleghaniensis   /   Rose Family

Familiar, thicket-forming shrub. Leaves with three or five leaflets
palmately compound. Flowers white, slightly larger than raspberry.
Stem sometimes angled in cross-section, with stout thorns.
Fruit a sweet, black berry that does not separate from its base.
L 4–8 in. H 3–7 ft.

Habitat: Open areas and forest clearings.

Similar Species: See note above.

Poison Ivy

Toxicodendron radicans   /   Cashew (Sumac) Family

Erect or creeping shrub or vine. Extremely irritating; can cause
severe skin rashes. Leaves often glossy with three leaflets, the
uppermost extending on a distinct stalk above the lower two.
Leaflets with a few coarse teeth, turning conspicuously red in the
fall. Small greenish flowers loosely clumped along dangling stalks.
Small, white, berrylike fruit. L 2–4 in. H 1–3 ft.

Habitat: Roadsides and thickets. Uncommon along the trail
except at road crossings.

SHRUBS

Opposite Simple Leaves

Sheep Laurel

Kalmia angustifolia   /   Heath Family

Leathery, evergreen leaves often arranged in whorls of three.
Beautiful pink flowers clustered around the stem. Fruit a dry,
rounded capsule opening in five parts. Foliage poisonous
to livestock, giving another common name, lambkill.
L 1–2 in. H ½–3 ft.

Habitat: Wet and dry acidic soils.

Hobblebush

Wild Raisin

Maple-leaved Viburnum

Red Elderberry

Hobblebush
Viburnum alnifolium / Honeysuckle Family

Conspicuous shrub with pairs of large, round, finely toothed leaves. Stems sometimes arching over to root at the tip. Flowers in spring before leaves attain full size. White flowers in a large cluster. Tiny flowers in center of cluster, larger ones around the edge. Dark, purple, berrylike fruit. L 4–7 in. H 3–6 ft.

Habitat: Ubiquitous in all forest types along the trail except for krummholz.

Wild Raisin
Viburnum nudum var. cassinoides / Honeysuckle Family

Oval leaves with wavy, slightly toothed edges. Buds rusty orange. White flowers in a cluster resembling hobblebush except with no larger flowers on the cluster edges. Dark blue waxy berrylike fruit. L 3–5 in. H 2–10 ft.

Habitat: Wet woods and swamps; common at pond edges along the trail.

Maple-leaved Viburnum
Viburnum acerifolium / Honesuckle Family

Maple-like, coarsely toothed leaves. Small, white flowers in a cluster similar to wild raisin. Glossy, black, berrylike fruit. L 2½–5 in. H 3–6 ft.

Habitat: Moist or dry woods.

Opposite Compound Leaves

Red Elderberry
Sambucus racemosa / Honeysuckle Family

Erect shrub. Compound leaves with five to seven toothed leaflets. Leaf stalk purplish. Small, white flowers in a pyramid-shaped cluster. Fruit an inedible, red berry. L 5–8 in. H 3–9 ft.

Habitat: Rich woods and thickets.

Similar Species: Common elderberry (Sambucus canadensis) (not pictured) has edible, black berries in a flatter cluster.

Bunchberry

Partridgeberry

Partridgeberry

Creeping Snowberry

Flowers

Note that many of the species listed here are in bloom in the
early spring when the Long Trail system is closed for mud season.
Please respect the closures and prevent trail erosion by staying off
wet muddy trails. Flowers are arranged by color and petal number.

Key
P = plant height
F = flower width

White Flowers with Four Petals

Bunchberry
Cornus canadensis   /   Dogwood Family

Smooth, prominently veined, whorled leaves. Flower with four
petal-like bracts surrounding a group of small greenish flowers.
Most noticeable in the late summer and fall when it bears a tight
cluster of bright red fruits, which give it its name. Flowers June
to August. P 6 in. F 1 ½ in.

Habitat: Moist, often coniferous woods.

Partridgeberry
Mitchella repens   /   Madder Family

Creeping, sometimes mat-forming, evergreen plant with small,
round, shiny, opposite leaves. Flowers in pairs. Petals funnel-
shaped at the bottom and noticeably fringed near top. Fruit an
edible, asymmetrical, bright red berry. Flowers June to July.
P 3 in. F ½ in.

Habitat: Woods.

Creeping Snowberry
Gaultheria hispidula   /   Heath Family

Creeping plant with tiny, dark green, round evergreen leaves.
Tiny, white flowers. Fruit an edible, white berry. Flowers May to
June. P 3–12 in. F < ¼ in.

Habitat: Moist mountain woods.

WHITE FLOWERS

Tall Meadow Rue

Canada Mayflower

Goldthread

Three-toothed Cinquefoil

Tall Meadow Rue

Thalictrum pubescens   /   Buttercup Family

Tall, spindly plant with alternate compound leaves. Tiny clustered flowers with prominent stamens that look almost fluffy. Flowers June to July. P 3–8 in. F ¼ in.

Habitat: Wet woods and riverbanks.

Canada Mayflower (False Lily of the Valley)

Maianthemum canadense   /   Lily Family

Sometimes in dense colonies. Nonflowering stalks with a single smooth leaf are ubiquitous. Flowering stalks with two or three alternate clasping leaves. Small clusters of tiny white flowers. Fruit a red berry. Flowers May to July. P 3–6 in. F ¼ in.

Habitat: Woods.

White Flowers with Five Petals

Goldthread

Coptis trifolia   /   Buttercup Family

Single flower with five to seven petals and many stamens perched on slender stem. Evergreen leaves are three parted and very toothed. Thin, gold roots, visible if the soil around the base of the plant is pulled back slightly, give this plant its name. Roots can be boiled to make a mouthwash. Flowers May to July. P 3–6 in. F ¼ in.

Habitat: Wet woods and swamps, often with conifers.

Three-toothed Cinquefoil

Potentilla tridentata   /   Rose Family

Short, often alpine plant with several flowers on a branched stem. Evergreen, three-part leaves. Each leaflet with three teeth. Flowers June to Aug. P 2–3 in. F ½ in.

Habitat: Rocky open areas, often on mountaintops.

Starflower

Indian Pipe

Pringle Herbarium/UVM

Wintergreen

Shinleaf

Starflower

Trientalis borealis   /   Primrose Family

Bright, white, star-shaped flowers usually with seven petals.
One to two flowers on slender stems emerge from a whorl of
long narrow leaves. Flowers May to June (later on mountaintops).
P 3–9 in. F ¾ in.

Habitat: Cool moist woods.

Indian Pipe

Monotropa uniflora   /   Indian Pipe Family

Waxy white all over. Plant absorbs nutrients, with the help of a
closely associated root fungus, from decaying matter in the soil or
from the roots of other living plants. This unusual energy supply
accounts for the plant's lack of green chlorophyll, the pigment
that most plants use to get energy from sunlight. Bell-shaped,
nodding flower. Small, scalelike leaves along the stem. Flowers
June to September. P 4–10 in. F 1 in.

Habitat: Shady woods.

Wintergreen

Gaultheria procumbens   /   Heath Family

Tiny, bell-shaped flowers hang down below leaves. Evergreen
leaves with tiny teeth that smell strongly of wintergreen when
crushed. Older leaves can be used to make a tea. Fruit an
edible, mint-flavored, bright red berry. Flowers July to Aug.
P 3–6 in. F ¼ in.

Habitat: Dry, often coniferous woods.

Shinleaf

Pyrola elliptica   /   Pyrola Family

Nodding flowers attached at various point to a single stem.
Large (up to 3 in.) oval leaves at base of flower stem. Flowers June
to Aug. P 4–12 in. F ¾ in.

Habitat: Moist to dry woods.

WHITE FLOWERS

WHITE FLOWERS

Wild Sarsaparilla

Susan Shea

Dwarf Ginseng   **Sweet Cicely**

Diapensia

Wild Sarsaparilla
Aralia nudicaulis   /   Ginseng Family

Extremely common plant with conspicuous, three-parted leaves, each part with five toothed leaflets. Tiny flowers in ball-shaped clusters. Typically, three flowers cluster to a stem somewhere below the leaves. Fruit clusters of black berries. Extractions of the root used for medicinal purposes. Flowers May to June. P 20 in. F 2 in. (cluster)

Habitat: All woods.

Dwarf Ginseng
Panax trifolium   /   Ginseng Family

Inconspicuous plant except when blooming in the early summer. Three three-parted leaves whorled around stem. Tiny flowers clustered in a small ball. Flowers May to June. P 3–8 in. F < ¼ in.

Habitat: Deciduous woods.

Sweet Cicely
Osmorhiza claytonii   /   Parsley Family

Tall plant with conspicuous, finely divided leaves. Tiny flowers in loose clusters. Stem hairy. Flowers May to June. P 1–3 in. F ¼ in.

Habitat: Rich woods.

Diapensia
Diapensia lapponica   /   Diapensia Family

Low alpine plant takes on a dense, cushionlike form to protect itself from extreme wind and cold. Tiny, leathery evergreen leaves tufted onto stems. Endangered: only found in Vermont on the summit of Mt. Mansfield. Flowers June to July. P 3 in. F ½ in.

Habitat: Exposed alpine summits.

Mountain Sandwort

Foamflower

Miterwort

False Solomon's Seal

False Solomon's Seal

Mountain Sandwort
Arenaria groenlandica   /   Pink Family

Low, tufted plant with needlelike leaves crowded around stem, sometimes forms large mats. Often several flowers to a stem. Common in disturbed alpine areas, especially along trails. Flowers June to Aug. P 2–5 in. F ½ in.

Habitat: Alpine summits.

Foamflower
Tiarella cordifolia   /   Saxifrage Family

Low plant with hairy, maple-shaped leaves. Delicate flowers form "foamy" cluster at the top of a single stem. Flowers April to June. P 6–12 in. F ¼ in.

Habitat: Rich woods.

Miterwort (Bishop's Cap)
Mitella diphylla   /   Saxifrage Family.

Plant and basal leaves very similar to foamflower. Tiny, fringed flowers spread out along stem. One pair of opposite leaves on flower stalk. Flowers April to May. P 8–18 in. F ¼ in.

Habitat: Rich woods.

White Flowers with Six Petals

False Solomon's Seal
Smilacina racemosa   /   Lily Family

Plant with medium (3–6 in. long), elliptical, opposite, prominently veined leaves on unbranched stem. Small flowers in an arching elongated cluster. Fruit are red berries. Flowers May to July. P 1–3 ft. F ¾ in.

Habitat: Rich woods.

Similar Species: True Solomon's seal (Polygonatum pubescens) with green flowers paired along the stem.

WHITE FLOWERS

Wild Leeks

Wild Leeks

Whorled Aster

White Snakeroot

Susan Shea

White Baneberry

White Baneberry

Wild Leeks (Ramps)
Allium tricoccum / Lily Family

Large (6–12 in. long) smooth, bright green, elliptical leaves appear in early spring and wither before flowering time; edible onionlike bulb. Tiny, star-shaped flowers in a spherical cluster perched atop a long slender stem. This plant, called winooski by the native Abenaki, lends its name to many local landmarks. Flowers June to July. P 6–18 in. F ¼ in.

Habitat: Rich moist woods.

White Flowers with Many Petals

Whorled Aster
Aster acuminatus / Aster Family

Sharply pointed, coarsely toothed leaves appear whorled; hairy stem. Flowers sometimes tinged purple in loosely branching cluster. Flowers July to Sept. P 1–2 ft. F 1–½ in.

Habitat: Woods, common at mid-elevations in mountains.

White Snakeroot
Eupatorium rugosum / Aster Family

Leaves pointed at tip, broadly rounded at base. Tiny flowers in branched, flat-topped clusters. Flowers July to Sept. P 1–4 ft. F ¼ in.

Habitat: Rich woods.

White Baneberry (Doll's Eyes)
Actaea alba / Buttercup Family

Leaves coarsely toothed and divided. Tiny, filamentous flowers in slightly elongated clusters. Fruit a white berry with conspicuous dark dots on thick stalks reminiscent of old-fashioned doll's eyes. Berries poisonous. Flowers May to June. P 1–3 ft. F ¼ in.

Habitat: Rich woods.

Similar Species: Red baneberry (Actaea rubra) (not pictured) with similar flowers and red berries.

WHITE FLOWERS

Hepatica

Canada Violet

Dutchmen's Breeches

Hepatica
Hepatica acutiloba   /   Buttercup Family

Three-lobed leaves at the base of the plant. Old leaves become mottled resembling liver (hence the name). Flowers with five to twelve petals are solitary on the stalk. On the trail, flowers are most often white but can also be pink or purple. Flowers April to May. P 2–6 in. F 1 in.

Habitat: Rich Woods.

White Flowers with Irregular Petals

Canada Violet
Viola canadensis   /   Violet Family

Alternate, heart-shaped leaves on slender stem. Flowers yellow inside, tinged with purple outside. Flowers May to July. P 6–18 ft. F 1 in.

Habiat: Rich woods.

Dutchmen's Breeches
Dicentra cucullaria   /   Fumitory Family

Very finely divided, fragile leaves wither soon after flowering. Odd-shaped flowers resemble their namesake hung on a laundry line. Flowers April to May. P 4–12 in. F ½–1 in.

Habitat: Rich woods.

Similar Species: Squirrel corn (Dicentra canadensis) (not pictured). Flowers more heart-shaped; yellow cornlike tubers at plant base.

White or Sometimes White Flowers Listed Elsewhere

- **Wild oats** (yellow)
- **Painted trillium** (pink)
- **Mountain wood sorrel** (pink)
- **Spring beauty** (pink)
- **Twinflower** (pink)
- **Twisted stalk** (see rose twisted stalk, pink)

Marsh Marigold

Bluebead Lily

Wild Oats

Trout Lily

Yellow Flowers with Five Petals

Marsh Marigold
Caltha palustris / Buttercup Family

Heart-shaped, long-stalked leaves emerging from plant base. Showy flowers with mostly five but up to nine petals. Flowers April to June. P 6–24 in. F ½–1 ½ in.

Habitat: Wet woods, meadows, and swamps.

Yellow Flowers with Six Petals

Bluebead Lily
Clintonia borealis / Lily Family

Large, dark green, smooth, elliptical leaves cupped around the base of a leafless flower stalk. Three to eight nodding flowers. Fruit a conspicuous dark blue, slightly poisonous berry. Flowers May to July. P 6–16 in. F ¾–1 in.

Habitat: Woods from lowlands up to mountain forests.

Trout Lily
Erythronium americanum / Lily Family

Elliptical leaves mottled with brown, perhaps resembling its namesake, wither soon after flowering. Leaves often carpet the forest floor in early spring. Nodding flowers on leafless stems. Flowers April to May. P 4–8 in. F 1–2 in.

Habitat: Woods.

Wild Oats
Uvularia sessilifolia / Lily Family

Delicate, smooth, parallel-veined leaves on branched stem. Nodding, solitary, light yellow flower. Flowers May to June. P 4–12 in. F ½–1 in.

Habitat: Woods.

Similar Species: Large-flowered bellwort.

Large-flowered Bellwort

Zigzag Goldenrod

Large-leaved Goldenrod

Rough-stemmed Goldenrod

Large-flowered Bellwort
Uvularia grandiflora / Lily Family

Plant similar to wild oats, but bigger. Large, yellow flowers with spiraling petals. Flowers April to May. P 1–2 ft. F 2 in.

Habitat: Rich woods.

Similar Species: Wild oats.

Yellow Flowers with Many Petals

Zigzag Goldenrod
Solidago flexicaulis / Aster Family

Egg-shaped, sharply toothed leaves with flowers in the axils where the leaf attaches to the stem. Stems bend at each leaf giving it its name. Flowers Aug. to Oct. P 1–3 ft. F ¼ in.

Habitat: Rich woods.

Large-leaved Goldenrod
Solidago macrophylla / Aster Family

Basal leaves large, egg shaped, and long stalked. Flowers in an elongated, unbranched cluster. Flowers July to Sept. P ½–3 ft. F ¼–½ in.

Habitat: Moist subalpine woods.

Rough-stemmed Goldenrod
Solidago rugosa / Aster Family

Very tall, hairy-stemmed plant. Leaves toothed, slightly fuzzy, and without three noticeable veins. Flowers Aug.–Oct. P 1–7 ft. F ¼ in.

Habitat: Roadsides and fields.

Similar Species: Late goldenrod (Soldago gigantea) and Canada goldenrod (Solidago canadensis) (not pictured) both have similar flower clusters and height, but are not nearly so hairy.

Early Yellow Violet

Red Trillium

Spotted Touch-me-not

Yellow Flowers with Irregular Petals

Early Yellow Violet
Viola rotundifolia / Violet Family

Heart-shaped leaves at the base of the plant. Leaves are one inch long at flowering time; over the summer they become larger and rounder. Flowers April to May. P 3–4 in. F ½ in.

Habitat: Rich woods.

Yellow Flowers Listed Elsewhere

• **Pale touch-me-not** (see spotted touch-me-not, orange and red)

Orange and Red Flowers

Red Trillium (Wake Robin)
Trillium erectum / Lily Family

Flower with three petals; three broad leaves whorled around the stem. Stinky flowers have the color and smell of raw meat to attract carrion flies, which pollinate them. One of our most noticeable spring flowers. Flowers May to June. P 8–16 in. F 2–3 in.

Habitat: Moist, slightly enriched woods.

Similar Species: Painted trillium (Trillium undulatum) is a white flower with a dark pink center.

Spotted Touch-me-not (Jewelweed)
Impatiens capensis / Touch-me-not Family

Irregular, orange flower hangs below delicate, coarsely toothed leaves. Fruit is a dry pod that releases its seeds explosively. Flowers July to Sept. P 2–5 ft. F 1 in.

Habitat: Wet woods, streams, and roadsides.

Similar Species: Pale touch-me-not (Impatiens pallida) (not pictured) has yellow flowers.

ORANGE AND RED FLOWERS

Wild Red Columbine   **Painted Trillium**

Mountain Wood Sorrel

Wild Red Columbine

Aquilegia canadensis   /   Buttercup Family

Alternate, compound leaves with rounded, toothed leaflets.
Delicate, nodding flowers. Petals shaped into elongated tubes
specially adapted for pollination by hummingbirds. Flowers
April to June. P 1–2 ft. F 1–½ in.

Habitat: Rocky slopes and ledges.

Pink Flowers with Three Petals

Painted Trillium

Trillium undulatum   /   Lily Family

White flowers with dark pink veins and center. Three egg-shaped,
slightly stalked leaves in whorled around flower stem. Flowers
May to June. P 8–16 in. F 1–2 in.

Habitat: Mixed and deciduous woods, sometimes quite high up
on mountain trails.

Similar Species: Red trillium (Trillium erectum).

Pink Flowers with Five Petals

Mountain Wood Sorrel
(Common Wood Sorrel)

Oxalis acetosella   /   Wood Sorrel Family

White flower with pink veins. Cloverlike leaves have three heart-
shaped leaflets. Often forms large patches in higher elevation
forests. Leaves edible in small quantities but large amounts
should be avoided as they contain poisonous oxalic acid.
Flowers June to Aug. P 3–5 in. F 1 ½ in.

Habitat: Moist coniferous and mixed woods, often on
mountain slopes.

PINK FLOWERS

Spring Beauty

Pringle Herbarium/UVM

Twinflower   **Pink Lady's Slipper**

Rose Twisted Stalk

Spring Beauty

Claytonia virginica / Purslane Family

One of the earliest spring flowers. Narrow, dark green leaves paired on a delicate flower stem. Flowers with pink (sometimes white) veins that guide pollinating bees and flies into the center of the flower. Flowers close when cold or dark to protect them against early spring weather. Flowers April to May. P 3–8 in. F ½–1 in.

Habitat: Deciduous woods.

Twinflower

Linnaea borealis / Honeysuckle Family

Small, round, opposite leaves paired along trailing stem. Small twin pink or white flowers perched atop a delicate stem. Reputedly the favorite flower of the great taxonomist Linnaeus. Flowers June to Aug. P 3–6 in. F ½ in.

Habitat: Cool, usually coniferous woods.

PINK FLOWERS

Pink Flowers with Six Petals

Rose Twisted Stalk

Streptopus roseus / Lily Family

Alternate, prominently veined leaves; stems usually branched. Bell-shaped flowers hang below the leaves on bent (twisted) stalks. Flowers May to June. P 1–2 ft. F ½ in.

Habitat: Moist slightly enriched woods.

Similar Species: Twisted stalk (Streptopus amplexifolius) has white flowers and is a larger plant.

Pink Flowers with Irregular Petals

Pink Lady's Slipper

Cypripedium acaule / Orchid Family

Exotic-looking, uncommon flower with large, pink, pouchlike petal (the slipper). Two broad leaves surround the base of the flower stalk. Flowers May to June. P 6–15 in. F 1 ½–2 ½ in.

Habitat: Acidic woods, bogs.

Spotted Joe-Pye Weed

Susan Shea

Pringle Herbarium/UVM

Virginia Waterleaf   **Harebell**

Pink Flowers with Many Petals

Spotted Joe-Pye Weed

Eupatorium maculatum / Aster Family

Plant with coarsely toothed leaves in whorls of four or five around the deep purple stem. Tiny flowers in a large, hairy-looking cluster. Flowers July to Sept. P 2–6 ft. F ¼ in.

Habitat: Wet meadows and pond shores.

Pink Flowers Listed Elsewhere

• **Hepatica** (white)

Purple and Blue Flowers with Five Petals

Virginia Waterleaf

Hydrophyllum virginianum / Waterleaf Family

Coarsely toothed, compound leaves. Clustered, bell-shaped flowers with noticeably long stamens. Young plants reportedly used as salad by early settlers. Flowers May to July.
P 1–2 ½ ft. F ½ in.

Habitat: Rich moist woods.

Harebell

Campanula rotundifolia / Bluebell Family

Plant with long narrow leaves and thin delicate stalks. Nodding bell-shaped flower. Flowers June to Sept. P 4–30 in. F ½–1 in.

Habitat: Rocky ledges and alpine areas.

PURPLE AND BLUE FLOWERS

GREEN AND BROWN FLOWERS

Blue Cohosh

Heart-leaved Aster

Wild Ginger

Purple and Blue Flowers with Six Petals

Blue Cohosh
Caulophyllum thalictroides   /   Barberry Family

Leaves appear bluish and shriveled when young, becoming more open and green. Odd-looking flowers in loose clusters. Plant reportedly used to stimulate childbirth, but may be poisonous. Flowers April to May. P 1–2 ½ ft. F ½–1 in.

Habitat: Rich woods.

Purple and Blue Flowers with Many Petals

Heart-leaved Aster
Aster cordifolius   /   Aster Family

Lower leaves large, heart-shaped, and conspicuously toothed. Small flowers in a loose cluster. Flowers Aug. to Oct. P 1–5 ft. F ½ in.

Habitat: Woods and thickets.

Purple and Blue Flowers Listed Elsewhere

• **Hepatica** (white)

Green and Brown Flowers with Three Petals

Wild Ginger
Asarum canadense   /   Birthwort Family

One or two large, kidney-shaped leaves on long furry stems. Inconspicuous brown flowers hidden below the leaves. Pollinated by flies looking for carrion in early spring. Root with a distinct ginger flavor (although unrelated to the common spice) often candied in pioneer days. Flowers April to May. P 6–12 in. F 1–2 in.

Habitat: Rich woods.

GREEN AND BROWN FLOWERS

Plants and Fungi

GREEN AND BROWN FLOWERS

Indian Cucumber

Solomon's Seal

Jack-in-the-pulpit

False Hellebore

Green and Brown Flowers with Six Petals

Indian Cucumber
Medeola virginiana   /   Lily Family

Tall stem with two whorls of leaves. Lower whorl of five to eleven
elongated leaves; upper whorl of three to four smaller leaves.
Inconspicuous greenish flowers nod below upper whorl of leaves.
Root edible. Flowers May to June. P 1–2 ft. F ½–1 in.

Habitat: Moist deciduous woods.

Solomon's Seal
Polygonatum pubescens   /   Lily family

Slender stem with opposite elongated leaves. Prominently veined
leaves hairy underneath. Pairs of greenish flowers hang down
below each leaf. Flowers May to July. P 1 ½–3 in. F ¼–½ in.

Habitat: Moist woods.

Similar Species: False Solomon's seal (Smilacina racemosa)
has an elongated cluster of white flowers.

False Hellebore
Veratrum viride   /   Lily Family

Stout stem with large, prominent, ribbed leaves. Large branching
cluster of yellow-green flowers. Very common in mountain
wetlands. Flowers June to July. P 2–6 ft. F ¼–½ in.

Habitat: Swamps and wet woods.

Green and Brown Flowers with Irregular Petals

Jack-in-the-pulpit
Arisaema triphyllum   /   Arum Family

Erect leaves with three leaflets. Tiny densely packed flowers
wrapped by a specialized purple- or green-striped structure called
a spathe. Pollinated by small insects, which can only exit from the
base of the flower. Flowers May to July. P 1–3 ft. F 2–4 in.

Habitat: Rich wet woods.

GREEN AND BROWN FLOWERS

Wood Nettle

Common Polypody

Sensitive Fern

Wood Nettle

Laportea canadensis   /   Nettle Family

Erect plant with stinging hairs. Leaves alternate and egg shaped.
Tiny, green flowers with indistinguishable petals on arching
branches. Flowers July to Sept. P 2–4 ft. F < ¼ in.

Habitat: Moist woods and stream banks.

Ferns

An important characteristic for identifying ferns is how divided the
leaf is. An undivided leaf has leaves without smaller subsections.
A once-divided leaf has leaflets arranged along the main axis of
the leaf stem. A twice-divided leaf has tiny leaflets arranged on
the axes of larger leaflets, which are in turn arranged on the main
axis of the leaf. A thrice-divided or lacy leaf has one more set of
leaf subdivisions. Ferns are generally arranged by how divided the
leaves are. Another important fern characteristic is the shape and
location of the sori. These are the structures that hold the spores,
by which a fern reproduces. They can be either on the backs of
the regular leaves or on specialized leaves with no green tissue.

Key

P = Blade, the length of the leafy, expanded portion of the frond,
not including stem.

Common Polypody

Polypodium virginianum

Small, evergreen, once-divided fern. Round sori on the backs
of regular leaves. P 4–15 in.

Habitat: Rocks and rocky woods.

Sensitive Fern

Onoclea sensibilis

Once-divided, spreading fern. Black, beadlike sori are on a separate
erect stalk and often very noticeable against the snow in wintertime.
Plant sensitive to early frost, hence its name. P 1–2 1 / 5 ft.

Habitat: Wet open areas and wooded swamps.

FERNS

Christmas Fern

Long Beech Fern

Maidenhair Fern

Bracken Fern

Royal Fern

Christmas Fern
Polystichum acrostichoides

Evergreen, once-divided fern with scaly stem. Leaflets have a thumblike projection pointing up the stem. Round sori on backs of regular leaves. P 8–24 in.

Habitat: Deciduous woods and rocky slopes.

Long Beech Fern
Thelypteris phegopteris

Small, almost twice-divided fern. Lowest leaflets stick up like rabbit ears. Round sori on the back of regular leaves. P 8–18 in.

Habitat: Moist woods and cliffs.

Maidenhair Fern
Adiantum pedatum

Unusual-looking, delicate, fan-shaped, twice-divided fern with wiry, black stem. Elongated sori on the outer edges of the leaflets. P 1–2 ½ ft.

Habitat: Rich woods.

Bracken Fern
Pteridium aquilinum

Large, coarse fern mostly twice divided. Generally triangular leaf divided into three main parts. Elongated sori on the edges of the leaflets. P 1–5 ft.

Habitat: Dry to moist woods and clearings.

Royal Fern
Osmunda regalis

Large, twice-divided fern. Leaflets widely spaced. Sori massed on the ends of separate leaves. P 2–5 ft.

Habitat: Bogs, swamps, and low wet woods.

FERNS

Interrupted Fern

Cinnamon Fern

Ostrich Fern

New York Fern

Interrupted Fern

Osmunda claytoniana

Large, twice-divided fern, leaves in clumps. Sori massed in the middle of green leaves "interrupting" them. P 2–4 ft.

Habitat: Low wet woods, swamps, and roadsides.

Cinnamon Fern

Osmunda cinnamomea

Very similar to interrupted fern except that sori are on separate erect stalks arranged in the middle of a clump of green leaves. Leaf stalks with distinct orange-brown sori and hairy when young. P 2–5 ft.

Habitat: Swamps, stream banks and moist woods.

Ostrich Fern

Matteuccia struthiopteris

One of our largest ferns with twice-divided, broad, coarse leaves arranged in a distinctive vase shape. Sori on separate stiff woody stalks. P 2–5 ft.

Habitat: Floodplains and wooded swamps.

Marginal Wood Fern (not pictured)

Dryopteris marginalis

Twice-divided fern. Leaves arranged in clumps with brown scales on the stalks. Round sori on the back edge (margin) of each leaflet. P 1–2 ft.

Habitat: Rocky woods.

New York Fern

Thelypteris noveboracensis

Delicate fern whose leaf narrows at the bottom and at the top. Round sori on the backs of the leaflets. P 1–2 ft.

Habitat: Moist deciduous woods.

Intermediate Fern   **Hay-scented Fern**

Running Clubmoss

Intermediate Wood Fern
Dryopteris intermedia

One of our most common ferns. Evergreen almost thrice-divided leaves arranged in clumps. Brown scales on leaf stalks. Round sori on the back of each leaflet. P 1 ½–3 ft.

Habitat: Woods.

Similar Species: Mountain wood fern (Dryopteris campyloptera) (not pictured) has a slight difference in the structure of the lowest leaflets, but otherwise looks the same. Grows at higher elevations.

Hay-scented Fern
Dennstaedtia punctilobula

Very lacy fern. Sori on the back edge of the leaflets. Leaves are very aromatic when crushed. P 1–2 ½ ft.

Habitat: Open woods and clearings.

Clubmosses

Clubmosses are small, mosslike plants that resemble tiny trees or pipe cleaners stuck in the ground. Like ferns, they reproduce by releasing tiny spores instead of seeds. The spores are either collected on erect clubs, which stand up above the plant, or are densely clustered on the backs of the leaves.

Key
H = plant height

Running Clubmoss
Lycopodium clavatum   /   Clubmoss Family

Resembles bristly, green pipe cleaners. Stalks run along the ground and also stand erect. Spore club on a long stalk above the plant. H 4–8 in.

Habitat: Dry or rocky acidic woods.

Tree Clubmoss

Shining Clubmoss

Sphagnum

Big Redstem Moss

Tree Clubmoss (Princess Pine)

Lycopodium obscurum   /   Clubmoss Family

Erect stalk with several many-forked flattened branches all covered with tiny needlelike leaves. Spore club close to the top-most branch. Often used for winter decorations. H 3–12 in.

Habitat: Moist woods and bog edges.

Shining Clubmoss

Lycopodium lucidulum

Single or only occasionally branched, erect stalks. Leaves larger and fleshier than the previous two species. Spores on the leaf backs not on erect clubs. H 3–6 in.

Habitat: Moist woods; common in montane spruce-fir forests along the trail.

MOSSES

Mosses

Mosses are small plants that lack distinct veins to carry water and nutrients. A small representation of the diversity of mosses along the trail is shown here.

Sphagnum

Sphagnum spp.

Common moss of boggy areas. Star shaped when viewed from the top. Various species, some with different colorations, occur on the trail.

Habitat: Wet hollows and bogs, especially in spruce-fir forest.

Big Redstem Moss

Pleurozium schreberi

One of our most common mosses with conspicuous red stems.

Habitat: Found on soil in dry open woods and in wet coniferous forests.

MUSHROOMS

Haircap Moss

Alex Kopista

Turkey Tail

Artist's Conk

Tinder Conk

Haircap Moss
Polytrichum spp.

A small, stiff, wiry moss with thin threads standing erect above the green foliage.

Habitat: Wet soils throughout, particularly in the spruce-fir forest.

Stairstep Moss (not pictured)
Hylocomnium splendens

Stiff and wiry with flat, ferny branches coming out at regular, steplike intervals from the stem.

Habitat: Common in spruce-fir forest and in damp ravines.

Mushrooms

Mushrooms are not plants at all, but are instead classified as fungi.

Key
W = plant width

Turkey Tail
Trametes versicolor

Striking, bracket-forming fungus striped in concentric bands that range from gray to reddish brown. Visible year-round. W 1–3 in.

Habitat: Hardwood logs and stumps.

Artist's Conk
Ganoderma applanatum

Large, bracket-forming, gray to brown woody fungus. Often used as a medium for carving. Visible year-round. W < 20 in.

Habitat: Living or dead hardwood trees.

Tinder Conk
Fomes fomentarius

Very common bracket fungus. Light to dark gray, half conical. Visible year-round. W < 6 in.

Habitat: Dead hardwood trees and logs.

MUSHROOMS

MUSHROOMS

Birch Polypore

Russula

Platterful Mushroom

Alex Kopista

Fly Agaric

King Bolete

Birch Polypore
Piptoporus betulinus

Rounded, thick, semicircular, light gray to brown bracket fungus. Visible year-round. W < 9 in.

Habitat: Dead birch trees.

Russula
Russula emetica

Shiny, bright red, convex to flat caps. White stalk. Poisonous. Visible Aug. to Sept. W 2–4 in. H 2 ½ in.

Habitat: Soil or rotten wood.

Platterful Mushroom
Tricholomopsis platyphylla

Abundant, light gray-brown, fleshy mushroom. Convex, flattening and splitting with age. Visible June. W 2 ½–8 in. H < 6 in.

Habitat: Logs and stumps.

Fly Agaric
Amanita muscaria

Flat to slightly convex, yellow-orange caps covered with white, cottony bumps. Very poisonous. Visible June to Sept. W 2 ½–8 in. H < 6 in.

Habitat: On the ground in woods.

King Bolete
Boletus edulis

Large, soft, spongy mushroom. Cap tan to red brown. Stalk stout and beige. Visible June to Oct. W 4–8 in. H < 6 in.

Habitat: On the ground in coniferous or mixed woods.

MUSHROOMS

LICHENS

Old Man's Beard

Reindeer Lichen

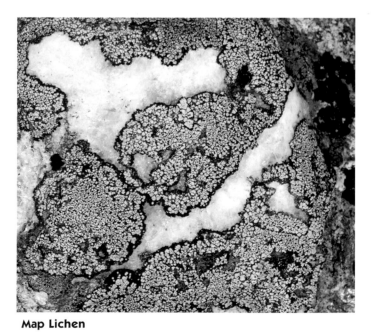

Map Lichen

Lichens

Although they appear to be individual species, lichens are actually two organisms, algae and fungi, that are mutually dependent on each other. Each lichen species is a unique pair of one alga and one fungus. The fungus provides structure while the alga provides energy through photosynthesis.

Old Man's Beard

Usnea spp.

Gray-white, hairlike lichen that hangs down in long strands from living and dead trees. If a single strand is pulled apart, the outer sheath breaks, but the strong inner cord remains intact.

Habitat: On trees living and dead.

Reindeer Lichen

Cladina rangiferina

Rather stiff, gray-white, very branched lichen. Each branch looks almost like a miniature tree.

Habitat: Sandy soil in woodlands and thin soil over rocks.

Map Lichen

Rhizocarpon geographicum

A thick yellowish crust cracked into flakes. Black underneath.

Habitat: On rocks above timberline.

Green Mountain Club

The mission of the Green Mountain Club is to make the Vermont mountains play a larger part in the life of the people by protecting and maintaining the Long Trail system and fostering, through education, the stewardship of Vermont's hiking trails and mountains.

For information, call (802)244-7037 or visit www.greenmountainclub.org

Part V:

The Animals of the Long Trail

The Animals of the Long Trail

Mammals

For most hikers, mammals are harder to spot than birds or insects. Although you may not often see them, once you know what to look for, their signs abound. Tracks frequently crisscross the trail; shoots show signs of nibbling; and the chattering of a squirrel echoes down from the canopy. The mammals listed here range from the commonplace squirrels to the elusive but iconic bobcat and fisher. They are arranged by family: shrew, rabbit, rodent, weasel, dog, cat, bear, and deer.

Key
L = length from nose to tail tip

MAMMALS

Snowshoe Hare

Chipmunk

Red Squirrel

Short-tailed Shrew (not pictured)

Blarina brevicauda / Shrew Family

Small, rounded animal with gray fur, pointy nose, and very short tail. Active day and night. Generally a four-print bounding track, sometimes with a slight tail drag. L 3½–5 in.

Habitat: Deciduous and mixed forests and open areas in loose leaf litter and low vegetation.

Snowshoe Hare

Lepus americanus / Rabbit Family

Very large rabbit with oversized feet to give flotation in snow. Light brown in summer; white in winter. Large four-print bounding track often seen in snow. L 15–21 in.

Habitat: Coniferous and mixed forests with brushy areas.

Chipmunk

Tamias striatus / Rodent Family

Familiar animal with reddish brown sides and back, gray stripe from crown to back, and black-and-white stripes on sides. Not active most of the winter except for occasional forays to their food stores. Small four-print bounding track. L 8–11 in.

Habitat: Brushy areas, primarily in deciduous forests.

Red Squirrel

Tamiasciurus hudsonicus / Rodent Family

Small, rusty-red squirrel with fluffy tail. Very territorial, often emits a loud chatter when hikers (and others!) come near. Eats red spruce buds. Often clips off the tips of the branches to eat the buds and leaves them in a pile under the tree. L 12 in.

Habitat: Coniferous and mixed forest.

Gray Squirrel

Beaver

White-footed Mouse

Southern Red-backed Vole

Gray Squirrel

Sciurus carolinensis / Rodent Family

Familiar, gray animal with long fluffy tail. Builds large leafy nests
often visible in treetops. Eats nuts, primarily acorns, walnuts,
and hickories. L 18–20 in.

Habitat: Deciduous forest with adequate food trees,
also residential areas.

Beaver

Castor canadensis / Rodent Family

Dark brown, thick, waterproof fur and a large, scaly,
paddle-shaped tail. Tail is used to store fat, as a swimming aid,
and for support when on land. Mainly nocturnal.
Common sign include cut logs, dams, and lodges. L 3–4 ft.

Habitat: Brooks, streams, and ponds.

White-footed Mouse

Peromyscus leucopus / Rodent Family

One of the most common mammals along the trail, though
infrequently seen. Brown above; stomach, throat, and feet are
white. Track is a four-footed hopping pattern commonly seen
in the snow. Nocturnal. L 6–9 in. (including tail)

Habitat: Interiors and edges of mixed and deciduous forest .

Similar Species: Deer mouse (not pictured) is very similar to the
white-footed mouse, though more common in coniferous forests.

Southern Red-backed Vole

Clethrionomys gapperi / Rodent Family

Distinctive, reddish brown back. Body rounder than a mouse,
with a shorter tail and smaller ears. Track is a hopping pattern
where the front and back prints often merge to appear
two footed. In winter, vole trails commonly lead under the snow.
Mainly nocturnal. L 4–8 in.

Habitat: Cool moist forests.

Similar Species: Several other similar species of voles and
lemmings occur on the trail, but they are not as common.

MAMMALS

Porcupine

MAMMALS

Fisher

Short-tailed Weasel

Mink

Porcupine

Erethizon dorsatum / Rodent Family

Distinctive, slow-moving animal. Quills, actually highly modified hairs, cover the animal. Feeds on foliage and inner bark of trees, particularly hemlock and pine. Can cause considerable damage to trees and wooden structures (including shelters). Mostly nocturnal. L 26–41 in.

Habitat: Mixed and coniferous forests with adequate den sites in rock ledges or trees.

Fisher

Martes pennanti / Weasel Family

Our largest forestland weasel. Extremely competent predator. One of the few things that can kill porcupines. Also eats snowshoe hare, birds, deer, and carrion. Track variable. Often similar to short-tailed weasel, but much larger. Nocturnal. L 33–41 in.

Habitat: Coniferous and mixed forests.

Short-tailed Weasel (Ermine)

Mustela erminea / Weasel Family

In summer, coat is brown above and white underneath. In winter, all white with black tail tip. Feeds on mice, voles, and other small mammals. Track is a two-footed hopping pattern. Distance between track sets alternates short and long. L 7–14 in.

Habitat: Forests and open areas with dense brush.

Similar Species: Long-tailed weasel (Mustela fremata) (not pictured) is bigger, but not as common.

Mink

Mustela vison / Weasel Family

Long, thin, dark, curious weasel. Feeds on a wide variety of prey, including small mammals, birds, fish, and frogs. Nocturnal. L 18–29 in.

Habitat: Streams, rivers, lakeshores, and other wetlands.

MAMMALS

MAMMALS

Steven D. Faccio

Red Fox

Susan C. Morse

Coyote

Susan C. Morse

Bobcat

Susan C. Morse

Black Bear

Red Fox
Vulpes vulpes / Dog Family

Secretive animal. Reddish brown back and sides, bushy white-tipped tail, pointy ears. Feeds on a wide variety of food from insects, to small mammals, to berries. Track is alternating prints nearly in a line. L 32–45 in.

Habitat: Prefers a mix of forest and open land.

Similar Species: Gray fox (Urocyon cinereoargenteus) (not pictured) is much less commonly seen.

Coyote
Canis latrans / Dog Family

Gray to brown above, paler underneath, bushy tail. Its call, a long series of yipping barks, is occasionally heard on quiet nights on the trail. Track similar to a dog's, typically alternating between walking and trotting. Nocturnal. L 42–53 in.

Habitat: Forest edges and fields. Habitat has expanded greatly in New England over the last century.

Bobcat
Lynx rufus / Cat Family

Gray to reddish brown mottled fur above, lighter below. Very rarely seen. Feeds on snowshoe hare, squirrels, and other small mammals and birds. Track similar to a house cat, though twice the size. Nocturnal. L 26–50 in.

Habitat: Deciduous and mixed forests often in rocky, brushy, or swampy areas.

Black Bear
Ursus americanus / Bear Family

Generally black in our area. Rarely seen in Vermont, though claw marks on beech trees and other signs are quite common. Feeds on a wide variety of berries, nuts, vegetation, carrion, small mammals, and human garbage when available. Inactive in winter. Mostly nocturnal. L 65–75 in.

Habitat: Forested areas.

MAMMALS / BIRDS

Steven D. Faccio

White-tailed Deer

Steven D. Faccio

Moose

Steven D. Faccio

Broad-winged Hawk

White-tailed Deer

Odocoileus virginianus / Deer Family

Reddish brown with tail that is prominently white when erect.
Feeds on foliage, twigs, bark, grasses, ferns, and other vegetation.
L 46–82 in.

Habitat: Forests and forest edges. In heavy snow, will pack down
snow and seek shelter in groups in stands of coniferous trees
known as deeryards.

Moose

Alces alces

Bulky creature with humped back. Coat dark brown. Feeds on
leaves, twigs, bark, aquatic vegetation, and grasses. Piles of
cylindrical pellets up to one inch long commonly seen.
L >100 in.

Habitat: Swamps, ponds (particularly in summer), coniferous
and mixed forests.

Birds

Wherever you hike, birds, sometimes seen only as splashes
of color flitting in the treetops, will accompany you. The birds
in this guide are arranged in the traditional manner. Falcons
are first, followed by grouse, owls, woodpeckers, and finally
the numerous songbirds.

Key:
L = length from beak to tail tip

Broad-winged Hawk

Buteo platypterus / Family: Hawk
Most likely hawk that would be seen along the trail.
Underwings generally white with dark edges. L 15 in.

Habitat: Decidous or mixed woods; most abundant during
fall migration.

MAMMALS / BIRDS

BIRDS

Elinor Osborn/www.agpix.com/osborn/

Ruffed Grouse

Steven D. Faccio

Barred Owl

Steven D. Faccio

Yellow-bellied Sapsucker

Elinor Osborn/www.agpix.com/osborn/

Elinor Osborn/www.agpix.com/osborn/

Downy Woodpecker

Hairy Woodpecker

Ruffed Grouse

Bonasa umbellus   /   Family: Grouse

Frequently heard on the trail. If surprised on a nearby nest, the bird will stagger through the woods with a "broken wing" display to lure potential predators away from the chicks. Makes a low-pitched drumming noise that gets progressively faster. L 17 in.

Habitat: Deciduous and mixed forest with dense understory.

Barred Owl

Strix varia   /   Family: Owl

Our most common owl, mostly heard and not seen. Dark bars on its chest and neck. Occasionally heard during the daytime. Often thought to sing "Who cooks for you, who cooks for you all?" L 21 in.

Habitat: Dense coniferous and mixed forest.

Yellow-bellied Sapsucker

Sphyrapicus varius   /   Family: Woodpecker

Red forehead and chin (forehead only in females). Drills neatly spaced holes in trees to eat the sap and the insects caught in it. Makes a distinctive drumming that gradually slows down. L 8 ½ in.

Habitat: Mixed deciduous and coniferous forest.

Downy Woodpecker

Picoides pubescens   /   Family: Woodpecker

Our most common and our smallest woodpecker. Has a very short bill. L 6 ¾ in.

Habitat: Deciduous and mixed forest.

Hairy Woodpecker

Picoides villosus   /   Family: Woodpecker

Very similar to downy woodpecker, though larger and less common. Bill noticeably longer than downy, almost as long as the head. L 9 ¼ in.

Habitat: Deciduous and mixed forest.

BIRDS

Eastern Wood-pewee

Red-eyed Vireo

Least Flycatcher

Blue-headed Vireo

Blue Jay

Eastern Wood-pewee

Contopus virens   /   Family: Flycatcher

Widespread small, dark grayish brown bird. Song is a distinctive slow "pee-a-wee" that sounds a little like a cat-call. L 6 ¼ in.

Habitat: Deciduous and mixed forests and woodlands.

Least Flycatcher

Empidonax minimus   /   Family: Flycatcher

Small olive-brown bird with large head and noticeable white eye-ring. Song is a series of quick two-noted chirps. L 5 ¼ in.

Habitat: Deciduous and mixed woods including suburbs.

Red-eyed Vireo

Vireo olivaceus   /   Family: Vireo

Larger than solitary vireo with gray crown and white line above the eyes. Very distincitive ubiquitous song in short phrases: "Here I am. Where are you?" Sings all day long. L 6 in.

Habitat: Deciduous forests and woodlands.

Blue-headed Vireo

Vireo solitarius   /   Family: Vireo

Blue-gray head with white "spectacles." Song is similar to but slower than red-eyed vireo. L 5 ½ in.

Habitat: Coniferous or mixed woods.

Blue Jay

Cyanocitta cristata   /   Family: Crows and Jays

Well-known strikingly pretty bird. Seen on the trail as well as at home. Has a strident descending call. L 11 in.

Habitat: Just about anywhere except spruce-fir forest.

BIRDS

U.S. Fish & Wildlife Service

Common Raven

Steven D. Faccio

American Crow

Steven D. Faccio

Black-capped Chickadee

Elinor Osborn/www.agpix.com/osborn/

Red-breasted Nuthatch

Elinor Osborn/www.agpix.com/osborn/

White-breasted Nuthatch

Common Raven

Corvus corax / Family: Crows and Jays

Large all-black bird with long wedge-shaped tail. Call is a low croak. L 24 in.

Habitat: Mostly at higher elevations.

American Crow

Corvus brachyrhynchos / Family: Crows and Jays

Common all-black bird. Less common in unbroken forest. Call is the familiar, not very musical "caw, caw, caw." L 17 ½ in.

Habitat: Woodlands and forest edges.

Black-capped Chickadee

Poecile atricapillas / Family: Chickadee

Very common familiar bird. Song is a clear, two-toned whistle. L 5.25 in.

Habitat: Deciduous or mixed forest and woodland.

Red-breasted Nuthatch

Sitta canadensis / Family: Nuthatch

Small, gray bird with striking black-and-white eye stripes and reddish breast. Has a high-pitched, nasal call. Creeps up and down tree-trunks foraging. L 4 ½ in.

Habitat: Coniferous and mixed forest.

White-breasted Nuthatch

Sitta carolinensis / Family: Nuthatch

Similar in shape to red-breasted nuthatch, though somewhat larger. Without the black eye stripe or reddish breast. Song is a series of rapid nasal notes that sounds almost like a cackle. L 5 ¾ in.

Habitat: Deciduous and mixed forest.

Cornell Lab of Ornithology

Cornell Lab of Ornithology

Brown Creeper

Winter Wren

U.S. Fish & Wildlife Service

Cornell Lab of Ornithology

Golden-crowned Kinglet

Veery

U.S. Fish & Wildlife Service

American Robin

Brown Creeper

Certhia americana   /   Family: Creeper

Small brown bird well camouflaged against tree trunks.
Creeps spirally up the tree foraging. Song is two high thin notes
followed by several faster ones. L 5 ¼ in.

Habitat: All mature forests.

Winter Wren

Troglodytes troglodytes   /   Family: Wren

Small nondescript brown bird. More often seen than heard.
Has a gorgeous long complicated trilling song. L 4 in.

Habitat: Dense coniferous forest; nests in stumps or the roots
of fallen trees.

Golden-crowned Kinglet

Regulus satrapa   /   Family: Kinglet

Small, active bird with noticeably striped face and yellow crown.
Similar to ruby-crowned kinglet (not pictured here), which
has a red crown and is seen during migration. Song is a series
of very high-pitched whistles ending in a trill. L 4 in.

Habitat: Open coniferous forest.

American Robin

Turdus migratorius   /   Family: Thrush

Well-known red-breasted bird. Song is a series of warbling rising
and falling phrases: "cheerily cheer-up cheerio." L 10 in.

Habitat: Nests in overgrown fields; seen along the trail during
migration.

Veery

Catharus fuscescens   /   Family: Thrush

Reddish brown back and wings. Lightly spotted breast.
Has a descending distinctive multitonal song. L 7 in.

Habitat: Deciduous and mixed forest.

BIRDS

BIRDS

Steven D. Faccio

Bicknell's Thrush

Steven D. Faccio

Hermit Thrush

Elinor Osborn/www.agpix.com/osborn/

Magnolia Warbler

Elinor Osborn/www.agpix.com/osborn/

Black-throated Blue Warbler

Elinor Osborn/www.agpix.com/osborn/

Yellow-rumped Warbler

Bicknell's Thrush

Catharus bicknelli / Family: Thrush

Very similar to the hermit thrush with less distinct eye-ring.
Globally rare bird due to its limited habitat. Song is a three-parted
wheezy trill. L 6¾ in.

Habitat: Restricted to northeastern fir forests above 3,000 feet.

Hermit Thrush

Catharus guttatus / Family: Thrush

Vermont's state bird. Drab brown bird with black-spotted breast
and white eye-ring; best known for its song, which is an ethereal
flutelike phrase. L 6¾ in.

Habitat: Mixed or coniferous woods.

Magnolia Warbler

Dendroica magnolia / Family: Wood-warbler

Yellow throat and breast with black streaks. Male has a black face
and white eye-brow. Female similar with gray face. Song is a
series of several twitters. L 5 in.

Habitat: Open coniferous forest.

Black-throated Blue Warbler

Dendroica caerulescens / Family: Wood-warbler

Dark blue wings and back with black face and throat and a
prominent white wing patch. Song is a three- or four-noted
buzzing song higher pitched at the end: "zee zee zee zeeeee."
L 5¼ in.

Habitat: Shrubby deciduous forests.

Yellow-rumped Warbler

Dendroica coronata / Family: Wood-warbler

One of our most common warblers during migration.
Yellow rump, crown, and side patch; white throat. Song is a slow,
high warble. L 5½ in.

Habitat: Coniferous and mixed forest.

BIRDS

Bryan Pfeiffer / Wings Photography

Black-throated Green Warbler

Steven D. Faccio

Steven D. Faccio

Blackpoll Warbler

Black-and-white Warbler

Bryan Pfeiffer / Wings Photography

U.S. Fish & Wildlife Service

Ovenbird

Scarlet Tanager

Black-throated Green Warbler

Dendroica virens   /   Family: Wood-warbler

Olive-green back and yellow face. Song similar to black-throated blue warbler, but with an extra note: "zee zee zee zoo zeeee."
L 5 in.

Habitat: Open coniferous and mixed woods.

Blackpoll Warbler

Dendroica striata   /   Family: Wood-warbler

Striking black cap and white cheeks. Song is a series of rapid high-pitched notes. L 5 ½ in.

Habitat: Dense spruce-fir forest at high elevation.

Black-and-white Warbler

Mniotilta varia   /   Family: Wood-warbler

Streaked black and white over entire body. Song is a series of high-pitched phrases that sound like a squeaky wheel.
L 5 ¼ in.

Habitat: Deciduous and mixed forest.

Ovenbird

Seiurus aurocapillus   /   Family: Wood-warbler

Very common woodland bird that is often heard but hard to see. Drab olive back and wings. White eye-ring and rusty-red crown. Song is a series of two-syllable phrases getting progressively louder: "teacher teacher teacher teacher." L 6 in.

Habitat: Deciduous or mixed forest.

Scarlet Tanager

Piranga olivacea   /   Family: Tanager

Male has striking scarlet body and black wings. Widespread across Vermont. Song is a series of rising and falling phrases. Said to sound like a robin with a cold. L 7 in.

Habitat: Mature deciduous and mixed forest.

BIRDS

Elinor Osborn/www.agpix.com/osborn/

Rose-breasted Grosbeak

Elinor Osborn/www.agpix.com/osborn/

White-throated Sparrow

Elinor Osborn/www.agpix.com/osborn/

Dark-eyed Junco

Elinor Osborn/www.agpix.com/osborn/

Purple Finch

Elinor Osborn/www.agpix.com/osborn/

American Goldfinch

Rose-breasted Grosbeak

Pheucticus ludovicianus / Family: Cardinal

Adult male with a striking black head and reddish breast.
Song is a very musical series of rising and falling phrases,
like a robin's song but richer. L 8 in.

Habitat: Mature deciduous forest.

White-throated Sparrow

Zonotrichia albicollis / Family: Sparrow

Black-and-white striped head and white chin. Song is a clear
series of whistles: "Oh sweet Canada, Canada, Canada."
L 6¾ in.

Habitat: Coniferous or mixed forest; often heard at
high elevations.

Dark-eyed Junco

Junco hyemalis / Family: Juncos

Slate colored; darker around the eyes. Song is a high-pitched
trill. L 6¼ in.

Habitat: Coniferous and mixed forest including high
elevation areas.

Purple Finch

Carpodacus purpureus / Family: Finch

Rose-red breast and head. Song is a complicated warble.
L 6 in.

Habitat: Coniferous and mixed woods at all elevations.

American Goldfinch

Carduelis tristis / Family: Finch

Male has yellow body with black wings and forehead. Song is
a series of trills and twitters. L 5 in.

Habitat: Generalist found in forests, fields, and gardens.

REPTILES

Elinor Osborn/www.agpix.com/osborn

Common Garter Snake

Jim Andrews

Northern Redbelly Snake

Jim Andrews

Eastern Milk Snake

Jim Andrews

Northern Brown Snake

Reptiles

Reptiles are cold blooded, egg-laying, animals covered with scales. Along the trail, they are limited to snakes and turtles. None of the snakes found on the Long Trail are poisonous.

Key
L = length

Northern Redbelly Snake

Storeria occipitomaculata   /   Snake suborder

Inconspicuous brownish snake with a distinct red belly and yellow spots on the back of the head. L 10–14 in.

Habitat: Moist woods and swampy areas.

Common Garter Snake

Thamnophis sirtalis   /   Snake suborder

Our most common snake. Dark, slightly mottled body with three yellow stripes: one along the back and one on each side. L 18–44 in.

Habitat: Wide variety of habitats including woods and fields.

Eastern Milk Snake

Lampropeltis triangulum   /   Snake suborder

Light colored with large, reddish brown splotches bordered in black. L 30 in.

Habitat: Woods and fields with brushy cover on the southern half of the trail.

Northern Brown Snake

Storeria dekayi   /   Snake suborder

Light brown snake with rows of darker brown dots. L 12–28 in.

Habitat: Woods, fields, swamps, and roadsides on the southern half of the trail.

AMPHIBIANS

Snapping Turtle

Painted Turtle

Wood Turtle

Eastern Newt

Snapping Turtle
Chelydra serpentina   /   Turtle Order

Our largest turtle. Rough, brown shell. Powerful head and tail. Can inflict a painful bite. L 10–18 in.

Habitat: Lakes and ponds with muddy bottoms.

Wood Turtle
Clemmys insculpta   /   Turtle Order

Brown, deeply grooved shell. Orange neck and legs. L 7–9 in.

Habitat: Wet meadows, woods, stream banks, and swamps.

Painted Turtle
Chrysemys picta   /   Turtle Order

Very common turtle. Smooth, brown shell with red markings along the edges. Head and neck yellow striped. L 5–6 in.

Habitat: Shallow ponds, marshes, pools, and wet meadows.

AMPHIBIANS

Amphibians

Amphibians, such as salamanders and frogs, are creatures that spend the first part of their lives dependent on water, and later are able to travel on land.

Key:
L = length from nose to tail tip

Eastern Newt
Notophthalmus viridescens   /   Salamander Order

Most commonly seen in the immature terrestrial form: red eft (shown here). Adults return to water. The eft is prominently orange with bright red spots. L 2½ in.

Habitat: Common in moist woods.

AMPHIBIANS

Spotted Salamander

Northern Dusky Salamander

Red-backed Salamander

American Toad

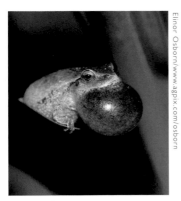

Spring Peeper

Green Frog

Spotted Salamander

Ambystoma maculatum   /   Salamander Order

Dark gray body with bright yellow spots. Stocky body. L 7 in.

Habitat: Moist woods; requires fish-free pools for breeding.

Northern Dusky Salamander

Desmognathus fuscus   /   Salamander Order

Inconspicuous dark, mottled skin. Throat and legs orange.
L 3 ½ in.

Habitat: Stream banks and woodland springs.

Red-backed Salamander

Plethodon cinereus   /   Salamander Order

Dark body with wide orange-red strip along the back. L 3 in.

Habitat: Under logs and rocks in coniferous and mixed woods.

American Toad

Bufo americanus   /   Frog and Toad Order

Gray-brown with rusty brown "warts." Be careful if you pick
one up; it exudes very irritating secretions as protection.
L 2 ¾ in.

Habitat: Found in almost any habitat from woods to gardens.

Spring Peeper

Pseudacris crucifer   /   Frog and Toad Order

Light brown with a darker X on its back. Rarely seen but often
heard. Has a high-pitched musical call heard on spring evenings.
L 1 in.

Habitat: Woodland swamps

Green Frog

Rana clamitans   /   Frog and Toad Order

Green with dark spots and yellowish throat. Our most abundant
frog. L 2–4 in.

Habitat: Shores of ponds and streams.

BUTTERFLIES & DRAGONFLIES

Wood Frog

Pickerel Frog

Canadian Tiger Swallowtail

Wood Frog
Rana sylvatica   /   Frog and Toad Order

Dull brown with a distinctive dark patch behind the eye and white stripe on the upper lip. L 1 ½–3 in.

Habitat: Moist woods, often far from water; breeds in temporary woodland pools.

Pickerel Frog
Rana palustris   /   Frog and Toad Order

Olive-green to brown skin with striking dark brown rectangular spots. L 2–4 in.

Habitat: Stream and pond shores and wet meadows; breeds in shallow woodland ponds.

Butterflies and Dragonflies

Insects have three main body parts: the head, the thorax or midsection, and the abdomen. For dragonfly descriptions, the thorax is the main body part. The abdomen, which extends behind the thorax, looks somewhat like a tail.

Key

W = width from wing tip to wing tip

L = length from head to the tip of the abdomen

Canadian Tiger Swallowtail
Papilio canadensis   /   Swallowtail Family

Boldly colored yellow with black stripes. Feeds on birches and aspen. Visible late May to mid-July. W 3 ¼ in.

Habitat: Deciduous and mixed open forests and forest edges.

Cabbage White

Atlantis Fritillary

Clouded Sulphur

Milbert's Tortoiseshell

Common Ringlet

Cabbage White

Pieris rapae / White and Sulphur Family

One of our most common butterflies. Cream colored with either one (in males) or two (in females) black spots on the wing. Feeds on mustard family plants. Visible spring to fall. W 2 in.

Habitat: Open areas, roadsides. and fields.

Clouded Sulphur

Colias philodice / White and Sulphur Family

Yellow with black wing tips. Feeds on clover. Visible spring to fall. W 2 in.

Habitat: Fields and roadsides; found in most openings along the trail, including ski slopes.

Atlantis Fritillary

Speyeria atlantis / Brushfoot Family

Wings gray brown toward the center, orange with black markings farther out. Feeds on violets. Visible mid-June to mid-September. W 2 in.

Habitat: Open mixed-aged woods and along higher forest edges.

Milbert's Tortoiseshell

Nymphalis milberti / Brushfoot Family

Very dark body with bright orange and yellow wing bands. Feeds on nettles. Visible spring to fall. W 1 ½ in.

Habitat: High open areas including summits and ski slopes.

Common Ringlet

Coenonympha tullia / Brushfoot Family

Reddish orange on upper side with small dot on wingtips. Feeds on grasses. Visible June to Aug. W 1 ½ in.

Habitat: Low grassy fields.

BUTTERFLIES & DRAGONFLIES

White Admiral

Canada Darner

Cherry-faced Meadowhawk

Marsh Bluet

Eastern Forktail

White Admiral
Limenitis arthemis   /   Brushfoot Family

Striking white bands on black wings. Feeds on birch and aspen.
Visible June to Aug. W 3 in.

Habitat: Forests, especially near open areas.

Canada Darner
Aeshna canadensis   /   Dragonfly Suborder

Brown thorax with side stripes. Abdomen brown with blue
markings. Visible June to October. L 2 ¾ in.

Habitat: Marshy bogs and pond edges.

Cherry-faced Meadowhawk
Sympetrum internum   /   Dragonfly Suborder

Brownish thorax. Abdomen dark red with long black side stripe.
Visible mid-June to Oct. L 1 ¼ in.

Habitat: Ponds and marshes.

Marsh Bluet
Enallagma ebrium   /   Damselfly suborder

Iridescent blue thorax, abdomen, and wings. Visible May to July.
L 1 ¼ in.

Habitat: arshy ponds and bog

Eastern Forktail
Ischnura verticalis   /   Damselfly suborder

Thorax black with green sides. Abdomen black with blue at
the tip. Visible May to Sept. L 1 in.

Habitat: Ponds and streams.

BUTTERFLIES & DRAGONFLIES

204

Bibliography

Alden, Peter et al. 1998. *National Audubon Society Field Guide to New England.* Alfred A. Knopf, New York.

Barron, George. 1999. *Mushrooms of Northeast North America.* Lone Pine Publishing, Edmonton, AB.

Borror, Donald J. and Richard E. White. 1998. *A Field Guide to Insects: America North of Mexico.* Second edition. The Peterson Field Guide Series, Houghton Mifflin, Boston.

Brady, Nyle. 1984. *The Nature and Property of Soils.* Macmillan, New York.

Burns, G. P. and C. H. Otis. 1979. *The Handbook of Vermont Trees.* First Tuttle edition. Charles E. Tuttle Company, Rutland, VT.

Burns, Russell M. and Barbara Honkala, tech cords. 1990. *Silvics of Forest Trees of North American: 1. Conifers; 2. Hardwoods.* Agriculture Handbook 654. U.S.D.A. Forest Service, Washington, DC.

Carter, Kate. 2001. *Wildflowers of Vermont.* Cotton Brook Publications, Waterbury Center, VT.

Christman, Robert A. 1956. *The Geology of Mt. Mansfield State Forest.* Vermont Geological Survey, Montpelier, VT.

Dann, Kevin T. 1988. *Traces on the Appalachians: A Natural History of Serpentine in Eastern North America.* Rutgers University Press, New Brunswick, NJ.

DeGraaf, Richard M. and Deborah D. Rudis. 1983. *Amphibians and Reptiles of New England: Habitats and Natural History.* University of Massachusetts Press, Amherst.

DeGraaf, Richard M. and Mariko Yamasaki. 2000. *New England Wildlife: Habitat, Natural History and Distribution.* University Press of New England, Hanover, NH.

Doll, Charles G., David P. Stewart, and Paul Maclintock. 1971. *Surficial Geologic Map of Vermont.* Vermont Geological Survey, Montpelier, VT.

Doll, Charles G. et al. 1961. *Centennial Geologic Map of Vermont*. Vermont Geological Survey, Montpelier, VT.

Doolan, Barry. 1996. The Geology of Vermont. *Rocks and Minerals* 71:218–25, Heldref Publications, Washington, DC.

Dunkle, Sidney W. 2000. *Dragonflies Through Binoculars: A Field Guide to Dragonflies of North America*. Oxford University Press, USA.

Ehrlich, Paul R., D. S. Dobkin, and Darryl Wheye. 1988. *The Birder's Handbook: A Field Guide to the Natural History of North American Birds*. Simon & Schuster, New York.

Forrest, Louise R. 1988. *Field Guide to Tracking Animals in the Snow*. Stackpole Books, Harrisburg, PA.

Glassberg, Jeffrey. 1999. *Butterflies Through Binoculars, The East: A Field Guide to the Butterflies of Eastern North America*. Oxford University Press, USA.

Gleason, Henry A. and Arthur Cronquist. 1991. *Manual of Vascular Plants of Northeastern United States and Adjacent Canada*. Second edition. New York Botanical Garden, New York.

Hallowell, Anne C. and Barbara G. Hallowell. 1981. T*he Fern Finder*. Nature Study Guild, Rochester, NY.

Heinrich, Bernd. 1997. *The Trees in My Forest*. First Cliff Street Books/Harper Perennial, New York.

Himmelman, John. 2006. *Discovering Amphibians: Frogs and Salamanders of the Northeast*. Down East Books, Camden, ME.

Holmgren, Noel H. Kathleen M. McCauley, and Laura Vogel, illustrators. 1998. *Illustrated Companion to Gleason and Cronquit's Manual*. New York Botanical Garden, New York.

Johnson, Charles W. 1985. B*ogs of the Northeast*. University Press of New England, Hanover, NH.

———. 1999. *The Nature of Vermont*. Second edition. University Press of New England, Hanover, NH.

Kimmerer, Robin Wall. 2003. *Gathering Moss: A Natural and Cultural History of Mosses*. Oregon State University Press, Corvalis, OR.

Klyza, Chirstopher M. and Steven T. Trombulak. 1999. *The Story of Vermont: A Natural and Cultural History*. University Press of New England, Hanover.

Magee, Dennis W. and Harry. E. Ahles. 1999. *Flora of the Northeast: A Manual of the Vascular Flora of New England and Adjacent New York*. University of Massachusetts Press, Amherst.

Marchand, Peter J. 1987. *North Woods: An Inside Look at the Nature of Forests in the Northeast*. Appalachian Mountain Club Books, Boston.

Marchand, Peter J. 1991. *Life in the Cold: An Introduction to Winter Ecology.* Second Edition. University Press of New England, Hanover.

Murie, Olaus J. 1982. *A Field Guide to Animal Tracks.* Second edition. The Peterson Field Guide Series, Houghton Mifflin, Boston.

Murin, Ted and Bryan Pfeiffer. 2002. *Birdwatching in Vermont.* University Press of New England, Hanover, NH.

Nearing, G. G. 1962. *The Lichen Book: Hand book of Lichens of the Northeastern United States.* E. Lundberg, Ashton, MD.

Newcomb, Lawrence with Gordon Morrison illustrator. 1977. *Newcomb's Wildflower Guide.* Little, Brown, Boston.

Odum, Eugene P. and Gary W. Barrett. 2004. *Fundamentals of Ecology. Fifth edition.* Brooks Cole, Stamford, CT.

Petrides, George A. 1988. *A Field Guide to Eastern Trees.* The Peterson Field Guide Series, Houghton Mifflin, Boston.

Reid, Fiona. 2006. *A Field Guide to Mammals of North America.* Fourth edition. The Peterson Field Guide Series, Houghton Mifflin, Boston.

Rezendes, Paul. 1992. *Tracking and the Art of Seeing: How to Read Animal Tracks and Signs.* Camden House Publishing, Charlotte, VT.

Rimmer, Christopher C. and Kent P. McFarland. 1999. Sky Island Songbirds. *Natural History* 108.7:34–38

Sanders, Jack. 2003. *The Secrets of Wildflowers.* Lyons Press, Guilford, CT.

Sibley, David A. 2000. *National Audubon Society: The Sibley Guide to Birds.* Alfred A. Knopf, New York.

Slack, Nancy G. and Allison W. Bell. 1995. *Field Guide to the New England Alpine Summits.* Appalachian Mountain Club Books, Boston.

Symonds, George W. D. 1958. *The Tree Identification Book.* William Morrow & Company, New York.

———. 1963. T*he Shrub Identification Book.* William Morrow & Company, New York.

Thompson, Elizabeth H. and Eric R. Sorenson. 2000. *Wetland, Woodland, Wildland: A Guide to the Natural Communities of Vermont.* Vermont Department of Fish and Wildlife, and the Nature Conservancy of Vermont, Montpelier, VT.

Van Diver, Bradford B. 1987. *Roadside Geology of Vermont and New Hampshire.* Mountain Press, Missoula, MT.

Wessels, Tom. 1997. *Reading the Forested Landscape: A Natural History of New England.* Countryman Press, Woodstock, VT.

Index

Note: Page numbers in italic refer to photographs.

214

About the Author

Lexi Shear has a degree in botany from the Field Naturalist Program at the University of Vermont and has worked as an ecologist for The Trust for Public Land. A veteran long-distance hiker, she has through-hiked the 2,700-mile Pacific Crest Trail and section-hiked Vermont's Long Trail. Her numerous other hikes include a journey on the Salzburger Almenweg with her husband and twelve month-old daughter. She lives with her family in Montpelier where she teaches biology and chemistry at Montpelier High School.

Green Mountain Club

Providing and Protecting Vermont's Hiking Trails Since 1910

Your membership or gift supports hiking in Vermont and protection of the Green Mountains.

Thank you for considering a contribution to the GMC at 4711 Waterbury-Stowe Road, Waterbury Center, Vermont 05677.

Call (802)244-7037 or visit www.greenmountainclub.org

Mixed Sources
Product group from well-managed forests and other controlled sources
www.fsc.org Cert no. BV-COC-080420
© 1996 Forest Stewardship Council
FSC